6/03

D0664695

The Psychology of Self-Esteem

A Revolutionary Approach to Self-Understanding That Launched a New Era in Modern Psychology

Nathaniel Branden

JOSSEY-BASS
A Wiley Company
San Francisco

Jossey-Bass books and products are available through most bookstores. To contact Jossey-Bass directly, call (888) 378-2537, fax to (800) 605-2665, or visit our website at www.josseybass.com.

Substantial discounts on bulk quantities of Jossey-Bass books are available to corporations, professional associations, and other organizations. For details and discount information, contact the special sales department at Jossey-Bass.

Manufactured in the United States of America.

Library of Congress Cataloging-in-Publication Data

Branden, Nathaniel.
    The psychology of self-esteem: a revolutionary approach to self-understanding that launched a new era in modern psychology /Nathaniel Branden.—32nd anniversary ed.
        p. cm.
Includes bibliographical references and index.
    ISBN 0-7879-4526-9 (alk. paper)
    1. Self-esteem. I. Title.
    BF697 .B7 2000
    155.2—dc21   00-010734

FIRST EDITION
PB Printing   10 9 8 7 6 5 4 3

155.2
BRANDEN

Contents

Preface to the 32nd Anniversary Edition

I wrote this book during the 1960s and it was published in 1969. It is a source of immense satisfaction to have this opportunity to write a new Preface for the 32nd anniversary edition. Although I have written many books since this one, for a significant number of my readers it remains their favorite of my works. Certainly it laid the foundation for everything I wrote subsequently about self-esteem.

Are there things that I would do differently if I were writing the book today? Of course. It is impossible for an author to reread a book written more than three decades ago and not feel, "Today I could do it better." However, I have chosen to leave the book in its original form—unedited and unchanged—for this edition. It has, I am convinced, an integrity, or internal logic, that would be undermined if I attempted to co-mingle it with perspectives arrived at later.

This book is more philosophical than most of my subsequent writings, which I do not regret, and more moralistic, if only by implication—which I do regret. Its ethical vision is narrower than that offered in such books of mine as *The Six Pillars of Self-Esteem* (1995) and *The Art of Living Consciously* (1997). And yet people in the fields of publishing and psychology tell me repeatedly that this book has done more to awaken consciousness concerning the importance of self-esteem to human well-being than any other single work. If true, I am proud of that. I struggle to make real, at the age of seventy, that I made my first notes on self-esteem while still in my twenties and began writing this book when I was thirty-three.

Wanting to offer the reader some sense of how my thinking about self-esteem has developed, I offer an Epilogue entitled

"Working with Self-Esteem in Psychotherapy." A single essay cannot retrace all the steps involved in my evolving and expanding vision of the dynamics of self-esteem, but it will convey a good (if highly distilled) introduction to my more recent thinking, and it will disclose how the basic conceptual structure first presented in *The Psychology of Self-Esteem* still stands.

To comment on one small linguistic change: in the present volume I speak of the two components of self-esteem as self-confidence and self-respect. In my later work, I speak of *self-efficacy* and *self-respect*. The reason for the change is that *self-confidence* is too general, too abstract, too vague. What I wanted to convey was specifically the experience of being *efficacious* in the face of life's challenges.

I have learned what I know about self-esteem from several sources—from reasoning about human experience that is more or less available to everyone, from working with clients in psychotherapy for more than four decades and having to constantly test my ideas against the challenge of needing to achieve specific results, and from working on my own development. In *The Six Pillars of Self-Esteem* (which I regard as the grandchild of the present volume), I tell a number of stories about myself, about mistakes I made, and about the lessons I learned from those mistakes—all of which deepened my understanding of what strengthens self-esteem and what undermines it. It is difficult to help others grow in self-esteem if we do not understand how its dynamics operate in ourselves.

One of the most important things this book makes clear is that self-esteem is not a feel-good phenomenon. Our need of it is rooted deep in our nature, and if we understand that need, we understand that it cannot be satisfied arbitrarily or capriciously by just any pursuit that might happen to attract us. Self-esteem rests on the appropriate exercise of mind, and what that means specifically is examined in the pages that follow. We will see that self-esteem, rationality, perseverance, self-responsibility, and personal integrity are all intimately related.

We will also see that even though others may help us or obstruct us on the path to self-esteem, especially when we are young, no one can literally *give* us self-esteem. It must be generated from within.

The best analogy I can think of is to physical fitness—getting in shape. Others can encourage us or teach us principles of exercise and healthy nutrition, but no one can make us a gift of being physically fit. That is a state we must achieve ourselves—through the actions and practices we cultivate. Precisely the same is true of self-esteem. We make a muscle strong by using it. That is how we make a mind strong.

Aristotle taught us that we build a good character through the discipline of converting virtuous practices into habits. How this idea applies to building self-esteem, we shall shortly proceed to consider. But first we must look at the context in which the need for self-esteem arises. What is it in the nature of reality and of mind that makes self-esteem an urgent concern?

This is where our inquiry begins.

Los Angeles, California   NATHANIEL BRANDEN
October 2000

Introduction

In his quest to understand the universe in which he lives, man is confronted with three fundamental facts of nature: the existence of matter, of life, and of consciousness.

In response to the first of these phenomena, he developed the sciences of physics and chemistry; in response to the second, he developed the science of biology; in response to the third, he developed the science of psychology. It is notorious that, to date, the greatest advances in knowledge have been achieved in the field of physics—the least, in the field of psychology.

The explanation of this difference in the comparative rates of progress lies, at least in part, in the respective challenges posed by these three sciences. In seeking to identify laws of nature, man basically is seeking to identify the *principles of action* exhibited by entities in their behavior: to grasp *what* entities do in different contexts and *why*. Given this task, the job of the physicist is simpler than that of the biologist: the number of variables with which he must cope in studying the action of inanimate matter, the variety of actions possible to inanimate entities, is far less than that encountered in the behavior of living organisms. But the job of the biologist is simpler than that of the psychologist: a *conscious* living organism such as man exhibits a complexity and variety of behavior greater by far than that exhibited by any other entity, living or nonliving.

As a being who possesses the power of self-consciousness—the power of contemplating his own life and activity—man experiences a profound need for a conceptual frame of reference from which to view himself, a need for a self-intelligibility which it is the task of psychology to provide. This book is offered as a step toward the achievement of that goal.

It is no part of my intention, in this context, to engage in polemics against contemporary psychology or to argue that it has failed to provide man with the self-knowledge he needs. So I will simply say that such is my conviction—and that my reasons, as well as the nature of my differences with current schools of psychology, will become clear as we proceed.

If the science of psychology is to achieve an accurate portrait of man, it must, I submit, question and challenge many of the deepest premises prevalent in the field today—must break away from the anti-biological, anti-intellectual, automaton view of human nature that dominates contemporary theory. Neither the view of man as an instinct-manipulated puppet (psychoanalysis), nor the view of him as a stimulus-response machine (behaviorism), bears any resemblance to man the biological entity whom it is the task of psychology to study: the organism uniquely characterized by the power of conceptual thought, propositional speech, explicit reasoning and self-awareness.

The central theme of this book is the role of self-esteem in man's life: the need of self-esteem, the nature of that need, the conditions of its fulfillment, the consequences of its frustration— and the impact of a man's self-esteem (or lack of it) on his values, responses, and goals.

Virtually all psychologists recognize that man experiences a need of self-esteem. But what they have not identified is the nature of self-esteem, the reasons why man needs it, and the conditions he must satisfy if he is to achieve it. Virtually all psychologists recognize, if only vaguely, that there is some relationship between the degree of a man's self-esteem and the degree of his mental health. But they have not identified the nature of that relationship, nor the causes of it. Virtually all psychologists recognize, if only dimly, that there is some relationship between the nature and degree of a man's self-esteem and his motivation, i.e., his behavior in the spheres of work, love, and human relationships. But they have not explained why, nor identified the principles involved. Such are the issues with which this book deals.

More precisely, such are the issues dealt with in Part Two of this book. Part One is concerned with the psychological foundations of my theory of self-esteem—with the view of man on which it rests. This entails an examination of the nature of living organisms, with special reference to the concept of biological and psychological needs; the nature of man's mind, as contrasted with the consciousness of lower animals; the issue of psychological freedom and self-responsibility; the nature and source of emotions, the relationship of reason and emotion, the problem of emotional repression; and, finally, the concepts of mental health and illness.

Some of the material in this book originally appeared in *The Objectivist* (formerly *The Objectivist Newsletter*), a journal of ideas of which I was co-founder with Ayn Rand, and, from 1962 to 1968, coeditor. Some of the material in one chapter originally appeared in my book *Who Is Ayn Rand?*[1] Although I am no longer associated with Miss Rand, I welcome this opportunity to acknowledge the invaluable contribution which her work as a philosopher has made to my own thinking in the field of psychology. I indicate, throughout the text, specific concepts and theories of Miss Rand's philosophy, Objectivism, which are crucially important to my own ideas. The Objectivist epistemology, metaphysics, and ethics are the philosophical frame of reference in which I write as a psychologist.

Indeed, for many years, when lecturing on my psychological theories, it was my practice to designate my system as "Objectivist Psychology." I knew, however, that this was only a temporary designation—a working title—and that it is not appropriate to name a system of psychology, or any science, after a philosophy. One would not, for instance, speak of "Objectivist Physics," even if a physicist were to make use of tenets of Objectivist epistemology or metaphysics.

The name I eventually selected arose from my conviction that psychology must be firmly rooted in a biological orientation; that a study of the nature of man must begin with a study of the nature of life; that man's psychological nature can only be understood in the context of his nature as a living organism; and that man's nature and needs as a specific kind of organism are the source both of his unique achievements and of his potential problems. The biocentric approach (i.e., the biologically oriented, life-centered approach) is basic to my thinking and to my method of analyzing psychological problems. For this reason, I call my system: Biocentric Psychology.

It is, of course, an indication that a science is at an early stage of development when that science is still divided into schools, each with its own name. In this sense, I regret that it is necessary to designate my work by any name at all.

And, in truth, in my own mind I do not call what I am doing Biocentric Psychology. I call it psychology.

Part One

The Foundations

Chapter One

| Psychology as a Science

The Definition of Psychology

There are two questions which every human being—with rare exceptions—asks himself through most of his life. The rare exceptions are the persons who know the answer to the first of these questions, at least to a significant extent. But everyone asks the second, sometimes in wonder, often in despair. These two questions are: How am I to understand myself? and: How am I to understand other people?

Historically—in the development of the human race and in the life of an individual—these questions constitute the starting point of, and initial impetus to, psychological investigation.

The inquiry implicit in these questions can be cast in a wider, more abstract form: Why does a person act as he does? What would be required for him to act differently?

Writing in the early years of this century, the German psychologist Hermann Ebbingaus made an observation that has become famous: "Psychology has a long past, but only a short history." His statement was intended to acknowledge the fact that, throughout recorded history, men have been intensely concerned with issues and problems of a psychological nature, but that psychology, as a distinct scientific discipline, emerged only in the second half of the nineteenth century. Up to that time, the domain of psychology had not been isolated as such and studied systematically; it existed only as a part of philosophy, medicine, and theology. The establishment of Wilhelm Wundt's experimental laboratory in 1879 is often regarded as the formal beginning of scientific psychology. But when one considers the views of man and the theories of his nature that have been put forth as knowledge in the past hundred years, it remains a moot question whether the starting date of the science of psychology lies behind us—or ahead.

Science is the rational and systematic study of the facts of reality; its aim is to discover laws of nature, to achieve a comprehensive, integrated knowledge that will make the universe intelligible to man. Man requires such knowledge in order to deal with reality successfully, in order to live. If "nature, to be commanded, must be obeyed"—then the purpose of science is to provide man with the intellectual means of his survival.

A new science is born when, out of the countless questions that man asks concerning the nature of things, certain questions are isolated and then integrated into a distinct category—isolated and integrated by a defining principle that distinguishes these questions from all others and identifies their common characteristics. It took many centuries before physics, chemistry, biology, and physiology, for instance, were conceptualized as specific sciences.

What is the science of psychology? How is it to be defined? What is its specific domain?

Consider the following problems; they are typical of those with which psychology deals; and consider by what principle one is able to recognize that they *are* psychological.

A scientist struggles to answer some difficult question that has arisen in his work. After months of effort, he feels no closer to a solution than when he began. Then, one day, while he is out for a walk, the solution unexpectedly flashes into his mind. What mental processes underlie and account for this phenomenon, the phenomenon of sudden "insight" or "inspiration"?

Among our acquaintances we note that one person characteristically is serene, confident, even-tempered; that another is irritable, nervous, unsure of himself; that a third is tense, brooding, emotionally frozen; that a fourth is emotionally explosive, volatile, elated one moment and depressed the next. What accounts for such differences? What are the causes of a person's character and personality? What *are* character and personality?

A man awakens in the middle of the night, his body trembling and his heart beating violently. To the best of his knowledge, he has no cause to be afraid. Yet what he feels is terror. Through a sleepless night, then through the days and weeks that follow, the sense of impending disaster persists: the dread invades him, as if some alien power had taken possession of his body. Finally, he seeks the help of a psychotherapist. He learns that his problem is shared, in varying degrees of intensity, by millions of people. It is called pathological anxiety. What is its cause? What does it signify? How is it to be cured?

These examples pertain to human beings, but psychology is not restricted exclusively to the study of man—it includes the study of animals. When a scientist investigates the learning processes of a dog, or the relative effectiveness of reward and punishment on a monkey, or the "family life" of a chimpanzee—his pursuit and concern are distinctly psychological. If, on the other hand, a scientist studies the actions of astronomical bodies or the heliotropic action of a plant, his investigation is clearly *not* psychological. How do we recognize this? What is the principle of the difference?

Psychology is confined to the study of living organisms. Of *all* living organisms? No—of those living organisms which are *conscious,* which exhibit *awareness.*

If one wishes to understand the definition and distinctive nature of a particular science, the question to answer is: *What are the specific facts of reality that give rise to that science?* For example, the basic fact of reality that gives rise to the science of biology is that certain entities in nature are *alive.* Thus, biology is the science that studies the attributes and characteristics which certain entities possess by virtue of being alive.

That certain living organisms are conscious—that they are able to be aware of existence—is the basic fact of reality which gives rise to the science of psychology. *Psychology is the science that studies the attributes and characteristics which certain living organisms possess by virtue of being conscious.*

This definition subsumes the study of behavior; of motivation; and of the structure, categories, and functions of consciousness. As such, it subsumes the areas covered by the traditional definitions of psychology as "the science of consciousness" or "the science of mind" or "the science of mental activity" or "the science of behavior."

"Consciousness" is used here in its widest and most general sense, to indicate the faculty and state of *awareness,* of *any* form of awareness—from the complex mode of cognition possible to man, to the far more limited range of awareness possible to a frog.

The more complex and highly developed the nervous system of a given species, the greater is the range of its consciousness—measured in terms of ability to discriminate, versatility of action or response, general capacity to cope with the external environment. Man's is the most highly developed nervous system and his is the widest range of awareness; the chimpanzee's is less, the cat's still less, the frog's still less.

Living species differ not only in their overall range of awareness but also in the sensitivity of specific sense modalities; a dog's sense of smell, for instance, is more developed than man's. In judging a given species' range of awareness, one does not consider the sensitivity of a particular sense modality out of context; one judges in terms of the species' overall capacity to discriminate and to vary action in coping with the environment. (In the case of man, of course, his greatly superior power of discrimination is a product of his *conceptual* faculty.)

The fundamental question to be asked about any existing thing is: Is it living or inanimate? The fundamental question to be asked about any living organism is: Is it conscious or not? The fundamental question to be asked about any conscious organism is: What is its distinctive form of consciousness? Every living species that possesses awareness survives by the guidance of its consciousness; *that* is the role and function of consciousness in a living organism. One cannot understand the characteristic behavior of a particular species without reference to its specific form and range of awareness. Thus, the study of the psychology of any given species is the study of the attributes and characteristics which that species possesses by virtue of its distinctive form and range of consciousness.

While psychology is concerned with all conscious organisms, it is primarily concerned with the study of *man*. The psychologist's interest in other species lies, predominantly, in the light his investigation might cast on human beings. The science of human psychology is the study of the attributes and characteristics which man possesses by virtue of his distinctive form and range of consciousness.

The central and basic task of psychology is to understand the nature and consequences of man's distinctive form of awareness;

this holds the key to understanding man behaviorally, motivationally, and characterologically.

Man's defining attribute, which distinguishes him from all other living species, is his ability to reason. This means: to extend the range of his awareness beyond the perceptual concretes immediately confronting him, to abstract, to integrate, to grasp principles—to apprehend reality on the *conceptual* level of consciousness (Chapter Three).

An animal's range is only as wide as its percepts. The rudimentary forms of inference of which it may be capable are entirely bound by and dependent on the physical cues within its immediate sensory field (in the context, of course, of past experience). It cannot conceptualize, it cannot initiate a process of question-asking, it cannot project a chain of inference that is independent of immediate sensory stimuli. But man can chart, on the back of an envelope, the motion of planets through the outer reaches of space.

Like every other species that possesses awareness, man survives by the guidance of *his* distinctive form of consciousness, i.e., by the guidance of his conceptual faculty.

This is the first fact about man's nature that must be understood, *this* is the starting point of any scientific study of man—the basic principle without which no aspect of the distinctively *human* can be understood. Whether one is seeking to understand the nature of emotion, or the psychology of family relationships, or the causes of mental illness, or the meaning of love, or the significance of productive work, or the process of artistic creativeness, or sexual behavior—one must begin by identifying the fact upon which any subsequent analysis of man necessarily rests: that man is a rational being, a being whose distinctive form of consciousness is *conceptual.*

Thus, psychology, as it pertains to man, is properly conceived and defined as *the science that studies the attributes and characteristics which man possesses by virtue of his rational faculty.*

Consciousness

Consciousness is an attribute of living organisms—an attribute of life at a certain level of development and organization.

"Consciousness" denotes both a faculty and a state.

As a faculty, "consciousness" means: the attribute of certain living organisms which enables them to be aware of existence. (I use "faculty" in the Aristotelian sense, to designate a power or ability.)

As a state, "consciousness" is: *awareness*—the condition of an organism in cognizing, perceiving, or sensing.

The concept of consciousness as a state, the state of awareness, is a primary; it cannot be broken down any further or defined by reference to other concepts; there are no other concepts to which it can be reduced. It is the basic psychological concept and category to which all other psychological terms ultimately must refer; only in the context of the phenomenon of awareness as one's root concept can such concepts as "thought," "idea," "perception," "imagination," "memory," "emotion," or "desire" be intelligible. One can investigate the structural and functional conditions in an organism that are necessary for the existence of consciousness; one can inquire into the neurophysiological *means* of consciousness (such as sensory receptors, afferent nerves, etc.); one can differentiate levels and forms of consciousness. But the concept of *consciousness* as such is an irreducible primary.

It is what Ayn Rand has termed an *"axiomatic concept."* She writes:

> Axioms are usually considered to be propositions identifying a fundamental, self-evident truth. But explicit propositions as such are not primaries: they are made of concepts. The base of man's knowledge—of all other concepts, all axioms, propositions and thought—consists of axiomatic concepts.
>
> An axiomatic concept is the identification of a primary fact of reality, which cannot be analyzed, i.e., reduced to other facts or broken into component parts. . . . It is the fundamentally given and directly perceived or experienced, which requires no proof or explanation, but on which all proofs and explanations rest.
>
> The first and primary axiomatic concepts are "existence," "identity" (which is a corollary of "existence") and "consciousness." One can study what exists and how consciousness functions; but one cannot analyze (or "prove") existence as such, or consciousness as such. These are irreducible primaries. (An attempt to "prove" them is self-contradictory: it is an attempt to "prove" existence by means of non-existence, and consciousness by means of unconsciousness).[1]

That mental processes are correlated with neural processes in the brain, in no way affects the status of consciousness as a unique and irreducible primary. It is a species of what philosophers term "the reductive fallacy" to assert that mental processes are "nothing but" neural processes—that, for example, the perception of an object *is* a collection of neural impulses, or that a thought *is* a certain pattern of brain activity. A perception and the neural processes that mediate it are not identical, nor are a thought and the brain activity that may accompany it. Such an equation is flagrantly anti-empirical and logically absurd.

As one philosopher observes:

> [Reductive materialism] maintains that consciousness *is a form of brain activity;*—that it is either some fine and subtle kind of matter, or (more commonly) some form of energy, either kinetic or potential. . . . To say that consciousness *is* a form of matter or of motion is to use words without meaning. . . . Argument against any given position must regularly take the general form of the *reductio ad absurdum.* He therefore, who chooses at the beginning a position which is as absurd as any that can be imagined is in the happy situation of being armor proof against all argument. He can never be "reduced to the absurd" because he is already there. If he cannot see that, though consciousness and motion may be *related* as intimately as you please, we *mean* different things by the two words, that though consciousness may be *caused* by motion, it *is* not itself what we mean by motion any more than it is green cheese—if he cannot see this there is no arguing with him.[2]

To quote another philosopher:

> We speak of an idea as clear or confused, as apposite or inapposite, as witty or dull. Are such terms intelligible when applied to those motions of electrons, atoms, molecules, or muscles, which for [the reductive materialist] are all there is to consciousness? Can a motion be clear, or cogent, or witty? What exactly would a clear motion be like? What sort of thing is a germane or cogent reflex? Or a witty muscular reaction? These adjectives are perfectly in order when applied to ideas; they become at once absurd when applied to movements in muscle or nerve. . . .
>
> On the other side, movements have attributes which are unthinkable as applied to ideas. Movements have velocity; but what is the average velocity of one's ideas on a protective tariff?

> Movements have direction; would there be any sense in talking of
> the north-easterly direction of one's thought on the morality of
> revenge?[3]

It is true that whereas matter can exist apart from consciousness, consciousness cannot exist apart from matter, i.e., apart from a living organism. But this dependence of consciousness on matter does not in any way support the claim that they are identical. On the contrary: as more than one critic of reductive materialism has pointed out, it is reasonable to speak of one thing being dependent on another only if they are *not* identical.

In the writings of Aristotle, one finds a treatment of consciousness (and of life) that is signally superior to the approach of most "moderns." There are many respects in which, when one studies the history of philosophy, moving from Aristotle to Descartes to the present, one feels as though history were moving backward, not forward—as if most of Aristotle's successors down through the ages have been pre-Aristotelians. Aristotle is neither a mystic nor a "materialist"; he does not regard consciousness as *supernatural,* as an incomprehensible and irksome presence in a mechanistic universe, to be banished by reduction to the blind motion of inanimate particles, like an exile whom the authorities found discomfiting. To Aristotle, consciousness is a natural fact of reality, the characteristic attribute of certain entities. In this issue, his approach is far more "empirical" than that of most "empiricists." His example should serve as a lead to those who desire to pursue a genuinely scientific study of conscious living organisms.[4]

The only consciousness of which one has direct and immediate knowledge is one's own. One knows the consciousness of other beings only indirectly, inferentially, through outward physical expression in action. This does not mean that one can achieve exhaustive knowledge of the nature and laws of mental activity, merely by introspection. It means that each man can directly experience only his *own* consciousness; the consciousness of other beings can never be the object of his direct perception of experience.

Communication among men concerning psychological states is possible because each man has his own inner psychological laboratory to which he can refer.

To clarify this metaphor: if a man has never had the experience of sight, there is no way to communicate the experience to him. No discussion of light waves, retinas, rods, and cones could make sight meaningful to a man who has been blind since birth. Like the basic attributes of physical objects, such as extension and mass, the basic categories of consciousness can be defined only *ostensively*, i.e., by reference to direct experience. Just as *extro*spective ostensive definitions are indispensable to any communication among men concerning the physical world, so *intro*spective ostensive definitions are indispensable to any communication concerning the psychological realm. These extrospective and introspective observables are the base on which all more complex concepts, and all subsequent, inferential knowledge, are built.

Introspection is the first source of one's psychological knowledge; and without introspection no other avenue of psychological knowledge could be significant or meaningful, even if it were possible. The study of behavior, or of the descriptive self-reports of other men, or of cultures and cultural products, would yield one nothing—if one had no apprehension of such phenomena as ideas, beliefs, memories, emotions, desires, to which one could relate one's observations and in terms of which one could interpret one's findings. (Strictly speaking, of course, it is absurd to imagine that, if one had no awareness of such categories, one could be engaged in the study of *anything*.)

While introspection is a necessary condition and source of psychological knowledge, it is not sufficient by itself—neither one's own introspection nor the introspective reports of others. Psychology requires the study of the outward manifestations and expressions of mental activity: behavior. Consciousness is the regulator of action. Consciousness cannot be fully understood without reference to behavior, and behavior cannot be understood without reference to consciousness; man is neither a disembodied ghost nor an automaton. Scientific psychology requires that the data of introspection and the observations of beings in action be systematically integrated into coherent knowledge. A theory, to be valid, must integrate all and contradict none of the relevant evidence or data; and this entails the necessity of taking cognizance of everything that *is* relevant.

In the light of the foregoing, it is appropriate to comment briefly on a curious phenomenon in modern psychology: the doctrine of behaviorism.

The Revolt Against Consciousness

In order, allegedly, to establish psychology as a "genuine science," on a part with the physical sciences, behaviorism proposes the following program: to dispense with the concept of consciousness, to abandon all concern with "mythical" mental states, and to study exclusively an organism's behavior—i.e., to restrict psychology to the study of physical motions. For this reason, a writer on the history of psychology aptly entitled his chapter on behaviorism, "Psychology out of its Mind."[5]

Sometimes a distinction is made between "radical behaviorism" and "methodological behaviorism." Radical behaviorism is explicit reductive materialism; it holds that mind *is* a series of bodily responses, such as muscular and glandular reactions. The gross untenability of this doctrine has already been noted. The advocates of methodological behaviorism frequently repudiate this doctrine as "unsophisticated" and "philosophical." *Their* form of behaviorism, they insist, makes no metaphysical commitment whatever, i.e., no commitment about the fundamental nature of man or of mind; it is entirely *procedural;* it merely holds that consciousness—whatever that might be—is not an object of scientific study; and that scientific psychology must confine itself to an analysis of observed behavior without reference to mentalistic data and without recourse to any concepts derived by means of introspection.

A methodology, however, to be valid, must be appropriate to its subject. Therefore, it necessarily entails a view of the nature of its subject. Methodological behaviorism implies that the organisms which psychology studies are such that their behavior *can be understood* without reference to consciousness. And this, clearly, is a metaphysical position.

Methodological behaviorists may wish to deny that they are reductive materialists. But then, as a minimum, their doctrine entails a belief in another, no more promising version of materialism: *epiphenomenalism*—the doctrine that consciousness is merely an incidental by-product of physical processes (as smoke is a by-product of a locomotive), and that conscious events have no causal efficacy, neither with regard to bodily events nor to other mental events, i.e., one's thoughts do not have the power to affect either one's actions or one's subsequent thoughts. Thus, epiphenomenalism commits its advocates to the position that the history of the human race would be exactly the same if no one had ever been conscious of anything, if no one had any perceptions or thoughts. As a philosophical position, epiphenomenalism is scarcely more defensible than reductive materialism; neither is very impressive in the light of even a cursory logical analysis.

The difference between these two variations of behaviorism is, for any practical purpose, nonexistent. Both agree that consciousness is *irrelevant* to psychology and to behavior; this is the essence of their position.

The behaviorist has been conspicuously reluctant to enunciate the conclusions to which his theory leads. He has not, for instance, felt obliged to declare: "Since phenomena of consciousness are illusory or irrelevant to explanations of behavior, and since this includes *my* behavior, nothing that I may think, understand or perceive (whatever these terms mean) bears any causal relation to the things I do or the theories I advocate."

When a person puts forth a doctrine which amounts to the assertion either that he is not conscious or that it makes no difference to him (and should make no difference to others) whether he is conscious or not—the irresistible temptation is to agree with him.

Many writers, of the most varied and divergent viewpoints, have exposed the arbitrariness, the contradictions, and the epistemological barbarism of the behaviorist theory.[6] It is unnecessary to review their criticisms here. Behaviorists, in line with their general policy of dismissing those aspects of reality which they find it inconvenient to consider, have not attempted, for the most part, to answer these criticisms; they have ignored them.

The chief focus of the behaviorists' attack is on the psychologist's use of introspection. Their argument is as follows: Psychology has failed to establish itself as a science or to produce any genuine knowledge; the fault lies in the psychologist's reliance on introspection; the physical sciences, which are far more advanced, do not employ introspection; therefore, psychology should abandon introspection and emulate the methods of the physical sciences; it should, like physics, study the actions of material entities, i.e., study observable behavior.

This program has led, on the part of behaviorists, to an orgy of "experiments" and "measurements," with only this difference from the physical sciences: that behaviorists have been notoriously unclear as to what their experiments are to accomplish, *what* they are measuring, *why* they are measuring it, or what they expect to *know* when their measurements are completed. The practical success of their program has been nil. (This does not mean that every experiment performed by an advocate of behaviorism necessarily has been valueless; but that its value, if any, bears no intrinsic relation to the behaviorist thesis, i.e., the experiment did not require or depend on the experimenter's commitment to behaviorism. Behaviorists were scarcely the first to recognize that psychology requires, among other things, the study of behavior under experimentally controlled conditions.)

It is true that psychology has failed as yet to establish itself as a science; it is also true that classical introspectionists, such as Wundt, Titchener, and members of the so-called Würzburg school, were guilty of grave errors in their concept of the nature, scope, and methods of psychology. But the behaviorist program represents, not a solution or a step forward, but the abdication of psychology as such.

While posturing as the expression of scientific *objectivity*, behaviorism, in fact, represents a collapse to methodological *subjectivism*. To be objective is to be concerned with *facts*, excluding one's wishes, hopes, or fears from cognitive consideration; objectivity rests on the principle that that which is, *is*, that facts are not created or altered by the wishes or beliefs of the perceiver. If, therefore, a scientist decides to study a given aspect of reality, objectivity requires that he adjust his methods of investigation to the nature of the field being studied; ends determine means; he does *not*, arbitrarily, because it suits his convenience, select certain methods of investigation and then decree that only those facts are relevant which are amenable to his methods.

No one, including the behaviorist, can escape the knowledge (a) that he is conscious and (b) that *this is a fact about himself of the greatest importance*, a fact which is indispensable to any meaningful account of his behavior. If the behaviorist is unequal to the task of formulating scientific epistemological principles for the use of introspection and for the integration of introspective data with psychological data obtained by other means, he is not justified in seeking to reduce an entire field to the level of his inadequacy. Arbitrarily to define the nature of conscious organisms in such a way as to justify one's preferred method of study, is subjectivism.

Behaviorists frequently attempt to defend their position by means of an epistemological confusion which they did not originate, but which is very common today among psychologists and philosophers: the argument that since states of consciousness are "private," and since, therefore, they are not "publicly observable," they cannot be the subject of objective, scientific knowledge.

Phenomena of consciousness *are* "private," in the sense indicated earlier, namely, that the only consciousness a man can experience *directly* is his own. But, as was also indicated, the inferences a psychologist makes, on the basis of his introspection, concerning the nature and functions of consciousness, may be checked by his fellow workers, who also have recourse to introspection—just as one scientist checks on the reported findings of another by repeating the other's experiment in his own laboratory. If psychologists sometimes disagree about what they perceive, or about the correct interpretation of what they perceive, this is true of physical scientists also. And the method of resolving such differences is, in principle, the same: to investigate further, to compare data more carefully, to define terms more precisely, to explore other, possibly relevant facts, to check their conclusions in the light of the rest of their knowledge, to search for contradictions or *non sequiturs* in their reports.

The objectivity of one's conclusions depends, not on whether they are derived from "publicly observable" data, but on (a) whether they are true (i.e., consonant with the facts of reality), and on (b) the rationality of one's method of arriving at them. Conclusions arrived at by a rational method can be confirmed by other men and are, in this sense, "publicly verifiable." But the objective and the publicly observable (or verifiable) are not synonymous.

Whatever men may learn from one another, each man, epistemologically, is alone; *knowing* is not a social process. If one man's judgment is unreliable and nonobjective, because it is his own, a hundred unreliable, nonobjective judgments will not yield a reliable, objective one.

So much for the mystique of the "publicly observable."

The behaviorist assault on consciousness merely represents the extreme of a more general trend in modern psychology and philosophy: the tendency to regard consciousness or mind with suspicious hostility, as a disturbing, "unnatural" phenomenon which somehow must be explained away or, at the last, barred from the realm of the scientifically knowable.

For centuries, *mystics* have asserted that phenomena of consciousness are outside the reach of reason and science. The modern "scientific" apostles of the anti-mind agree. While proclaiming themselves exponents of reason and enemies of supernaturalism, they announce, in effect, that only insentient matter is "natural"— and thereby surrender man's consciousness to mysticism. They have conceded to the mystics a victory which the mystics could not have won on their own.

It is from such *neo*mysticism that a genuinely scientific psychology must reclaim man's mind as a proper object of rational study.

Chapter Two

| Man: A Living Being

Needs and Capacities

From the simplest unicellular animal to man, the most complex of organisms, all living entities possess a characteristic structure, the component parts of which function in such a way as to preserve the integrity of that structure, thereby maintaining the life of the organism.

An organism has been described, correctly, as being not an aggregate, but an integrate. When an organism ceases to perform the actions necessary to maintain its structural integrity, it dies. Death is *dis*integration. When the life of the organism ends, what remains is merely a collection of decomposing chemical compounds.

For all living entities, action is a necessity of survival. Life is motion, a process of self-sustaining action that an organism must carry on constantly in order to remain in existence. This principle is equally evident in the simple energy-conversions of the plant and in the long-range, complex activities of man. Biologically, inactivity is death.

The action that an organism must perform is both internal, as in the process of metabolism, and external, as in the process of seeking food.

The pattern of all self-preserving action is, in essence, as follows: *an organism maintains itself by taking materials which exist in its environment, transforming or rearranging them, and thereby converting them into the means of its own survival.*

Consider the processes of nutrition, respiration, and synthesis, which, together with their related functions, comprise metabolism.

17

Through the process of nutrition, the raw materials the organism needs are brought into its system; through respiration (oxidation), energy is then extracted from these raw materials; a part of this energy is then used in the process of synthesis which transforms the raw materials into structural components of living matter. The remaining energy, together with all the structural components, makes possible the continuation of the organism's self-maintaining activity. Metabolism characterizes all living species.

But now consider an example of the wider principle involved, that is peculiar to man: the activity of harnessing a waterfall in order to obtain the electric energy needed to power a factory engaged in the manufacture of farm equipment or clothing or automobiles or drugs. Here, the action is external rather than internal, behavioral rather than metabolic; but the basic principle of life remains the same.

The existence of life is conditional; an organism always faces the possibility of death. Its survival depends on the fulfillment of certain conditions. It must generate the biologically appropriate course of action. What course of action is appropriate, is determined by the nature of the particular organism. Different species survive in different ways.

An organism maintains itself by exercising its *capacities* in order to satisfy its *needs*. The actions possible to and characteristic of a given species, are to be understood in terms of its *specific* needs and capacities. These constitute its basic behavioral context.

"Need" and "capacity" are used here in their fundamental, metaphysical sense (by "metaphysical," I mean: pertaining to the nature of things); in this context, "need" and "capacity" refer to what which is innate and universal to the species, not to that which is acquired and peculiar to the individual.

An organism's *needs* are those things which the organism, by its nature, requires for its life and well-being—i.e., for its efficacious continuation of the life-process. An organism's *capacities* are its inherent potentialities for action.

The concept of needs and capacities is fundamental to biology and psychology alike. Biology is concerned with the needs and capacities of living organisms *qua* physical entities. Psychology is concerned with the needs and capacities of living organisms *qua* conscious entities.

Just as man possesses specific psychological capacities, by virtue of his distinctive form of consciousness, his conceptual faculty—so, by virtue of this same faculty, he possesses specific psychological needs. (I shall discuss some of these needs in Part Two.)

When a physical or psychological need fails to be fulfilled, the result is danger to the organism: pain, debilitation, destruction. However, needs differ (a) in the degree of their temporal urgency, and (b) in the form of the threat which they potentially pose. This is most easily seen in the case of physical needs, but the principle applies to all needs.

(a) Man has a need of oxygen and of food; but whereas he can survive for days without food, he can survive for only minutes without oxygen. Man can survive much longer without Vitamin C than without water; but both are needs. In some cases, the frustration of a need results in immediate death; in other cases, the process can take years.

(b) Man has a need to maintain his body temperature at a certain level; he has internal adaptive mechanisms which adjust to changes in the external environment. If he is exposed to extreme temperatures beyond the power of his adaptive mechanisms to cope with, he suffers pain and, within a few hours, dies. In such a case, the disastrous consequences of need-frustration are direct and readily discernible; similarly with oxygen deprivation, food deprivation, etc. But there are instances of need-frustration in which the sequence of disaster is much less direct. For example, man has a need of calcium; there are regions in Mexico where the soil contains no calcium; the inhabitants of these regions do not perish outright, but their growth is stunted, they are generally debilitated, and they are prey to many diseases to which the lack of calcium makes them highly susceptible. *They are impaired in their general ability to function.* Thus, a need-frustration does not have to result in the organism's destruction *directly;* instead, it can undermine the organism's overall capacity to live, and thus make the organism vulnerable to destruction from many different sources. (This principle is important to remember in considering the frustration of *psychological* needs; we will have occasion to recall it in Chapter Twelve.)

Science comes to discover man's various needs through the consequences that occur when they are frustrated. Needs announce themselves through signals of pain, illness, and death. (If, somehow, a need were always and everywhere satisfied automatically—if no one ever suffered from any frustration of the need—it is difficult to surmise how scientists would be able to isolate and identify it.)

Even when symptoms do appear, it is often a long process to discover the underlying need-deprivation. Men died of scurvy for many centuries before scientists traced the causal connection to a lack of green vegetables; and only in comparatively recent history did they learn that the crucial ingredient supplied by the vegetables is Vitamin C.

Man is an integrated organism, and it is not surprising that the frustration of physical needs sometimes produces psychological symptoms—and that the frustration of psychological needs sometimes produces physical symptoms. As an example of the first: the hallucinations and loss of memory that can result from a deficiency of thiamin. As an example of the second: any psychosomatic illness—migraine headaches, peptic ulcers, etc.

It is the conditional nature of life that gives rise to the concept of need. If a being were indestructible—if it were not confronted with the alternative of life or death—it would have no needs. The concept could not be applicable to it. Without the concept of *life*, the concept of *need* would not be possible.

"Need" implies the existence of a goal, result, or end: the survival of the organism. Therefore, *in order to maintain that something is a physical or psychological need, one must demonstrate that it is a causal condition of the organism's survival and well-being.*

While biologists recognize this fact, many psychologists do not. They ascribe to man a wide variety of psychological needs, without offering any justification for their claims, as though the positing of needs were a matter of arbitrary choice. They seldom specify by what criterion they judge what are or are not needs; nor do they show how or why their lists of alleged needs are entailed by man's nature as a living organism.

Among the things that various psychologists have asserted to be inherent needs of man are the following: to dominate other men, to submit to a leader, to bargain, to gamble, to gain social prestige, to snub someone, to be hostile, to be unconventional, to be a conformist, to deprecate oneself, to boast, to murder, to suffer pain.

These so-called needs, it must be emphasized, are held by their advocates to be *innate and universal to the human species.*

A *desire* or a *wish* is not the equivalent of a *need.* The fact that a great many men may desire a thing, does not prove that it represents a need inherent in human nature. Needs must be *objectively demonstrable.* This should be obvious. But there are few facts that have been more recklessly ignored by most psychologists.

Perhaps the most remarkable "need" ever posited by a psychologist is the one propounded by Sigmund Freud in his theory of the "death instinct."[1] According to Freud, human behavior is to be understood in terms of instincts—specifically, the life instinct and the death instinct. The latter is the more powerful, says Freud, since all men eventually do die. These instincts, he claims, represent innate biological needs; man has a biological need to experience pain and to perish; in every cell of man's body there is a "will to die," an urge to "return" to an inorganic condition, to "re-establish a state of things which was disturbed by the emergence of life."[2]

This theory represents the extreme of what can happen when psychologists permit themselves to speculate about needs while ignoring the context in which the concept arises and the standard by which needs are to be established.

A need is that which an organism requires for its survival; the consequence of frustrating a need is pain and/or death; the postulate of a death instinct, of a need to die, of a need to experience pain, is literally meaningless. It is only on the premise of life as the goal that the concept of a biological need can be meaningful. The concept of a need to die—like the concept of a square circle—is a contradiction in terms.

If man fails to fulfill his *actual* needs, nature threatens him with pain and death—but what does nature threaten him with if he fails to fulfill his alleged need to suffer and die?

To move from the observation that all living things die to the conclusion that there exists within every cell of man's body a "will to die," is grotesque anthropomorphism. And to speak of an organism's urge to "return" to an inorganic condition, "to re-establish a state of things which was disturbed by the emergence of life," is to be guilty of the crudest violation of logic: an organism does not exist prior to its existence; it cannot "return" to non-existence; it cannot be "disturbed" by the emergence of itself. *Beyond the Pleasure Principle*—the monograph in which Freud presents his theory of the death instinct—is surely one of the most embarrassing productions in all psychological literature.

While the task of isolating and identifying man's physical needs is far from completed, biology has made enormous advances in this direction. With regard to the task of isolating and identifying man's mental needs, psychology is in a state of chaos.

This chaos serves, however, to emphasize the fact that the nature of man's needs has to be *discovered*. Needs are not self-evident. Alleged needs must be *proven* by relating them to the requirements of man's survival.

That man possesses psychological needs is indisputable. The widespread phenomenon of mental illness is evidence both of the existence of needs (which are being thwarted) and of the failure of psychology to understand the nature of these needs.

Needs, Goals, and "Instincts"

The psychologist, seeking to understand the principles of human behavior, observes (a) that man, as a biological entity, possesses various needs, and (b) that man characteristically acts to achieve various ends or goals.

It is the existence of needs that creates the necessity of action—i.e., of goal-seeking. Even when the goals a particular man selects are incompatible with his needs, so that he is pursuing a course of self-destruction, this principle still remains true.

The basic problem of motivational psychology may be formulated as follows: to bridge the gap between needs and goals—to trace the steps from the former to the latter—to understand the connection between them, i.e., to understand how needs get translated into goals.

It should be obvious that the solution of this problem requires a consideration of man's distinctive *capacities*. Yet in large measure, the history of motivational psychology represents an attempt to bypass man's most distinctively *human* capacity, his conceptual faculty, and to account for his behavior without reference to the fact that man can reason or that his mind is his basic means of survival.

The behaviorist projection of man as a stimulus-response machine is one version of this attempt. The projection of man as a conscious automaton, activated by *instincts,* is another.

The function which the concept of "demon" served for the primitive savage and the concept of "God" serves for the theologian, is served for many psychologists by the concept of "instinct"—a term denoting nothing scientifically intelligible, while creating the illusion of causal understanding. What a savage could not comprehend, he "explained" by postulating a demon; what a theologian cannot comprehend, he "explains" by postulating a God; what many psychologists cannot comprehend, they "explain" by postulating an instinct.

"Instinct" is a concept intended to bridge the gap between needs and goals, bypassing man's cognitive (i.e., reasoning and learning) faculty. As such, it represents one of the most disastrous and sterile attempts to deal with the problem of motivation.

Instinct theory enjoyed an enormous vogue in the eighteenth and nineteenth centuries and in the early years of the twentieth. Although its influence has been declining for the past several decades, it is still a major pillar of the (orthodox) Freudian school of psychoanalysis.

Observing certain types of behavior which they believed to be characteristic of the human species, instinct theorists decided that the causes of such behavior are innate, unchosen, and unlearned tendencies which drive man to act as he does. Thus, they spoke of a survival instinct, a parental instinct, an acquisitive instinct, a pugnacity instinct, and so forth. They seldom attempted to define precisely what they understood an instinct to be; still less did they trouble to explain how it functioned; they vied with one another in compiling lists of the instincts their particular theory assumed man to possess, promising to account thereby for the ultimate sources of all human action.

The most prominent of these theorists were William James, William McDougall, and Sigmund Freud. "Instinct," writes James, "is . . . the faculty of acting in such a way as to produce certain ends, without foresight of the ends, and without previous education in the performance."[3] "We may, then," writes McDougall, "define instinct as an inherited or innate psycho-physical disposition which determines its possessor to perceive, and to pay attention to, objects of a certain class, to experience an emotional excitement of a particular quality upon perceiving such an object, and to act in regard to it in a particular manner, or, at least, to experience an impulse to such action."[4] If these definitions are less than illuminating, Freud's formulation is outstanding in its unclarity. Freud writes of "instinct" as "a borderland concept between the mental and the physical, being both the mental representative of the stimuli emanating from within the organism and penetrating to the mind, and at the same time a measure of the demand made upon the energy of the latter in consequence of its connection with the body."[5] In spite of the central role that instincts play in his system, this is as close as Freud ever comes to a definition.

That mysterious force, "instinct," is not a thought or an action or an emotion or a need. The attempt, on the part of some theorists, to identify an instinct as a "compound reflex" has been recognized as unsupportable and has collapsed. A reflex is a specific, definable neurophysiological phenomenon, the existence of which is empirically demonstrable; it is not a dumping ground for ununderstood behavior.[6]

To account for man's actions in terms of undefinable "instincts" is to contribute nothing to human knowledge: it is only to confess that one does not know why man acts as he does. To observe that men engage in sexual activities and to conclude that man has a "sex instinct"—to observe that men seek food when they are hungry and to conclude that man has a "hunger instinct"—to observe that some men act destructively and to conclude that man has a "destructive instinct"—to observe that men usually seek out one another's company and to conclude that man has a "gregarious instinct"—is to explain *nothing*. It is merely to place oneself in the same epistemological category as the physician in the anecdote who "explains" to a distraught mother that the reason why her child will not drink milk is that "the child is just not a milk-drinker."

The history of instinct theory, in the past fifty years, is the history of intense efforts, on the part of its supporters, to twist the meaning of language, of their formulations and of the facts of reality, in order to protect their doctrines from science's growing recognition that traits and activities alleged to be "instinctive" are either: (a) not universal to the species, but a product of particular men's acquired attitudes or beliefs, as in the case of pugnacity; or (b) the product of learning, as in the case of sexual behavior—which is so simple for the organism to attain, that virtually all members of the species who develop normally, exhibit it; and/or (c) the product of the interaction of simple reflexes and learning, as in the case of an infant's sucking behavior.

The concept of "instinct" was first used to account for complex patterns of animal behavior, such as migratory, mating, and maternal behavior, that appeared inexplicable. But the concept is no less misleading when applied to animals.

There are, in principle, three categories in terms of which animal behavior can be explained. 1. Actions which are neurophysiological responses to physical stimuli, i.e., reflexes, and which do not involve the faculty of consciousness—such as the patellar reflex (knee jerk) in response to tendon stretch. 2. Actions which are guided directly by an animal's pleasure-pain sensory apparatus, and which involve the faculty of consciousness but not a process of learning—such as moving toward warmth. (Some students of animal behavior use the term "instinct" exclusively to designate behavior of this second category; when thus restricted in meaning, the use of the term may be defensible; but I am inclined to think it inadvisable, in view of the many other meanings historically associated with the term; at any rate, when I speak of "instinct" in this discussion, I refer to the term as it is commonly used by clinical psychologists and personality theorists—to cover a good deal more than behavior of this second category.) 3. Actions which are the result of learning—such as hunting and fighting. (Sometimes—and this is especially relevant to allegedly instinctive behavior—the learning is instantaneous, within a given context, and is virtually inescapable to all normal members of a species; this is "one trial" learning; for instance, avoiding a traumatically painful stimulus after one encounter.)

Animal behavior that has not been traced to one of these categories, or (more usually) to some combination of them, *has not been explained.*[7]

The inadequacy of "explanation via instincts" is still more apparent when one considers the complex goal-seeking activity of *man.*

Man is born with needs, but he is not born with a knowledge of those needs and of how to satisfy them. Some of his simpler, vegetative body-maintenance needs are satisfied automatically, given the appropriate physical environment, by the function of his internal organs—such as the need of oxygen, which is satisfied by the automatic function of his respiratory system. But the broad range of his more complex needs—all those needs which require the integrated action of his total entity in relation to the external world—are *not* satisfied automatically. Man does not obtain food, shelter, or clothing "by instinct." To grow food, to build a shelter, to weave cloth, requires consciousness, choice, discrimination, judgment. Man's body does not have the power to pursue such goals of its own volition, it does not have the power purposefully to rearrange the elements of nature, to reshape matter, independent of his consciousness, knowledge, and values.

All purposeful action aims at the achievement of a value. Things which can satisfy needs become objects of action only when they are chosen (in some form) as values.

Value and *action* imply and necessitate each other: it is in the nature of a value that action is required to achieve and/or maintain it; it is in the nature of a consciously initiated action that its motive and purpose is the achievement and/or maintenance of a value.

But values are not innate. Having no innate knowledge of what is true or false, man can have no innate knowledge of what is for him or against him, what is to be pursued or avoided, what is good for him or evil.

Unsatisfied, unfulfilled needs can set up a state of tension or disquietude or pain in man, thus prompting him to seek biologically appropriate actions, such as protecting himself against the elements. But the necessity of learning what *is* the appropriate action cannot be bypassed.

His body provides man only with signals of pain or pleasure; but it does not tell him their causes, it does not tell him how to alleviate one or achieve the other. *That* must be learned by his mind.

Man must *discover* the actions his life requires: he has no "instinct of self-preservation." It was not an instinct that enabled man to make fire, to build bridges, to perform surgery, to design a telescope: it was his capacity to think. And if a man chooses *not* to think—if he chooses to risk his life in senseless dangers, to close his eyes rather than open his mind at the sight of any problem, to seek escape from the responsibility of reason in alcohol or drugs, to act in willfully stubborn defiance of his own objective self-interest—he has no instinct that will force his mind to function, no instinct that will compel him to value his life sufficiently to do the thinking and perform the actions which his life requires.

The flagrantly self-destructive practices in which so many men engage—and the suicidal course that characterizes so much of human history—are an eloquent refutation and mockery of the claim that man has an instinct of self-preservation.

Recognizing some of the difficulties which an alleged instinct of self-preservation presents, Freud sought a way out of the dilemma by announcing that, *in addition* to possessing a life instinct, man *also* possesses a death instinct. This theory has largely fallen into disrepute. But his fellow instinct theorists have no right to laugh at Freud. If one is determined to account for human behavior by reference to instincts, and if (as virtually all instinct theorists do) one holds that man has an instinct of self-preservation, one might well feel compelled to posit a counteracting death instinct—in order to make men's actions explicable.

If such a thing as an "instinct" could exist, it would have to be some sort of innate, automatic knowledge, some sort of frozen information inscribed in the nervous system at birth. Instinct theory thus amounts to a resurrection of the doctrine of innate ideas, which has been thoroughly discredited by both philosophy and biology as a legacy of mysticism.

The mythology of instinct is disastrous to scientific theory, because, by offering a *pseudo-*explanation, it halts further inquiry and thus stands as an obstacle to a genuine understanding of the causes of human behavior. It should be discarded as the last, dying convulsion of medieval demonology.

In place of recourse to such primitive constructs, motivational psychology requires an analysis of the implications of the fact that man's biological distinction and basic tool of need-satisfaction is his rational faculty.

| **Man: A Rational Being**

Mind

"Consciousness," in the primary meaning of the term, designates a state: the state of being conscious or aware of some aspect of reality. In a derivative usage, "consciousness" designates a faculty: that faculty in man by virtue of which he is able to be conscious or aware of reality.

The concept of "mind" has a narrower application than that of "consciousness" and is associated specifically with the concept of "reason" or "rational faculty." This association provides the key to its definition and appropriate usage.

In varying forms or degrees, consciousness is found in many species of animal (and perhaps all). But the capacity to reason—to perform explicit conceptual integrations, guided by logic—is unique to man. It is his rational or conceptual faculty that constitutes man's distinctive form of consciousness. It is to this form of consciousness that the term "mind" applies.

"Mind" designates specifically *man's* consciousness (or form of consciousness)—in contradistinction to the forms of consciousness exhibited by lower animals.

The Conceptual Level of Consciousness

It is characteristic of the state of contemporary thought that if one speaks of advocating a biologically oriented or biocentric psychology, the listener is very likely to assume that one is concerned with studying man with his head omitted, i.e., without reference to his mind or his power of conceptual thought.

Yet the behavioristic or physicalistic or "guillotine" approach to man is profoundly antibiological. In the study of a living species, the biologist is vitally interested in learning the nature of that species' distinctive means of survival—since he recognizes that such information constitutes an indispensable key to the species' behavior. In the case of man, it is clear that *his* distinctive way of dealing with reality, of maintaining his existence, is through the exercise of his conceptual faculty. All of his unique attainments—scientific knowledge, technological and industrial achievements, art, culture, social institutions, etc.—proceed from and are made possible by his ability to think. It is upon his ability to think that his life depends. A biocentric approach, therefore, requires that one grant prime importance to man's conceptual faculty in the study of his behavior.

The ultimate source of all man's knowledge is the evidence of reality provided by his senses. Through the stimulation of his various sensory receptors, man receives information which travels to his brain in the form of sensations (primary sensory inputs). These sensory inputs, as such, do not constitute knowledge; they are only the material of knowledge. Man's brain automatically retains and integrates these sensations—thereby forming *percepts*. Percepts constitute the starting point and base of man's knowledge: the direct awareness of entities, their actions and their attributes.

In our discussion of the nature of living organisms (Chapter Two), we saw that an organism sustains itself physically by taking materials from the environment, reorganizing them and achieving a new integration which converts these materials into the organism's means of survival. We can observe an analogous phenomenon in the process by which a consciousness apprehends reality. Just as integration is the cardinal principle of life, so it is the cardinal principle of knowledge. This principle is operative when, in the brains of men or animals, disparate sensations are automatically retained and integrated (by nature's "programming," in effect) in such a way as to produce a perceptual awareness of entities—an awareness which men and animals require for their survival. (The principle of integration is central, as we shall see, to the process of concept-formation also—except that here the integration is not automatic or "programmed" by nature; conceptual integration must be achieved volitionally by man.)

It has been an issue of controversy whether or not any animals under man have the ability to rise above the perceptual level and form even primitive concepts. Mortimer J. Adler, in his scholarly work *The Difference of Man and the Difference It Makes,* presents a comprehensive review and analysis of the evidence and arguments on both sides of the controversy, and argues persuasively for the negative view. In my judgment, he has provided an unanswerable case to support the conclusion that there are no valid grounds for attributing concepts to any animal other than man, that man is truly unique among living species in being the conceptualizing animal.[1]

It is extremely doubtful if the lowest forms of conscious organisms are capable even of perceptions. The likeliest hypothesis is that they are capable of receiving and reacting only to disparate, unretained, and unintegrated sensations.

The higher forms of conscious life, under man, exhibit the ability of forming not only separate, unconnected percepts, but, in addition, "perceptual residues" and "perceptual abstractions." Perceptual residues (or perceptual traces) are "memory-images that function representatively, i.e., in place of sensory stimuli that are no longer themselves operative."[2] Perceptual abstraction refers to the process whereby the animal is able to recognize similarities and differences among sensible particulars, to recognize that a number of sensible particulars are *of the same kind* and are different from other sensible particulars. This ability accounts for the highest expressions of "intelligence" that animals under man exhibit; but this ability does not, as such, require or imply the capacity to form concepts, which consists not merely of recognizing that a number of sensible particulars are of the same kind, but of identifying explicitly *of what the kind consists.*

In his illuminating analysis of the idea of perceptual abstractions, Adler writes:

> For example, when an animal has acquired the disposition to discriminate between triangles and circles—in spite of differences in their size, shape, color or position, and whether or not they are constituted by continuous lines or dots—that acquired disposition in the animal is the perceptual attainment I have called a perceptual abstraction. This disposition is only operative in the presence of an appropriate sensory stimulus, and never in its absence, i.e., the animal does not exercise its acquired disposition to recognize

certain shapes as triangles or certain colors as red when a triangular shape or a red patch is not perceptually present and actually perceived.[3]

What is the nature of the immense intellectual leap that takes place with the development in man of the ability to form concepts? What is the nature of the ascent from the ability to perceive various green-colored objects to the ability to form the concept "green"—to move from the perception of individual chairs to the concept "chair"—to move from the perception of individual men to the concept "man"?

To appreciate the nature of the tremendous increase of intellectual power made possible by man's conceptualizing ability, it is necessary to realize the extreme limitations of an exclusively perceptual form of awareness. The number of units that *any* consciousness—human or animal—can hold in its field of awareness at any given moment, is necessarily small. A consciousness that is restricted only to those sensible particulars it can immediately perceive is severely restricted in its ability to accumulate or expand its knowledge. This is the state of all animals under man.

The ascent to the conceptual level of consciousness entails two related factors: the ability to categorize numerous particulars into groups or classes, according to a distinguishing characteristic(s) they exhibit in common—and the ability to develop or acquire a system of symbols that represents these various classes, so that a single symbol, held in a man's mind, can stand for an unlimited number of particulars.

The method of classification is concept-formation. The system of symbols is language.

By way of illustration, let us consider one of the first and simplest concepts a child forms—that of "chair." The first stage consists of his perceptual recognition that several objects are similar, similar specifically in shape, and are different from all other objects in regard to that characteristic. He is aware of that similarity on a visual, nonverbal level, and his mind gropes for some way to hold that awareness in permanent form. The first form in which that awareness is retained is a vague image, an image that omits many of the differences that exist among the chairs that he has perceived (such as, say, color) and retains an approximation of the essential characteristic they have in common. The next stage is when he learns from his elders to call that particular kind of object (that particular class of objects) by the word "chair." Now, he has a much firmer form of retaining in his mind that awareness which previously he could capture only as an image. The final step takes place when and if he learns the *definition* of "chair." A definition expresses, explicitly and in words, the essential characteristic(s) of a number of existents, in virtue of which characteristic(s) those existents are differentiated from all other existents and united into a single class.

Although the concept involved is a very simple one, we may observe in the above example the essence of the process of concept-formation. It consists of the mental act of classifying a number of existents on the basis of a characteristic(s)—an attribute(s)—which is exhibited by those existents and which differentiates them from all other existents. (An "attribute" is an aspect of an entity which can be isolated conceptually for the purpose of identification, but which cannot exist independently of the entity—for example, shape, color, length, weight.) In this particular example, the concept was initially symbolized by means of a visual image; but this is not an essential of the concept-formation process; it occurs most frequently in children (and in the mind of primitive men). Most concepts are acquired directly in the form of words, without the intermediary stage of an image or other non-linguistic symbol.

Concept-formation moves from the apprehension of similarities and differences among existents (entities, attributes, actions, relationships) to an explicit identification of the nature of those similarities and differences.

Concept-formation involves a process of discrimination and integration. Discrimination entails the mind's power of abstraction, which is the ability to isolate, to distinguish and consider separately, a particular aspect or character of an existent. Integration entails the mind's ability to retain a number of instances of such abstracted concretes, to relate them, to unify them into a single awareness which is represented in consciousness by means of a symbol. This unification, as we have seen, occurs on a primitive level by means of a non-linguistic symbol. On a mature level, as a fully realized concept, it is achieved by means of a precisely defined word.

A concept, once formed, refers not merely to the particular concretes which happen to give rise to it, but to all concretes possessing the distinguishing characteristic(s) involved—all concretes of this kind that now exist, ever did exist, or ever will exist.

The first level of man's concepts involves the integration into distinct classes of perceptually-observable concretes. This level provides the base for the much more complex and far-reaching structure of concepts that rises from it. On the one hand, man proceeds to integrate his narrower concepts into wider concepts (again, by isolating and integrating distinguishing characteristics), and then his wider concepts into still wider concepts. On the other hand, he proceeds to refine his knowledge by subdividing wider concepts into narrower classifications or categories.

An example of the first process, the integration of narrower concepts into wider ones, may be observed when man moves from the concepts of "chair," "table," and "bed" to the concept "furniture"—then, by integrating such additional concepts as "household goods"—then, by integrating such additional concepts as "automobile," reaches the still wider concept of "manufactured utilitarian objects." An example of the second process, the subdividing of wider concepts into narrower ones, may be observed when man moves from the general concept of "tree" to the classification of various types of trees, such as "oak," "birch," "maple," etc.

As we have noted, the tool that makes it possible for man to retain and designate his concepts is language. Language consists of an organized system of auditory-visual symbols by means of which man retains his concepts in firm, precise form. By the use of words, i.e., by means of single units that stand for unlimited numbers of particulars, man's mind is able to hold and work with wide categories of entities, attributes, actions, and relationships—a feat that would not be possible if he had to form images of each concrete subsumed under those categories. Words enable man to deal with such broad, complex phenomena as "matter," "energy," "freedom," "justice"—which no mind could grasp or hold if it had to visualize all the perceptual concretes these concepts designate.

Not only does man need symbols to retain and designate his concepts, but he specifically needs an organized system of *linguistic* symbols. A random collection of images or other non-linguistic symbols could never permit the exactitude, clarity—and complexity—his thinking requires.

Entailed in the conceptual method of functioning is the ability to regard concretes as instances or units of the class to which they belong; this is essential to the concept-forming process. In a brilliantly original analysis of the nature of concept-formation, Ayn Rand writes:

> *The ability to regard entities as units is man's distinctive method of cognition.* . . . A unit is an existent regarded as a separate member of a group of two or more similar members. . . .[4]
>
> A *concept* is a mental integration of two or more units which are isolated according to a specific characteristic(s) and united by a specific definition. . . .[5]
>
> The range of what man can hold in the focus of his conscious awareness at any given moment, is limited. The essence of his cognitive power is the ability to reduce a vast amount of information to a minimal number of units; this is the task performed by his conceptual faculty.[6]

(For a detailed epistemological analysis of the nature and formation of concepts, Miss Rand's monograph is strongly recommended. My own brief discussion, above, leans heavily on Miss Rand's monograph, but does not begin to convey the scope of her work in this area.)

The process by which sensations are integrated into percepts is automatic; the integration of percepts into concepts is not. It is a volitional process that man must initiate, sustain, and regulate (Chapter Four). Perceptual information is the given, the self-evident; conceptual knowledge requires a volitionally initiated process of reason. "Reason," again quoting Miss Rand, "is the faculty that identifies and integrates the material provided by man's senses."[7]

To define man as a rational animal is not to imply that he is an animal who invariably functions rationally, but rather to identify the fact that his fundamental distinguishing characteristic, the attribute that essentially differentiates him from other animals, is his ability to reason—to apprehend reality on the conceptual level of consciousness. The hallmark of that ability is his power of propositional speech.

One of the most important consequences of man's possession of a conceptual faculty is his power of self-awareness. No other animal is capable of monitoring and reflecting on its own mental operations of critically evaluating its own mental activity, of deciding that a given process of mental activity is irrational or illogical—inappropriate to the task of apprehending reality—and of altering its subsequent mental operations accordingly.

The same conceptual faculty that confers on man a unique stature compels him to confront unique challenges.

No other animal is explicitly aware of the issue of life or death that confronts all organisms. No other animal is aware of its own mortality—or has the power to extend its longevity through the acquisition of knowledge. No other animal has the ability—and the responsibility—to weigh its actions in terms of the long-range consequences for its own life. No other animal has the ability—and the responsibility—to think and plan in terms of a life span. No other animal has the ability—and responsibility—to continually work at extending its knowledge, thereby raising the level of its existence.

No other animal faces such questions as: Who am I? How should I seek to live? By what principles should I be guided in my actions? What goals ought I to pursue? What is to be the meaning of my life? What should I seek to make of my own person?

The necessity of confronting such issues is essential to the "human condition"—to everything that is distinctive about man's life. All of man's unique achievements and all of his potential problems are consequences of his possession of the conceptual form of awareness. In the pages that follow, we shall consider some of these consequences.

Man: A Being of Volitional Consciousness

The Principle of Volition

One of the characteristics of the majority of modern psychological theories, aside from the arbitrariness of so many of their claims, is their frequently ponderous *irrelevance.* The cause, both of the irrelevance and of the arbitrariness, is the evident belief of their exponents that one can have a science of human nature while consistently ignoring man's most significant and distinctive attributes.

Psychology, today, is in desperate need of *epistemological* rehabilitation. It should be unnecessary, for example, to point out what is wrong with the attempt to prove that all learning is of a random, trial-and-error kind by placing a rat into a maze where random, trial-and-error learning is all that is possible, then adducing the rat's behavior as evidence for the theory. It should be still less requisite to point out what is wrong with accepting the underlying premise of such experiments: the groundless and flagrantly unempirical notion that the learning process in man is to be understood through a study of the behavior of rats.

In the writings of modern psychologists—whether or not the writers happen to show a predilection for the study of rats (or pigeons or earthworms)—*man* is the entity most conspicuously absent. One can read many textbooks today and never learn that man has the ability to think; if the fact is acknowledged at all, it is dismissed as unimportant. One would not learn from these books that man's distinctive form of consciousness is conceptual, nor that this is a fact of crucial significance. One would not learn that man's biologically distinguishing attribute and his basic means of survival is his rational faculty.

The relation of man's reason to his survival is the first of two basic principles of man's nature which are indispensable to an understanding of his psychology and behavior. The second is that the exercise of his rational faculty, unlike an animal's use of his senses, is not automatic—that the decision to think is not biologically "programmed" in man—*that to think is an act of choice.*

This principle was formulated by Ayn Rand as follows:

> The key to . . . "human nature" . . . is the fact that *man is a being of volitional consciousness.* Reason does not work automatically; thinking is not a mechanical process; the connections of logic are not made by instinct. The function of your stomach, lungs or heart is automatic; the function of your mind is not. In any hour and issue of your life, you are free to think or to evade that effort. But you are not free to escape from your nature, from the fact that *reason* is your means of survival—so that for *you,* who are a human being, the question "to be or not to be" is the question "to think or not to think." [1]

In her subsequent writing, Miss Rand does not provide a theoretical elaboration of this statement. Let us proceed to provide it here.

A full exposition of the principle of volition requires that we begin by placing the issue in a wider biological context—that we consider certain basic facts about the nature of living organisms.

An organism's life is characterized by and dependent upon a constant process of internally generated action. This is evident in the process of growth and maturation, in the process of self-healing—and in the actions of the organism in relation to its environment. The *goal-directedness* of living action is its most striking feature. This is not meant to imply the presence of *purpose* on the non-conscious levels of life, but rather to stress the significant fact that there exists in living entities a principle of self-regulating action, and that that action moves toward, and normally results in, the continued life of the organism. For example, the complex processes involved in metabolism, or the remarkable self-repairing activities of living structures, or the integrated orchestration of the countless separate activities involved in the normal process of an organism's physical maturation. Organic self-regulation is the indisputable, fascinating, and challenging phenomenon at the base of the science of biology.

Life exists on different levels of development and complexity, from the single cell to man. As life advances from simpler to higher levels, one may distinguish three forms or categories of self-regulatory activity, which I shall designate as: the *vegetative* level of self-regulation—the *conscious-behavioral* level—the *self-conscious* level.

The vegetative level is the most primitive. All the physiological-biochemical processes within a plant, by which the plant maintains its own existence, are of this order. This pattern of self-regulatory activity is operative within a single cell and in all higher life forms. It is operative in the non-conscious physiological-biochemical processes within the bodies of animals and men—as in metabolism, for example.

The conscious-behavioral level of self-regulation appears with the emergence of consciousness in animals. The vegetative level continues to operate within the animal's body—but a new, higher level is required to protect and sustain the animal's life, as the animal moves through its environment. This level is achieved by the animal's power of awareness. Its senses provide it with the knowledge it needs to hunt, to move around obstacles, to flee from enemies, etc. Its ability to be conscious of the external world enables the animal to regulate and direct its motor activity. Deprived of its senses, an animal could not survive. For all living entities that possess it, consciousness—the regulator of action—is the basic means of survival.

The sensory-perceptual level of an animal's consciousness does not permit it, of course, to be aware of the issue of life and death as such; but given the appropriate physical environment, the animal's sensory-perceptual apparatus and its pleasure-pain mechanism function automatically to protect its life. If its range of awareness cannot cope with the conditions that confront the animal, it perishes. But, within the limit of its powers, its consciousness serves to regulate its behavior in the direction of life. Thus, with the faculty of locomotion *and* the emergence of consciousness in animals, a new form of self-regulatory activity appears in nature, a new expression of the biological principle of life.

In man, both life and consciousness reach their most highly developed form. Man, who shares with animals the sensory-perceptual mode of consciousness, goes beyond it to the conceptual mode to the level of abstractions, principles, explicit reasoning, and *self-consciousness.* Unlike animals, man has the ability to be explicitly aware of his own mental activities, to question their validity, to judge them critically, to alter or correct them. Man is not rational automatically; he is aware of the fact that his mental processes may be appropriate or inappropriate to the task of apprehending reality; his mental processes are not, to him, an unalterable given. In addition to the two previous forms of self-regulating activity, man exhibits a third: *the power to regulate the action of his own consciousness.*

In one crucial respect, the nature of this regulatory activity differs radically from the two previous ones.

On the vegetative and conscious-behavioral levels, the self-regulation is "wired in" to the system. A living organism is a complex integrate of hierarchically organized structures and functions. The various components are controlled in part by their own regulators and in part by regulators on higher levels of the hierarchy. For example, the rhythm of the heart is directly under the control of the heart's own "pacemaker" system; the pacemaker system is regulated by the autonomic nervous system and by hormones; these are regulated by centers in the brain. The ultimate regulative principle, inherent in and controlling the entire system of subregulators, from the nervous system to the heart down to the internal action of a single cell, is, clearly, the life of the organism, i.e., the requirements of the organism's survival. The organism's life is the implicit standard or goal that provides the integrating principle of the organism's internal actions. This ultimate regulator is "programmed" into the organism by nature, so to speak, as are all the subregulators; the organism has no choice in the matter.

Just as, on the vegetative level, the specific nature of the self-regulation, the controlling and integrating principle, is "wired in" to the system—so, in a different form, this is equally true of the conscious-behavioral level in animals. The ultimate standard and goal, the animal's life, is biologically "programmed"—through the animal's sensory-perceptual apparatus and its pleasure-pain mechanism—to regulate its behavior.

Now consider the *self-conscious* level of self-regulation.

The basic function of consciousness—in animals and in man—is *awareness,* the maintenance of sensory and/or conceptual contact with reality. On the plane of awareness that man shares with animals, the sensory-perceptual plane, the integrative process is automatic, i.e., "wired in" to the nervous system. In the brain of a normal human being, sensations (primary sensory inputs) are automatically integrated into perceptions. On the sensory-perceptual level, *awareness* is the controlling and regulating goal of the integrative process—by nature's "programming."

This is *not* true of the conceptual level of consciousness. Here, the regulation is not automatic, not "wired in" to the system. Conceptual awareness, as the *controlling goal* of man's mental activity, is necessary to his proper survival, *but it is not implanted by nature.* Man has to provide it. He has to select that purpose. He has to direct his mental effort and integrate his mental activity to the goal of conceptual awareness—by choice. The capacity of conceptual functioning is innate; but the exercise of this capacity is volitional.

To engage in an active process of thinking—to abstract, conceptualize, relate, infer, to *reason*—man must *focus* his mind: he must *set* it to the task of active integration. The choice to focus, in any given situation, is made by choosing to make *awareness* one's goal—awareness of that which is relevant in the given context.

One activates and directs the thinking process by setting the goal: awareness—and that goal acts as the regulator and integrator of one's mental activity.

The goal of awareness is set by giving oneself, in effect, the order: "Grasp this."

That this goal is not "wired in" to man's brain by nature, as the automatic regulator of mental activity, scarcely needs to be argued. One does not need to design special laboratory experiments in order to demonstrate that thinking is not an automatic process, that man's mind does not automatically "pump" conceptual knowledge, when and as his life requires it, as his heart pumps blood. The mere fact of being confronted with physical objects and events will not force man to abstract their common properties, to integrate his abstractions, to apply his knowledge to each new particular he encounters. Man's capacity to default on the responsibility of thinking is too easily observable. He must *choose* to focus his mind; he must *choose* to aim at understanding. On the conceptual level, the responsibility of self-regulation is his.

The act of focusing pertains to the *operation* of a man's consciousness, to its method of functioning—*not* to its content.

A man is in focus when and to the extent that his mind is set to the goal of awareness, clarity, intelligibility, with regard to the object of his concern, i.e., with regard to that which he is considering or dealing with or engaged in doing.

To sustain that focus with regard to a specific issue or problem, is to *think*.

To let one's mind drift in will-less passivity, directed only by random impressions, emotions, or associations, or to consider an issue without genuinely seeking to understand it, or to engage in an action without a concern to know what one is doing—is to be out of focus.

What is involved here is not an issue of the degree of a man's intelligence or knowledge. Nor is it an issue of the productiveness or success of any particular thinking process. Nor is it an issue of the specific subject matter with which the mind may be occupied. It is an issue of the basic regulating principle that directs the mind's activity: Is the mind controlled by the goal of awareness—or by something else, by wishes, fears, or the pull of lethargic passivity?

To be in focus is to set one's mind to the purpose of *active cognitive integration*. But the alternative confronting man is not simply optimal consciousness or absolute unconsciousness. There are different levels of awareness possible to man's mind, determined by the degree of his focus. This will be manifested in (a) the clarity or vagueness of his mind's contents, (b) the degree to which the mind's activity involves abstractions and principles or is concrete-bound, (c) the degree to which the relevant wider context is present or absent in the process of thinking.

Thus, the choice to focus (or to think) does not consist of moving from a state of literal unconsciousness to a state of consciousness. (This, clearly, would be impossible. When one is asleep, one cannot suddenly choose to start thinking.) To focus is to move from a *lower* level of awareness to a *higher* level—to move from (relative) mental passivity to purposeful mental activity—to initiate a process of directed cognitive integration. In a state of passive (or relatively passive) awareness, a man can apprehend the need to be in full mental focus. His choice is to evade that knowledge or to exert the effort of raising the level of his awareness.

The decision to focus and to think, once made, does not continue to direct a man's mind unceasingly thereafter, with no further effort required. Just as the state of full consciousness must be initiated volitionally, so it must be maintained volitionally. The choice to think must be reaffirmed in the face of every new issue and problem. The decision to be in focus yesterday will not compel a man to be in focus today. The decision to be in focus about one question will not compel a man to be in focus about another. The decision to pursue a certain value does not guarantee that a man will exert the mental effort required to achieve it. In any specific thinking process, man must continue to monitor and regulate his own mental activity, to "keep in on the rails," so to speak. In any hour of his life, he is free to suspend the function of his consciousness, to abandon effort, to default on the responsibility of self-regulation and let his mind drift passively. He is free to maintain only a *partial* focus, grasping that which comes easily to his understanding and declining to struggle for that which does not.

Man is free not only to evade the effort of purposeful awareness in general, but to evade specific lines of thought that he finds disconcerting or painful. Perceiving qualities in his friends, his wife, or himself that clash with his moral standards, he can surrender his mind to blankness or switch it hastily to some other concern, refusing to identify the meaning or implications of what he has perceived. Dimly apprehending, in the midst of an argument, that he is being ridden by his emotions and is maintaining a position for reasons other than those he is stating, reasons that he knows to be untenable, he can refuse to integrate his knowledge, he can refuse to pause on it, he can push it aside and continue to shout with righteous indignation. Grasping that he is pursuing a course of action that is in blatant defiance of reason, he can cry to himself, in effect: "Who can be sure of anything?"—plunge his mind into fog and continue on his way.

In such cases, a man is doing more than defaulting on the responsibility of making awareness his goal: he is actively seeking *un*awareness as his goal. This is the meaning of evasion.

In the choice to focus or not to focus, to think or not to think, to activate the conceptual level of his consciousness or to suspend it—and in this choice alone—is man psychologically free.

Man's freedom to focus or not to focus, to think or not to think, is a unique kind of choice that must be distinguished from any other category of choice. It must be distinguished from the decision to think about a particular subject: *what* a man thinks about, in any given case, depends on his values, interests, knowledge, and context. It must be distinguished from the decision to perform a particular physical action, which again depends on a man's values, interests, knowledge, and context. These decisions involve causal antecedents of a kind which the choice to focus does not.

The primary choice to focus, to set one's mind to the purpose of cognitive integration, is causally irreducible: it is the highest regulator in the mental system; it is subject to man's direct, volitional control. In relation to it, all other choices and decisions are *sub*-regulators.

The capacity of volitional choice presupposes, of course, a normal brain. A condition of disease can render *any* human faculty inoperative. But this analysis assumes an intact, normally functioning brain and nervous system.

To recognize that man is free to think or not to think is to recognize that, in a given situation, a man is able to think and he is able to refrain from thinking. The choice to think (not the *process* of thinking, but the *choice* to think) and the process of focusing his mind are an indivisible action, of which man is the causal agent.

The choice to focus one's mind is a primary, just as the value sought, *awareness,* is a primary. It is awareness that makes any other values possible, not any other values that antecede and make awareness possible. Awareness is the starting-point and precondition of goal-directed (value-directed) human action—not just another goal or value along the way, as it were. The decision to focus one's mind (to value awareness and make it one's goal) or not to focus, is a basic choice that cannot be reduced further.

It must be stressed that volition pertains, specifically, to the conceptual level of awareness. A child encounters the need of cognitive self-regulation when and as he begins to move from the perceptual to the conceptual level, when and as he learns to abstract, to classify, to grasp principles, to reason explicitly. So long as he functions on the sensory-perceptual level, he experiences cognition as an effortless process. But when he begins to conceptualize, he is confronted by the fact that this new form of awareness entails mental *work*, that it requires an effort, that he must choose to generate this effort. He discovers that, on this new level of awareness, he is not infallible; error is possible; cognitive success is not automatically guaranteed to him. (Whereas, on the perceptual level, to look is to see—on the conceptual level, to ask a question is not automatically to know the answer; and to know what question to ask is not automatic, either.) He discovers the continual need to monitor and regulate his mind's activity. A child does not, of course, identify this knowledge verbally or explicitly. But it is implicit in his consciousness, by direct introspective awareness.

Just as a man cannot escape the implicit knowledge that the function of his mind is volitional, so he cannot escape the implicit knowledge that he *should* think, that to be conscious is desirable, that his efficacy as a living entity depends on it. But he is free to act on that knowledge or to evade it. To repeat: Nature has not "programmed" him to think automatically.

(In some cases, the "motive" of non-focusing or nonthinking is anti-effort, i.e., a disinclination to exert the energy and accept the responsibility that thinking requires. In other cases, the "motive" is some wish, desire, or feeling which one wants to indulge and which one's reason cannot sanction—and so one "solves" the problem by going out of focus. In other cases, the "motive" is escape from fear, a fear to which one knows one should not surrender, but to which one does surrender, suspending one's consciousness and negating one's knowledge. These "motives" are not causal imperatives; they are feelings which a man may choose to treat as decisive.)

As focusing involves expanding the range of one's awareness, so evasion consists of the reverse process: of *shrinking* the range of one's awareness. Evasion consists of refusing to *raise* the level of one's awareness, when one knows (clearly or dimly) that one should—or of *lowering* the level of one's awareness, when one knows (clearly or dimly) that one shouldn't. To evade a fact is to attempt to make it unreal to oneself, on the implicit subjectivist premise that if one does not perceive the fact, it does not exist (or its existence will not matter and will not entail any consequences).

Consciousness is man's tool for perceiving and identifying the facts of reality. It is an organ of integration. To focus is to set the integrative process in purposeful motion—by setting the appropriate goal: awareness. Nonfocus is nonintegration. Evasion is willful *dis*integration, the act of subverting the proper function of consciousness, of setting the cognitive function in reverse and reducing the contents of one's mind to disconnected, unintegrated fragments that are forbidden to confront one another.

Man's life and well-being depend upon his maintaining a proper cognitive contact with reality—and this requires a full mental focus, maintained as a way of life.

The act of focusing, as a primary mental set, must be distinguished from the act of problem-solving. Problem-solving entails the pursuit of the answer to some specific question; as such, it presupposes a state of focus, but is not synonymous with it. For example, a man who goes for a walk on a sunny day, intent only on the enjoyment of his activity, with no immediate concern for any long-range problems, may still be in mental focus—if he knows clearly what he is doing, and if he preserves a fundamental alertness, a readiness for purposeful thought, should the need for it arise.

To be in focus does not mean that one must be engaged in the task of problem-solving every moment of one's waking existence. *It means that one must know what one's mind is doing.*

The more consistently and conscientiously a man maintains a policy of being in full mental focus, of thinking, of judging the facts of reality that confront him, of knowing what he is doing and why, the easier and more "natural" the process becomes. The steadily increasing knowledge he acquires as a result of his policy, the growing sense of control over his existence, the growing self-confidence—the conviction of living in a universe that is open to him—all serve to put every emotional incentive on the side of his continuing to think. Further, they reduce the possibility of an incentive that could even tempt him to evade. It is too clear to him that reality is not and can never be his enemy—that he has nothing to gain from self-inflicted blindness, and everything to lose.

No, this does not mean that, for such a man, the policy of rationality becomes automatic; it will always remain volitional; but he has "programmed" himself, as it were, to have every emotional incentive for rationality and none for irrationality. To borrow a phrase from Aristotle, he has learned to make rationality "second nature" to him. That is the psychological reward he earns for himself. But—and this must be emphasized—his psychological state must be maintained *volitionally;* he retains the power to betray it. In each new issue he encounters, he still must *choose* to think.

Conversely, the more a man maintains a policy of focusing as little as possible, and of evading any facts he finds painful to consider—the more he sabotages himself psychologically and the more difficult the task of thinking becomes for him. The inevitable consequences of his policy of nonthinking are feelings of helplessness, of inefficacy, or anxiety—the sense of living in an unknowable and inimical universe. These feelings undercut his confidence in his ability to think, in the usefulness of thinking—and he tends to feel overwhelmed by the enormity of the mental chaos in himself which he has to untangle. Further, the countless fears to which his policy of evasion inevitably condemns him puts the weight of his emotions on the side of additional evasions, of growing self-deception, of an increasingly frantic flight from reality.

No, this does not mean that his evasion and irrationality become automatic; they remain volitional; but he has "programmed" himself to find rationality harder and harder, and the temptation to evasion stronger and stronger. That is the psychological punishment which his nature imposes on him for his default.

But he retains the power to change his course. This side of psychosis, and assuming no interfering structural or chemical disorders, every man retains that power, regardless of his previous mental practices. Volition pertains exclusively to one issue: Is awareness the goal of one's consciousness—or not? What repeated evasion and irrationality can affect is not the ability to choose to focus, but the efficiency, speed, and productiveness of a given thinking process. Since the habitual evader has spent his time, not on improving the efficacy of his mind, but on sabotaging it, he suffers the consequences in terms of mental strain, slowness, internal chaos, when he does decide to think. If he perseveres, he can redeem and raise the efficacy of his thinking. But the mental effort he refused to exert formerly must now be exerted tenfold.

In a given moment, a man may be so overcome by a violent emotion—particularly fear—that he may find it difficult or impossible to think clearly. But he has the power *to know that he is in this state*—and, unless instant action is required, to defer acting or drawing final conclusions until his mind has cleared. In this manner, he can remain in control even under acute stress. (It is worth mentioning, in passing, that the more a man surrenders to his emotions in *non*acute situations, when he could have easily done otherwise, the more susceptible he is to becoming psychologically incapacitated and helplessly blinded under pressure; he has no firmly established "habit" of rational self-discipline to support him.)

An incentive is not a necessitating cause. The fact that a man has a good reason to want to think about some issue, does not guarantee that he will do so; it does not *compel* him to think. And the fact that a man is afraid to think about some issue, does not make it impossible for him to do so; it does not *compel* him to evade.

A man's *behavior*, i.e., his actions, proceed from his values and premises, which in turn proceed, in the context of the knowledge available to him, from his thinking or nonthinking. His actions may be said to be free in that they are under the control of a faculty which is free, i.e., which functions volitionally. This is the reason why a man is held responsible for his actions.

As to a man's desires and emotions, a man cannot will them in or out of existence directly; but he is not compelled to act on them if and when he considers them inappropriate. A desire or an emotion is a value-response, the automatic product of an estimate (conscious or subconscious)—and an estimate is the product of an individual's values and premises (conscious or subconscious), as the individual applies them to a given situation (Chapter Five). Man can alter his desires and emotions only by revising the thinking or nonthinking that produced his values and premises.

Volition and the Social Environment

A man's social environment can provide incentives to think or it can make the task harder—according to the degree of human rationality or irrationality that a man encounters. But the social environment cannot *determine* a man's thinking or nonthinking. It cannot force him to exert the effort and accept the responsibility of cognition and it cannot force him to evade; it cannot force him to subordinate his desires to his reason and it cannot force him to sacrifice his reason to his desires. In this issue, man is inviolately a self-regulator. The social environment can provide him with incentives for good or for evil, but—to repeat—an incentive is not a necessitating cause.

The environment consists only of facts; the meaning of those facts—the conclusions and convictions to be drawn from them— can be identified only by a man's mind. A man's character, the degree of his rationality, independence, honesty, is determined, not by the things he perceives, but by the thinking he does or fails to do about them.

At any step of the way, a man can make honest mistakes of knowledge or judgment; he is not infallible; he may identify incorrectly the meaning or the significance of the events he observes. His power of volition does not guarantee him protection against errors; but it does guarantee that he need not be left helplessly at the mercy of his errors for the rest of his life: he is able to leave his mind open to new evidence that can inform him that his conclusions are wrong and must be revised.

If, for instance, a child is brought up by irrational parents who give him a bewildering, frightening, and contradictory impression of reality, he may decide that all human beings by their nature are incomprehensible and dangerous to him; and, if he arrests his thinking at this point, if, in later years, he never attempts to question or overcome his chronic feeling of terror and helplessness, he can spend the rest of his life in a state of embittered paralysis. But such does not *have* to be his fate: if he continues to struggle with the problem, or, as he grows older, if he decides to consider the new, wider evidence available to him, he can discover that he has made an unwarranted generalization and he can reject it in favor of a fully reasoned and conscious conviction.

Another child, in the same circumstances, may draw a different conclusion: he may decide that all human beings are unreliable and evil, and that *he* will beat them at their own game: he will act as ruthlessly and dishonestly as possible, to hurt them before they hurt *him*. Again, he can revise this conclusion later in the light of wider evidence, if he chooses to think about it. The facts of reality available to him will give him many opportunities to perceive that he is wrong. If he doesn't choose to think, he will become a scoundrel— not because his parents were irrational, but because he defaulted on the responsibility of forming his convictions consciously and of constantly checking them against the facts of reality.

A third child, in the same circumstances, may decide that his parents are wrong, that they are unjust and unfair, or at least that they do not act intelligibly, and that *he* must not act as they do; he may suffer at home, but keep looking for evidence of better human behavior, among neighbors or in books and movies, refusing to resign himself to the irrational and the incomprehensible as inevitable. Such a child will draw an enormous advantage out of his misfortune, which he will not realize until many years later: he will have laid the foundation of a profound self-confidence.

If an adolescent grows up in a neighborhood where crime flourishes and is cynically accepted as the normal, he can, abdicating the independence of his judgment, allow his character to be shaped in the image of the prevailing values, and become a criminal himself; or, choosing to think, he can perceive the irrationality and humiliating self-degradation of those who accept a criminal's mode of existence, and fight to achieve a better way of life for himself.

If a man is pounded from childhood with the doctrine of Original Sin, if he is taught that he is corrupt by nature and must spend his life in penance, if he is taught that this earth is a place of misery, frustration, and calamity, if he is taught that the pursuit of enjoyment is evil—he does not have to believe it: he is free to think, to question, and to judge the nature of a moral code that damns man and damns existence and places its standard of the good outside of both.

Of any value offered to him as the right, and any assertion offered to him as the true, a man is free to ask: *Why?* That "Why?" is the threshold that the beliefs of others cannot cross without his consent.

It is conceivable, of course, that a young child could be subjected, from the first months and years of his life, to such extraordinarily vicious irrationality—such bewildering, contradictory, and terrifying behavior on the part of his parents—that it would be impossible for him to develop normally, because of the limited evidence available to him; it might be impossible for him to establish any firm base of knowledge on which to build. It is conceivable that a child could be paralyzed psychologically—or severely retarded mentally—in this manner. But this would represent the *destruction,* not the "conditioning," of a child's mind; and this is *not* what is meant by those who claim that man is a product of his background.

Let us consider the case of the individual who *does* appear to be the product of his background, of his social environment. Let us analyze, as an example, the case of the boy who, brought up in a bad neighborhood, becomes a criminal.

In the actions of a boy who thus allows himself to be shaped by his environment, the most obviously apparent motive is the desire "to swim with the current." The root of that desire is the wish to escape the effort and responsibility of initiating his own course of action. In order to choose one's own actions, one has to choose one's own goals, and to do that, one has to choose one's own values, and to do that, one has to think. But thinking is the first and basic responsibility that such a boy rejects.

Having no values or standards of his own, he is led—by his desire for "security"—to accept whatever values are offered to him by the social group in which he finds himself. To swim with the current, one has to accept the ocean or the swamp or the rapids or the cesspool or the abyss, toward which that particular current is rushing. Such a boy will want to swim with the current, he will want to follow any course of action ready-made for him by others, he will want to "belong."

And so, if the boys in the neighborhood form a gang at the corner poolroom, he will join; if they start robbing people, he will start robbing people; if they begin to murder, he will murder. What moves him is his *feelings.* His feelings are all he has left, once he has abandoned his mind. He does not join the gang by a conscious, reasoned decision: he *feels* like joining. He does not follow the gang because he honestly thinks they are right: he *feels* like following. If his mother objects and tries to argue with him, to persuade him to quit the hoodlums, he does not weigh her arguments, he does not conclude that she is wrong—he does not *feel* like thinking about it.

If, at some point, he begins to fear that the gang may be going too far, if he recoils from the prospect of becoming a murderer, he realizes that the alternative is to break with his friends and be left on his own; he does not weigh the advantages or disadvantages of being left on his own; he chooses blindly to stick with the gang—because he *feels* terror at the prospect of independence. He may see, across the river or just a few blocks away, people who lead a totally different kind of life, and boys of his own age who, somehow, did *not* become criminals; he has many means of access to a wider view of the possibilities of life; but this does not raise in his mind the question whether a better kind of life is possible for him, it does not prompt him to inquire or investigate—because he *feels* terror of the unknown. If he asks himself what it is that terrifies him about breaking with his background, he will answer, in effect: "Aw, I don't know nobody out there and nobody knows *me*." In reason, this is not an explanation: there is nothing objectively terrifying in that statement; but it satisfies him—because he *feels* an overwhelming dread of loneliness, and *feelings* are his only absolute, the absolute not to be questioned.

And if, at the age of twenty, he is dragged to jail to await execution for some monstrously bloody and senselessly wanton crime—he will scream that he could not help it and that he never had a chance. He will not scream it because it is true. He will scream it because he *feels* it.

In a sense opposite to that which he intends, there is one element of truth in his scream: given his basic policy of *anti-thought*, he could *not* help it and he never had a chance. Neither has any other human being who moves through life on that sort of policy. But it is not true that he or any other human being could not help running from the necessity to think, could not help riding blindly on his feelings.

On every day of this boy's life and at every crucial turning point, the possibility of thinking about his actions was open to him. The evidence on which to base a change in his policy was available to him. He evaded it. He chose not to think. If, at every turning point, he had thought carefully and conscientiously, and had simply reached the wrong conclusions, he would be more justified in crying that he could not help it. But it is not helplessly bewildered, conscientious thinkers who fill reform schools and who murder one another on street corners—through an error in logic.

If one wishes to understand what destroyed this boy, the key lies, not in his environment, but in the fact that he let himself be moved, guided, and motivated by his feelings, that he tried to substitute his feelings for his mind. There was nothing to prevent him from thinking, except that he did not feel like it.

To the extent that a man defaults on the responsibility of thinking, he *is*, in significant measure, "the product of his environment." But such is not the nature of man. It is an instance of pathology.

The attempt of most psychologists to explain a man's behavior without reference to the degree of his thinking or non-thinking—by attempting to reduce all of a man's behavior to causes either in his "conditioning" or in his heredity—is profoundly indicative of the extent to which man is absent from and ignored by most current psychological theories. According to the view prevalent today, man is only a walking recorder into which his parents, teachers, and neighbors dictate what they please—such parents, teachers, and neighbors themselves being only walking recorders carrying the dictations of other, earlier recorders, and so on. As to the question of where *new* ideas, concepts, and values come from, it is left unanswered; the helpless chunk of putty, which allegedly is man, produces them by virtue of some chance concatenation of unknown forces. It is interesting to consider the personal confession contained in the social determinist's dismay, incredulity, *and indignation* at the suggestion that original, self-generated thinking plays any significant role in a man's life.

The Contradiction of Determinism

"Free will"—in the widest meaning of the term—is the doctrine that man is capable of performing actions which are not determined by forces outside his control; that man is capable of making choices which are not necessitated by antecedent factors. As one writer formulates it: "In the case of an action that is free, it must be such that it is caused by the agent who performs it, but such that no antecedent conditions were sufficient for performing just that action."[2]

The nature of these free choices, to what human faculty they pertain, how they operate and what are their limits—are questions on which various theories of free will differ. Predominantly, theories of free will have attempted to argue that certain *desires* or *physical actions* are "free," i.e., causally irreducible—a position that is flagrantly insupportable.

Man's free will consists of a single action, a single basic choice: to think or not to think. It is a freedom entailed by his unique power of self-consciousness. This basic choice—given the context of his knowledge and of the existential possibilities confronting him—controls all of man's other choices, and directs the course of his actions.

The concept of man as a being of volitional consciousness stands in sharp opposition to the view that dominates our culture in general and the social sciences in particular: the doctrine of psychological determinism.

Psychological determinism denies the existence of any element of freedom or volition in man's consciousness. It holds that, in relation to his actions, decisions, values, and conclusions, man is ultimately and essentially *passive;* that man is merely a *reactor* to internal and external pressures; that those pressures determine the course of his actions and the content of his convictions, just as physical forces determine the course of every particle of dust in the universe. It holds that, in any given situation or moment, only one "choice" is psychologically possible to man, the inevitable result of all the antecedent determining forces impinging on him, just as only one action is possible to the speck of dust; that man has no *actual* power of choice, no *actual* freedom or self-responsibility. Man, according to this view, has no more volition than a stone: he is merely confronted with more complex alternatives and is manipulated by more complex forces.

Although they usually do not care to have it formulated so explicitly, nor to accept its full implications, this is the view of man's nature that most contemporary psychologists accept. They accept it, many of them candidly admit, as "an article of faith." That is, the majority do not claim that this view has been proven, has been logically demonstrated. They profess a belief in psychological determinism because they regard it as "scientific." This is the single most prevalent and destructive myth in the field of psychology today.

The doctrine of determinism contains a central and insuperable contradiction—an *epistemological* contradiction—a contradiction implicit in any variety of determinism, whether the alleged determining forces be physical, psychological, environmental, or divine.

The determinist view of mind maintains that whether a man thinks or not, whether he takes cognizance of the facts of reality or not, whether he places facts above feelings or feelings above facts—all are determined by forces outside his control; in any given moment or situation, his method of mental functioning is the inevitable product of an endless chain of antecedent factors; *he* has no choice in the matter.

That which a man does, declare the advocates of determinism, he *had* to do—that which he believes, he *had* to believe—if he focuses his mind, he *had* to—if he evades the effort of focusing, he *had* to—if he is guided solely by reason, he *had* to be—if he is ruled instead by feeling or whim, he *had* to be—he *couldn't help it.*

But if this were true, no knowledge—no *conceptual* knowledge—would be possible to man. No theory could claim greater plausibility than any other—including the theory of psychological determinism.

Man is neither omniscient nor infallible. This means: (a) that he must work to *achieve* his knowledge, and (b) that the mere presence of an idea inside his mind does not prove that the idea is true; many ideas may enter a man's mind which are false. But if man believes what he *has* to believe, if he is not free to test his beliefs against reality and to validate or reject them—*if the actions and content of his mind are determined by factors that may or may not have anything to do with reason, logic, and reality*—then he can never know if his conclusions are true or false.

Knowledge consists of the correct identification of the facts of reality; and in order for man to know that the contents of his mind *do* constitute knowledge, in order for him to know that he has identified the facts of reality correctly, he requires a means of testing his conclusions. The means is the process of *reasoning*—of testing his conclusions against reality and checking for contradictions. But this validation is possible only if his *capacity* to judge is free—i.e., nonconditional (given a normal brain). If his capacity to judge is *not* free, there is no way for a man to discriminate between his beliefs and those of a raving lunatic.

But then how did the advocates of determinism acquire *their* knowledge? What is its validation? Determinists are conspicuously silent on this point.

If the advocates of determinism insist that their choice to think and their acceptance of reason is *conditional,* dependent on factors outside their control—which means: that they are *not* free to test their beliefs against the facts of reality—then they cannot claim to *know* that their theory is true; they can only report that they feel helpless to believe otherwise. Nor can they claim that their theory is highly probable; they can only acknowledge the inner compulsion that forbids them to doubt that it is highly probable.

Some advocates of determinism, evidently sensing this epistemological dilemma, have sought to escape it by asserting that, although they are determined to believe what they believe, the factor determining them is *logic*. But by what means do they know this? Their beliefs are no more subject to their control than those of a lunatic. They and the lunatic are equally the pawn of deterministic forces. Both are incapable of judging their judgments.

One of the defining characteristics of psychosis is *loss* of volitional control over rational judgment—but, according to determinism, that is man's normal, metaphysical state.

There *is* no escape from determinism's epistemological dilemma.

A mind that is not free to test and validate its conclusions—a mind whose judgment is not free—can have no way to tell the logical from the illogical, *no way to ascertain that which compels and motivates it*, no right to claim knowledge of any kind; such a mind is disqualified for such appraisals by its very nature. The very *concept* of logic is possible only to a volitional consciousness; an automatic consciousness could have no need of it and could not conceive of it.

The concepts of logic, thought, and knowledge are not applicable to machines. A machine does not reason; it performs the actions its builder sets it to perform, and those actions alone. If it is set to register that two plus two equal four, it does so; if it is set to register that two plus two equal five, it does so; it has no power to correct the orders and information given it. If "self-correctors" are built into it, it performs the prescribed acts of "self-correction," and no others; if the "self-correctors" are set incorrectly, it cannot correct itself; it cannot make any independent, self-generated contribution to its own performance. If man, who is not "set" invariably to be right, were merely a super-complex machine, engineered by his heredity and operated by his environment, pushed, pulled, shaped, and molded by his genes, his toilet training, his parental upbringing, and his cultural history, then no idea reached by him could claim objectivity or truth—including the idea that man is a machine.

Those who propound determinism must either assert that they arrived at their theory by mystical revelation, and thus exclude themselves from the realm of reason—or they must assert that *they* are an exception to the theory they propound, and thus exclude their theory from the realm of truth.

The fact that knowledge is possible to man cannot be contested without self-contradiction. It is a truth that must be accepted even in the act of seeking to dispute it. Any theory that necessitates the conclusion that man can know nothing, is self-invalidating and self-refuting by that very fact. Yet such is the conclusion to which the theory of determinism inescapably leads.

In appraising any theory of the nature of man's mind and its operations, it is necessary to consider that, since the theory is itself a product of man's mind, its claim to truth must be compatible with its own existence and content. Otherwise, the theory is contradictory and nonsensical (Bertrand Russell's theory of types notwithstanding). For example, if a man were to declare, as an alleged fact of reality: "Man is incapable of knowing any facts"—the logical absurdity of his statement would be obvious. The epistemological contradiction of determinism is—in a subtler and more complex way—of the identical order.

Determinism is a theory whose claim to truth is incompatible with its own content. It exhibits what may be termed *the fallacy of self-exclusion*.

A number of thinkers, attacking the theory of classical associationism, have pointed out that the associationist theory of mind does not allow the possibility of ever establishing associationism as true; that the theory does not allow the possibility of *any* knowledge. But associationism is merely one version of psychological determinism. What has not been recognized is that the same objection applies to—and invalidates—*any* version of determinism.

It does not matter whether man's mind is alleged to be passively under the sway of the "laws of association"—or of conditioned reflexes—or of environmental pressures—or of Original Sin. *Any* theory of mind that denies man's volitional control over his faculty of judgment, collapses under the weight of the same inescapable and insuperable contradiction.

Only because man *is* a being of volitional consciousness, only because he *is* free to initiate and sustain a reasoning process, is conceptual knowledge—in contradistinction to irresistible, unchosen beliefs—possible to him.

Volition and the Law of Causality

Two notions—both mistaken—are especially influential in propagating the mystique of psychological determinism. The first is the claim that psychological determinism is logically entailed by the law of causality, that volition contradicts causality. The second is the claim that, without determinism, no science of psychology would be possible, there could be no psychological laws and no way to predict human behavior.

What is involved, in the first of these claims, is a gross misapprehension of the nature of the law of causality. Let us begin by considering the exact meaning of this law.

As Ayn Rand writes:

> The law of causality is the law of identity applied to action. All actions are caused by entities. The nature of an action is caused and determined by the nature of the entities that act; a thing cannot act in contradiction to its nature.[3]

This is the first point that must be stressed: all actions are actions *of entities*. (The concept of "action" logically requires and presupposes *that which* acts, and would not be possible without it. The universe consists of entities that act, move, and change—not of disembodied actions, motions, and changes.)

The actions possible to an entity are determined by its nature: what a thing can *do*, depends on what it *is*. It is not "chance," it is not the whim of a supernatural being, it is in the inexorable nature of the entities involved, that a seed can grow into a flower, but a stone cannot—that electricity can run a motor, but tears and prayers cannot—that actions *consistent* with their natures are possible to entities, but *contradictions* are not.

Just as what a thing *can* do, depends on what it is—so, in any specific situations, what a thing *will* do, depends on what it is. If iron is exposed to a certain temperature, it expands; if water is exposed to the same temperature, it boils; if wood is exposed to the same temperature, it burns. The differences in their actions are caused by differences in their properties. If an automobile collides with a bicycle, it is not "chance" that the bicycle is hurled into the air, rather than the automobile; if an automobile collides with a train, it is not "chance" that the automobile is hurled into the air, rather than the train. Causality proceeds from identity.

Causality pertains to a relationship between *entities and their actions.*

The law of causality is a very wide abstraction; per se, it does not specify the *kind* of causal processes that are operative in any particular entity, and it does not imply that the *same* kinds of causal processes are operative in *all* entities. Any such assumption would be gratuitous and unwarranted.

The actions of a stone, for example, are only *re*actions to other objects or forces; a stone, which moves by a mechanistic type of causation, cannot *initiate* actions. It cannot start rolling down a hillside, unless it is pushed by a man's hand or by the wind or by some other force *outside* itself. It can generate neither actions nor goals. But an animal possesses the power of locomotion, it can initiate movement, *goal-directed* movement, it can start walking or running: the source of its motion is *within* itself. That the animal may start running in response to the perception of some stimulus-object is irrelevant in this context. What is relevant is that the animal has the capacity to respond in a manner impossible to a stone: by originating, within its own body, the motion of running—and by moving toward a goal. Different causal processes, different principles of action, are involved in these two cases.

The nature of a *living* entity gives it the capacity for a kind of action impossible to inanimate matter: self-generated, goal-directed action (in the sense defined above). Man's greatest distinction from all other living species is the capacity to originate an action of his consciousness—the capacity to originate a process of abstract thought.

Man's unique responsibility lies in the fact that this process of thought, which is man's basic means of survival, must be originated volitionally. In man, there exists the power of *choice*, choice in the primary sense, choice as a psychologically irreducible natural fact.

This freedom of choice is not a negation of causality, but a category of it, a category that pertains to man. A process of thought is not causeless, it is caused by a man. The actions possible to an entity are determined by the entity that acts—and the nature of man (and of man's mind) is such that it necessitates the choice between focusing and nonfocusing, between thinking and non-thinking. Man's nature does not allow him to escape this choice; it is his alone to make: it is not made for him by the gods, the stars, the chemistry of his body, the structure of his "family constellation" or the economic organization of his society.

If one is to be bound by a genuine "empiricism"—i.e., a respect for observable facts, without arbitrary commitments to which reality must be "adjusted"—one cannot ignore this distinctive attribute of man's nature. And if one understands the law of causality as a relationship between entities and their actions, then the problem of "reconciling" volition and causality is seen to be illusory.

But it is not thus that the law of causality is regarded today. That is the source of the confusion.

The historical turning-point came at the Renaissance. Windelband, in his *A History of Philosophy,* describes it as follows:

> The *idea of cause had acquired a completely new significance* through Galileo. According to the [earlier] conception . . . causes were *substances* or things, while effects, on the other hand, were either their activities or were other substances and things which were held to come about only by such activities: this was the Platonic-Aristotelian conception. . . . Galileo, on the contrary, went back to the idea of the older Greek thinkers, who applied the causal relation only to the *states*—that meant now to the *motions* of substances—not to the Being of the substances themselves. Causes are motions, and effects are motions.[4]

This was the view that dominated post-Renaissance science and philosophy: causality was seen as a relationship between *actions* and *actions*—not between entities and actions. The "model" of causality was mechanics: the essence of the causal relationship was identified with the relationship of impact and counter-impact, of action and reaction.

Long after the time when the mechanical "model" was recognized by physicists as inapplicable to many aspects of the physical world, i.e., inapplicable even to many inanimate, deterministic systems within the universe (electromagnetic phenomena, for example) a disastrous legacy remained: the insidiously persistent notion that every action, including every action of man, is only a *re*action to some antecedent action or motion or force.

The view of causality as a relationship between motions is entirely spurious. It is worth noting that, if one accepts this view, there is no way to prove or validate the law of causality. If all that is involved is motion succeeding motion, there is no way to establish *necessary* relationships between succeeding events: one observes that B follows A, but one has no way to establish that B is the *effect* or *consequence* of A. (This, incidentally, is one of the reasons why most philosophers, who accept this notion of causality, have been unable to answer Hume's argument that one cannot *prove* the law of causality. One can't—unless one grasps its relationship to the law of identity. But this entails rejecting the motion-to-motion view of causality.)

Furthermore, the motion-to-motion view obscures the explanatory nature of the law of causality. If one wishes to understand *why* entities act as they do, in a given context, one must seek the answer through an understanding of the properties of the entities involved. And, in fact, any explanation via references to antecedent actions always implies and presupposes this understanding. For example, if one states that the *action* of a wastebasket catching fire was *caused* by the *action* of a lighted match being thrown into it, this constitutes a satisfactory causal explanation only if one understands the *nature* of paper and of lighted matches; a description of the action sequence, in the absence of such knowledge, would explain nothing.

The premise that every action is only a reaction to an antecedent action, rules out, arbitrarily and against the evidence, the existence of self-generated, goal-directed action. The way in which this premise has impeded progress in the science of biology is outside the scope of this discussion. What is directly pertinent here is the disastrous consequences of this premise for psychology; it is this premise that forbids men to grasp the possibility of a volitional consciousness.

On this premise, thinking or non-thinking is merely a necessitated reaction to an antecedent necessitated reaction to an antecedent necessitated reaction, etc. Such a view makes man wholly passive. It is entirely incompatible with the fact of man as a cognitive self-regulator. But it is not the fact of cognitive self-regulation that must be questioned and rejected; it is the mistaken notion of causality.

(It is an error to demand: "What *made* one man choose to focus and another man choose to evade?" This question almost invariably reflects the mistaken notion of causality we have just discussed above. The question implies one's failure to grasp the meaning of *choice* in the primary sense involved in the act of focusing or thinking. The questioner is asking: "To what is the action of focusing or thinking a *reaction*?")

As applied to physical nature, determinism may be regarded, and commonly is regarded, as synonymous with universal causality. But as applied to man, i.e., in a psychological context, the term has a narrower meaning, as defined above, which is *not* entailed by the law of causality and which is demonstrably at variance with the facts.

Now, let us consider the issue of psychological law and prediction.

Man's consciousness or mind has a specific nature; it has a specific structure, it has specific attributes, it has specific powers. Its manner of functioning exhibits specific principles or laws which it is the task of psychology to discover and identify. None of this is contradicted by the fact that the exercise of man's reason is volitional.

His mind is an organ over which man has a specific, delimited, regulatory control. Just as the driver of an automobile can steer the car in a chosen direction, but cannot alter or infringe the mechanical laws by which the car functions—so man can choose to focus, to aim his cognitive faculty in a given direction, but cannot alter or infringe the psychological laws by which his mind functions. If a man does not steer his car properly, he has no choice about the fact that he will end in a smash-up; neither has the man who does not steer his mind properly.

For example, a man is free to think or not to think, but he is not free to escape the fact that if he fails to think, if he characteristically evades facing any facts or issues which he finds unpleasant, he will set in motion a complex chain of destructive psychological consequences, one of which will be a profound loss of self-esteem.

This is a matter of demonstrable psychological law (Chapter Seven).

Or again, if a man forms certain values—as a result of his thinking or non-thinking—these values will lead him to experience certain emotions in certain situations. He will not be able to command these emotions out of existence by "will." If he recognizes that a specific emotion is inappropriate, he can alter it by rethinking the value(s) that evokes it—but he can do so only in a specific, "lawful" manner, *not* by arbitrary whim (Chapter Five).

"Free will" does *not* mean arbitrary, omnipotent power—*unlimited* power—over the workings of one's own mind.

Thus, to the extent that one understands the principles by which man's mind operates, one can predict the psychological consequences of given ideas, values, conclusions, attitudes, and thinking policies. One can predict, for example, that a man of authentic self-esteem will find intellectual stagnation intolerable; that a man who regards sex, life, and himself as evil will not be attracted to a woman of intelligence, independence, and guiltless self-confidence, will not feel at ease and "at home" with her romantically; that a man whose guiding policy is "Don't antagonize anyone," will not be the first to stand up for and champion a radical new idea or theory.

One cannot predict with certainty that these men will not change their thinking. Therefore, one's predictions must take the form of "all other things being equal," or "assuming no new factors enter the situation." But this is true of prediction in the physical sciences also.

If one is to understand man psychologically, a cardinal requirement is that one identify the fact of volition. A genuinely scientific psychology must repudiate the mystique of determinism and the spurious theory of causality on which it rests.

Chapter Five

Emotions

Emotions and Values

Throughout the preceding discussion, I have stressed that his ability to reason is man's essential attribute—the attribute which explains the greatest number of his other characteristics.

This fact is often obscured by the widespread confusion about the nature and role of *emotions* in man's life. One frequently hears the statement, "Man is not merely a rational being, he is also an emotional being"—which implies some sort of dichotomy, as if, in effect, man possessed a *dual* nature, with one part in opposition to the other. In fact, however, the content of man's emotions is the product of his rational faculty; his emotions are a derivative and a consequence, which, like all of man's other psychological characteristics, cannot be understood without reference to the conceptual power of his consciousness.

As man's tool of survival, reason has two basic functions: cognition and evaluation. The process of cognition consists of discovering what things *are,* of identifying their nature, their attributes and properties. The process of evaluation consists of man discovering the relationship of things to himself, of identifying what is beneficial to him and what is harmful, what should be sought and what should be avoided.

"A 'value' is that which one acts to gain and/or keep."[1] It is that which one regards as conducive to one's welfare. A value is the object of an action. Since man must act in order to live, and since reality confronts him with many possible goals, many alternative courses of action, he cannot escape the necessity of selecting values and making value-judgments.

"Value" is a concept pertaining to a relation—the relation of some aspect of reality to man (or to some other living entity). If a man regards a thing (a person, an object, an event, a mental state, etc.) as good for him, as beneficial in some way, he *values* it—and, when possible and appropriate, seeks to acquire, retain, and use or enjoy it. If a man regards a thing as bad for him, as inimical or harmful in some way, he *dis*values it—and seeks to avoid or destroy it. If he regards a thing as of no significance to him, as neither beneficial nor harmful, he is *indifferent* to it—and takes no action in regard to it.

Although his life and well-being depend on man selecting values that are *in fact* good for him, i.e., consonant with his nature and needs, conducive to his continued efficacious functioning, there are no internal or external forces compelling him to do so. Nature leaves him free in this matter. As a being of volitional consciousness, he is not biologically "programmed" to make the right value-choices automatically. He may select values that are incompatible with his needs and inimical to his well-being, values that lead him to suffering and destruction. But whether his values are life-serving or life-negating, it is a man's values that direct his actions. Values constitute man's basic motivational tie to reality.

In existential terms, man's basic alternative of "for me" or "against me," which gives rise to the issue of values, is the alternative of life or death (Chapter Twelve). But this is an adult, conceptual identification. As a child, a human being first encounters the issue of values through the experience of physical sensations of *pleasure* and *pain*.

To a conscious organism, pleasure is experienced, axiomatically, as a value—pain, as a disvalue. The biological reason for this is the fact that pleasure is a life-enhancing state and that pain is a signal of danger, of some disruption of the normal life process.

There is another basic alternative, in the realm of consciousness, through which a child encounters the issue of values, of the desirable and the undesirable. It pertains to his cognitive relationship to reality. There are times when a child experiences a sense of cognitive *efficacy* in grasping reality, a sense of cognitive *control*, of mental *clarity* (within the range of awareness possible to his stage of development). There are times when he suffers from a sense of cognitive *inefficacy*, of cognitive *helplessness*, of mental *chaos,* the sense of being out of control and unable to assimilate the data entering his consciousness. To experience a state of efficacy is to experience it as a value; to experience a state of inefficacy is to experience it as a disvalue. The biological basis of this fact is the relationship of efficacy to survival.

The value of a sense of efficacy *as such,* like the value of pleasure *as such,* is introspectively experienced by man as a primary. One does not ask a man: "Why do you prefer pleasure to pain?" Nor does one ask him: "Why do you prefer a state of control to a state of helplessness?" It is through these two sets of experiences that man first *acquires* preferences, i.e., values.

A man may choose, as a consequence of his errors and/or evasions, to pursue pleasure by means of values that *in fact* can result only in pain; and he can pursue a sense of efficacy by means of values that can only render him impotent. But the value of pleasure and the disvalue of pain, as well as the value of efficacy and the disvalue of helplessness, remain the psychological base of the phenomenon of valuation.

A man's values are the product of the thinking he has done or has failed to do. Values can be a manifestation of rationality and mental health or of irrationality and neurosis. They can be an expression of psychological maturity or of arrested development. They can grow out of self-confidence and benevolence or out of self-doubt and fear. They can be motivated by the desire to achieve happiness or by the desire to minimize pain. They can be born out of the desire to use one's mind or the desire to escape it. They can be acquired independently and by deliberation or they can be uncritically absorbed from other men by, in effect, a process of osmosis. They can be held consciously and explicitly or subconsciously and implicitly. They can be consistent or they can be contradictory. They can further a man's life or they can endanger it. These are the alternatives possible to a being of volitional consciousness.

There is no way for man to regress to the state of an animal, no stereotyped, biologically prescribed pattern of behavior he can follow blindly, no "instincts" to whose control he can surrender his existence. If he defaults on the responsibility of reason, if he rebels against the necessity of thought—the distortions, the perversions, the corruption that become his values are still a twisted expression of the fact that his is a conceptual form of consciousness. His values are still the product of his mind, but of a mind set in reverse, set against its own proper function, intent on self-destruction. Like rationality, irrationality is a concept that is not applicable to animals; it is applicable only to man.

An animal's basic values and goals are biologically "programmed" by nature. An animal does not face such questions as: What kind of entity should I seek to become? For what purpose should I live? What should I make of my life? Man does—and men answer these questions in vastly different ways, depending on the quantity and quality of their thinking.

Differences in men's basic values reflect differences in their basic premises, in their fundamental views of themselves, of other men, of existence—their views of what is possible to them and what they can expect of life.

Since values involve the relation of some aspect of reality to the valuer, to the acting entity, a man's view of himself plays a crucial role in his value-choices. To illustrate this by means of a simple example: a man regards a falling bomb as bad for him because he is aware of his own mortality; if he were physically indestructible, he would appraise the bomb's significance differently. One's (conscious or subconscious) view of one's own person, one's nature and powers—whether one appraises oneself correctly or not—is implicit in one's value-judgments.

The degree of a man's self-confidence or lack of it, and the extent to which he regards the universe as open or closed to his understanding and action—will necessarily affect the goals he will set for himself, the range of his ambition, his choice of friends, the kind of art he will enjoy, etc. (Chapter Seven).

For the most part, the process by which a man's view of himself affects his value-choices, does not take place on a conscious level; it is *implicit* in his evaluations, reflecting earlier conclusions which, in effect, are "filed" in his subconscious.

The subconscious is the sum of mental contents and processes that are outside of or below awareness. Man's subconscious performs two basic tasks which are crucial to his intellectual development and efficient functioning. The subconscious operates as a storehouse of past knowledge, observations, and conclusions (it is obviously impossible for man to keep all of his knowledge in focal awareness); and it operates, *in effect,* as an electronic computer, performing super-rapid integrations of sensory and ideational material. Thus, his past knowledge (provided it has been properly assimilated) can be instantly available to man, while his conscious mind is left free to deal with the *new.*

This is the pattern of all human learning. Once, a man needed his full mental attention to learn to walk; then the knowledge became automatized—and he was free to pursue new skills. Once, a man needed his full mental attention to learn to speak; then the knowledge became automatized—and he was enabled to go forward to higher levels of accomplishment. Man moves from knowledge to more advanced knowledge, automatizing his identifications and discoveries as he proceeds—turning his brain into an ever more efficacious instrument, *if* and to the extent that he continues the growth process.

Man is a *self-programmer.* Just as this principle operates in regard to his cognitive development, so it operates in regard to his value development. As he acquires values and dis-values, these, too, become automatized; he is not obliged, in every situation he encounters, to recall all of his values to his conscious mind in order to form an estimate. In response to his perception of some aspect of reality, his subconscious is triggered into a lightning-like process of integration and appraisal. For example, if an experienced motorist perceives an oncoming truck veering toward a collision, he does not need a new act of conscious reasoning in order to grasp the fact of danger; faster than any thought could take shape in words, he registers the significance of what he perceives, his foot flies to the brake or his hands swiftly turn the wheel.

One of the forms in which these lightning-like appraisals present themselves to man's conscious mind is his *emotions.*

His emotional capacity is man's automatic barometer of what is *for* him or *against* him (within the context of his knowledge and values). The relationship of value-judgments to emotions is that of *cause* to *effect.* An emotion is a value-response. It is the automatic psychological result (involving both mental and somatic features) of a super-rapid, subconscious appraisal.

An emotion is the psychosomatic form in which man experiences his estimate of the beneficial or harmful relationship of some aspect of reality to himself.

The sequence of psychological events is: from perception to evaluation to emotional response. On the level of immediate awareness, however, the sequence is: from perception to emotion. A person may or may not be consciously aware of the intervening value-judgment. A separate act of focused awareness may be required to grasp it, because of the extreme rapidity of the sequence. That a person may fail to identify either the judgment or the factors involved in it, that he may be conscious only of the perception and of his emotional response, is the fact which makes possible men's confusion about the nature and source of emotions.

There are many reasons why a person may remain unaware of the evaluative processes underlying his emotions. Among the most important of these reasons are the following:

1. Competence at introspecting and identifying one's own mental processes has to be *acquired;* it has to be *learned.* Most people have not formed the habit of seeking to account to themselves for the reasons of their beliefs, emotions, and desires; consequently, when they do attempt it, they frequently fail—and do not persevere.

2. Most people do not hold their values and convictions in clearly defined form. Vagueness and obscurity characterize a good deal of their mental contents. Their beliefs and values have never been formulated in precise, objective language, and are stored in the subconscious only as *approximations,* by means of pre-verbal symbols, such as images, which their owners cannot easily translate into objective, articulate speech.

3. Sometimes, an emotion and the value-considerations underlying it are extremely complex. For example, suppose a wife is emotionally upset; she knows that the feeling involves her husband. Perhaps he has been inconsiderate of her in some way; but he is working very hard and is under a strain; but she, too, is under a strain and is tired of bearing the emotional burden of his work pressures; still, she knows she is inclined to be oversensitive; on the other hand, she wants to be honest with him about her feelings; but she does not want to upset him and, perhaps, make the situation worse. All of these considerations may be clashing in her subconscious. On the conscious level, she feels an emotion of diffuse irritation at the universe in general and at her husband in particular, plus some amount of guilt—and she cannot untangle the reasons.

4. Sometimes, one responds emotionally to things of which one is not aware. For example, one may meet a person for whom one feels an almost instant dislike; yet if one searches one's mind, one can think of nothing objectionable that he has said or done. It may be the case that one was *peripherally* aware of affectations in his posture and way of moving; or of some subtle insincerity in his voice; or of some negative implications in his remarks that one did not pause to identify fully—and one's subconscious reacted accordingly.

5. The single most formidable obstacle to identifying the roots of one's emotions is *repression*. Since the values that underlie some people's emotional reactions are offensive to their self-respect and conscious convictions, the causes of such reactions may be barred from awareness. An artist who has a block against admitting the envy he feels toward a more talented rival, may be quite unaware—and ferociously resistant to recognizing—that the elation he feels was caused by news of the failure of his rival's art show.

It is interesting to observe that those who are most prone to rhapsodize about their emotions and to speak disparagingly of reason, are those who are most incompetent at introspection and most ignorant of the *source* of their emotions. They regard their emotions as the given, as mystical revelations, as the voice of their "blood" or of their "instincts," to be followed blindly.

For example, consider the following statement by D. H. Lawrence: "My great religion is a belief in the blood, the flesh, as being wiser than the intellect. We can go wrong in our minds. But what our blood feels and believes and says, is always true. The intellect is only a bit and a bridle. What do I care about knowledge? All I want is to answer to my blood, direct, without fribbling intervention of mind or moral, or what not."[2]

Lawrence expresses the position in an extreme form. But, in a milder, less flamboyant manner, many people live by—more precisely, die by—this doctrine every day.

Man is an integrated organism, his nature (*qua* living entity) does not contain contradictory elements; reason and emotion—thinking and feeling—are not mutually inimical faculties. But they perform radically different functions, and their functions are not interchangeable. *Emotions are not tools of cognition.* To treat them as such is to put one's life and well-being in the gravest danger. What one *feels* in regard to any fact or issue is irrelevant to the question of whether one's judgment is true or false. It is not by means of one's emotions that one apprehends reality.

One of the chief characteristics of mental illness is the policy of letting one's feelings—one's wishes and fears—determine one's thinking, guide one's actions and serve as one's standard of judgment. This is more than a *symptom* of neurosis, it is a *prescription* for neurosis. It is a policy that involves the wrecking of one's rational faculty.

It is not accidental, but logical and inevitable, that the predominant emotions an irrationalist is left with—after he has put this policy into practice—are depression, guilt, anguish, and fear. The notion of the happy irrationalist, like that of the happy psychotic, is a myth—as any psychotherapist is in a position to testify.

Whether or not they regard their emotions as reliable guides to action, the majority of people tend to regard some of them, in effect, as primaries, as "just there." Yet the evidence to refute such an error is overwhelming and readily available.

The mere perception of an object has no power to create an emotion in man—let alone to determine the *content* of the emotion. The emotional response to an object is inexplicable, except in terms of the *value-significance* of the object to the perceiver. And this necessarily implies a process of appraisal. For example, three men look at a scoundrel: the first man recognizes to what extent this person, in his craven irrationality, has betrayed his status as a human being—and feels contempt; the second man wonders how he can be safe in a world where such persons can prosper—and feels fear; the third man secretly envies the scoundrel's "success"— and feels a sneaking admiration. All three men *perceive* the same object. The differences in their emotional reactions proceed from differences in their evaluation of the *significance* of what they perceive.

Just as emotions are not created by objects of perception as such, so they are not the product of any sort of innate ideas. Having no innate knowledge of what is true or false, man can have no innate knowledge of what is good for him or evil. A man's values— to repeat—are a product of the quantity and quality of his thinking.

An emotional response is always the reflection and product of an estimate—and an estimate is the product of a person's values, *as the person understands them to apply to a given situation.*

This last must be stressed. Quite aside from the question of the objective validity of his values, a man may misapply them in a given case, so that his appraisal is incorrect even by his own terms. For example, a man may misapprehend the nature of the facts to be judged. Or he may focus on one aspect of a situation, failing to grasp the full context, so that his involuntary evaluation is grossly inappropriate. Or his evaluative process may be distorted by internal pressures and conflicts that are irrelevant to the issue confronting him. Or he may not recognize that his past thinking and conclusions are inadequate to a judgment of the present situation, which contains new and unfamiliar elements.

In making value-judgments, man does not hold in mind automatically the full, appropriate context. Brief, out-of-context reactions are not uncommon. One of the penalties of an improper reliance on one's emotions, is a tendency to attach undue importance to such responses. People sometimes reproach themselves for momentary emotions, felt out of context, that have no significance whatever. Suppose, for example, a happily married man, deeply in love with his wife, meets another woman for whom he experiences a sexual desire; he is tempted, for the space of a few moments, by the thought of an affair with her; then, the full context of his life comes back to him and he loses his desire; the abstract sexual appreciation remains, but that is all; there is no temptation to take action. Such an experience can be entirely normal and innocent. But many men would mistakenly reproach themselves and wonder about possible defects in their character revealed by their sexual response. Enduring and persistent emotions that clash with one's conscious convictions *are* a sign of unresolved conflicts. Occasional, *momentary* feelings need not be.

As to enduring and persistent emotions that clash with one's convictions and/or one's other values, these can be made the means of increased self-understanding and self-improvement—*if* one recognizes the nature and source of emotions. By analyzing the roots of his feelings and desires, a man can discover ideas he has held without conscious awareness, he can be led to a knowledge of values he has formed without verbal identification, to concepts he has accepted without thought, to beliefs that represent the opposite of his stated conclusions.

Reason and emotion are not antagonists; what may seem like a struggle between them is only a struggle between two opposing ideas, one of which is not conscious and manifests itself only in the form of a feeling. The resolution of such conflicts is not always simple; it depends on the complexity of the issues involved. But resolutions are achievable—and the necessary first step is to recognize the actual nature of that which needs to be resolved.

The guiltless emotional spontaneity that men long for—the freedom from torturing self-doubts, enervating depression and paralyzing fears—is a proper and achievable goal. But it is possible only on the basis of a rational view of emotions and of their relation to thought. It is possible only if one's emotions are not a mystery, only if one does not have to fear that they may lead one to destruction. It is the prerogative and reward of a person who has assumed the responsibility of identifying and validating the values that underlie his emotions—the person for whom emotional freedom and openness do *not* mean the suspension of awareness.

Emotion and Actions

The pleasure-pain mechanism of man's consciousness—the capacity to experience joy and suffering—performs a crucial function in regard to man's survival. This function involves the *motivational* aspect of man's psychology.

Imagine a living entity so constituted that every time it took an action beneficial to its life, it experienced pain—and every time it took an action inimical to its life, it experienced pleasure. Clearly, such an entity could not exist; it would be a biological impossibility. But if, impossibly and miraculously, it were to come into existence, it would quickly perish. With its pleasure-pain mechanism set in reverse, against its own life, it could not survive. Nothing could prompt or motivate it to perform the actions its survival required.

Pleasure (in the widest meaning of the term, as both a physical and an emotional experience) is a concomitant of life—a concomitant of efficacious action. Pain is a signal of danger—a concomitant of *in*efficacious action.

Such is the basic biological function of pleasure and pain. Pleasure is the reward of successful (life-serving) action and is an incentive to act further. Pain is the penalty of unsuccessful (life-negating) action and is an incentive to act differently.

On the physical level, i.e., on the level of sensations, it is a man's physiology that determines what he experiences as pleasurable or painful (although psychological factors are often involved). On the level of emotions, it is a man's values that determine what gives him joy or suffering. His physiology is not open to his choice. His values are.

As I discussed above, it is through his values that man programs his emotional mechanism. Short-term, man can pervert this mechanism by programming irrational values. Long-term, he cannot escape the logic implicit in its biological function. The protector of the biological function of man's emotional mechanism is the law of contradiction. A man whose values were *consistently* irrational (i.e., incompatible with his nature and needs) could not continue to exist. Most men's values are a mixture of the rational and the irrational—which, necessarily, creates an inner conflict. Such a conflict means that the satisfaction of one value entails the frustration of another.

The simplest example of the foregoing is the "pleasure" of getting drunk—followed by the misery of a hangover. One of the cardinal characteristics of irrational values is that they *always* entail *some* form of "hangover"—whether the loss of one's health, one's job, one's wife, one's intellectual competence, one's sexual capacity or one's self-esteem. According to the values he selects, his emotions are a man's rewards—or his nemesis. Nature and reality always have the last word.

Happiness or joy is the emotional state that proceeds from the achievement of one's values. Suffering is the emotional state that proceeds from a negation or destruction of one's values. Since the activity of pursuing and achieving values is the essence of the life-process—happiness or suffering may be regarded as an *incentive system* built into man by nature, a system of reward and punishment, designed to further and protect man's life.

The biological utility, i.e., the survival value, of *physical* pain is generally recognized. Physical pain warns man of danger to his body and thus enables him to take appropriate corrective action. It is not sufficiently recognized that *psychological* pain—anxiety, guilt, depression—performs the same biological function in regard to man's consciousness. It warns him that his mind is in an improper state and that he must act to correct it. He may, of course, choose to ignore the warning—but not with impunity.

There is another aspect involved in the biological utility of emotions. Man can draw conclusions, can acquire many values and premises, *implicitly,* without conscious awareness of doing so. He would be in danger if he had no means of being aware of their existence, if they affected his actions with no warning signs available to his conscious mind. But it is via his emotions that man is given the evidence of such subconscious premises—so that he can revise or correct them if necessary.

The motivational power and function of emotions is evident in the fact that every emotion contains an inherent action tendency, i.e., an impetus to perform some action related to the particular emotion. Love, for example, is a man's emotional response to that which he values highly; it entails the action tendency to achieve some form of contact with the loved person, to seek the loved person's presence, to interact intellectually, emotionally, physically, etc. The emotion of fear is a man's response to that which threatens his values; it entails the action tendency to avoid or flee from the feared object. Values by their very nature entail action. So do value-responses, i.e., emotions.

The action involved is not always physical. For example, there are feelings of quiet happiness that invoke in a man the desire only to remain still and contemplate the source of his happiness—or the beauty of the world around him; his sought-for values have been achieved and all he wants is to dwell on and experience the reality of their existence. But every emotion carries *some* implication for action. (This does not mean, of course, that the action should necessarily be taken; it may not be possible or appropriate in a given context.)

The action implication of some emotions is *negative,* i.e., they tend specifically to retard or inhibit action. This is evident in the case of acute depression. The person feels that nothing is worth doing, that action is futile, that he is helpless to achieve happiness. The impulse is toward stillness, passivity, withdrawal.

Implicit in every emotional response is a *dual* value-judgment, both parts of which have action implications. Every emotion reflects the judgment "for me" or "against me"—and also "to what extent." Thus, emotions differ according to their *content* and according to their *intensity.* Strictly speaking, these are not two *separate* value-judgments, they are integral aspects of the same value-judgment; they may be separated only by a process of abstraction. They are experienced as one response. But the intensity aspect obviously influences the strength of the impulse to action as well as, sometimes, the nature of the action taken.

An action tendency, as an emotional experience, can be distinguished from the wider emotional field in which it occurs. Considered as a separate experience, it is the emotion of *desire* or of *aversion.*

Every emotion proceeds from a value-judgment, but not every value-judgment leads to an emotion. An emotion is experienced only when the value-judgment is considered, by the person involved, to have significance for his own life, to have *relevance to his actions.*

Suppose, for example, that a research scientist reads about some new discovery in a field remote from his own, unconnected to his professional or personal interests and having no implications for his own actions or goals. He may appraise the discovery as "good," but the appraisal would not invoke any significant or discernible emotion in him.

Now suppose that he sees in the discovery a possible lead to the solution of a research problem of his own—then his appraisal of "good" is accompanied by an emotion, a sense of excitement and an eagerness to pursue the lead.

If he sees in the discovery an *unmistakable* and *major* key to the solution of his own problem—then the emotion of elation is more intense and so is the urgency of his desire to rush to his laboratory.

Now consider a different kind of example. A man is in love with a woman and feels sexual desire for her. Then some physical accident renders him impotent. He does not lose the capacity to experience sexual desire, but that desire now has a significantly different emotional quality—because the alteration in his own physical state has affected the action implications of his evaluation of the woman. The estimate of her value as such has not changed; what has changed is its relevance to himself, to his own actions.

In order to feel love for some object, be it a human being, a pet, or a new house, a man must see some possibility of action he can take in regard to it; otherwise, his appraisal of "good" is merely an abstract judgment, without *personal* significance.

The same principle is clearly evident in the case of the emotion of fear. When, in response to the perception of some danger to his values, a person feels fear—he feels it on the premise that there is some counteraction he could or should or might be able to take. If he were firmly, fully convinced that no action was possible, he might feel sadness or regret, but not fear. (Observe that fear always involves uncertainty: if a person knows clearly what action to take and is able to take it, he does not feel fear.)

Sometimes, the emotions a person feels, and the action implications they entail, are very abstract; the value-response is, in effect, metaphysical in character. A person may respond to some great achievement or to a great work of art, and draw emotional inspiration from it: he sees in it an expression of man's creative power, he sees the triumph of man's efficacy, he sees the heroic, the noble, the admirable—and this sight provides emotional fuel for the pursuit of his own values.

It is interesting to observe that both profound happiness and profound suffering are experienced as "metaphysical." Implicit in a feeling of profound happiness is the sense of living in a "benevolent" universe, i.e., a universe in which one's values are attainable, a universe open to the efficacy of one's effort. Implicit in profound suffering is the opposite feeling: the sense of living in a universe in which one's values are unreachable, a universe in which one is helpless, where no action is worth taking because nothing can succeed.

Unresolved contradictions in a man's values lead to psychologically destructive consequences. The action tendency inherent in emotional responses is pertinent to an understanding of this issue.

Contradictions cannot exist in reality. But a man can hold ideas, beliefs, values which, with or without his knowledge, are contradictory. Contradictory ideas cannot be integrated; they sabotage the integrative function of man's mind and undercut the certainty of his knowledge in general.

The disastrous consequence of holding contradictory values is the short-circuiting of the value-emotion-action mechanism. *A man is hit by two contradictory and conflicting impulses to action.* He knows or senses, in effect, that the impossible is being demanded of him. The more profound the values involved, the worse the psychological disaster—if the conflict is evaded and repressed rather than identified and resolved.

Consider, as a classic illustration of this problem, a case such as the following. A priest has taken vows of celibacy and feels deeply committed to his vows. But a woman in his congregation begins to attract him sexually. Walking up to his pulpit one Sunday, he sees her—and suddenly feels violent sexual desire. For a brief moment, he feels himself driven to a course of action that conflicts intolerably with the course of action to which he has committed his life. In the next instant, he faints. When he regains consciousness, he has no memory of his desire for the woman (he has repressed it); but he feels acute, seemingly causeless anxiety.

In cases of value-conflict, the short-circuit occurs in the transition from consciousness to reality, i.e., via the emotional mechanism that translates evaluations (events of consciousness) into actions (events of reality).

Whether a man's emotional mechanism brings him happiness or suffering depends on its programming. It depends on the validity and consistency of his values. His emotional apparatus is a machine. Man is its driver. According to the values he selects, he makes the motivational power of his emotions work in the service of his life—or against it.

Emotions and Repression: The Repression of Negatives

Repression is a subconscious mental process that forbids certain ideas, memories, identifications, and evaluations to enter conscious awareness.

Repression is an *automatized avoidance reaction,* whereby a man's focal awareness is involuntarily pulled away from any "forbidden" material emerging from less conscious levels of his mind or from his subconscious.

Among the various factors that may cause a man to feel alienated from his own emotions, repression is the most formidable and devastating.

But it is not emotions as such that are repressed. An emotion as such cannot be repressed; if it is not *felt,* it is not an emotion. Repression is always directed at thoughts. What is blocked or repressed, in the case of emotions, is either evaluations that would lead to emotions or identifications of the nature of one's emotions.

A man can repress the knowledge of what emotion he is experiencing. Or he can repress the knowledge of its extent and intensity. Or he can repress the knowledge of its object, i.e., of who or what aroused it. Or he can repress the reasons of his emotional response. Or he can repress conceptual awareness that he is experiencing any particular emotion at all; he can tell himself that he feels nothing.

For example, hearing of the success of a friend who is also a business rival, a man may repress the awareness that the emotion he feels is envious resentment, and assure himself that what he feels is pleasure. Or, failing to be admitted to the college of his choice, a student may tell himself that he feels "a little disappointed," and repress he fact that he feels devastatingly crushed. Or, feeling sexually rebuffed by his sweetheart and repressing his pain out of a sense of humiliation, a youth may account to himself for his depression by the thought that no one understands him. Or, repressing her guilt over an infidelity, a wife can explain her tension and irritability by the thought that her husband takes no interest in her or their home. Or, burning with unadmitted frustration and hostility because he was not invited to join a certain club, a man may tell himself that the subject leaves him completely indifferent.

Repression differs from evasion in that evasion is instigated consciously and volitionally; repression is subconscious and involuntary. In repression, certain thoughts are blocked and inhibited from reaching conscious awareness; they are not *ejected* from focal awareness, they are prevented from *entering* it.

In order to understand the mechanism of repression, there are three facts pertaining to man's mind that one must consider.

1. All awareness is necessarily selective. In any particular moment, there is far more in the world around him than a man could possibly focus on—and he must choose to aim his attention in a given direction to the exclusion of others. This applies to introspection no less than to extrospection.

Focal awareness entails a process of *discriminating* certain facts or elements from the wider field in which they appear, and considering them *separately*. This is equally true of the perceptual and the conceptual levels of consciousness.

2. There are *degrees* of awareness. There is a gradient of diminishing mental clarity along the continuum from focal awareness to peripheral awareness to total unawareness or unconsciousness. To use a visual metaphor, the continuum involved is like that between two adjoining colors on the spectrum, say, blue and violet; the area of pure blue (focal awareness) shades off by almost imperceptible degrees to blue-violent (peripheral awareness), which shades into pure violet (unconsciousness).

The phenomenon of degrees of awareness makes it possible for a man not to let his left hand know what his right hand is doing. A man can be aware of something very dimly—but aware enough to know that he does not want to be aware more clearly.

The mind can contain material which, at a given moment, is neither subconscious nor in focal awareness, but is in that wider field of consciousness whose elements must be distinguished and identified by a directed effort which will *bring* them into focal awareness—an act that a man may or may not choose to perform.

3. Man is a self-programmer. To an extent immeasurably greater than any other living species, he has the ability to retain, integrate, and *automatize* knowledge.

As a man develops, as he learns to form concepts and then still wider concepts, the quantity of programmed data in his brain grows immeasurably, expanding the range and efficacy of his mind. Cognitions, evaluations, physical skills—all are programmed and automatized in the course of normal human development. It is this programming, retained on a subconscious level, that makes possible not only man's continued intellectual growth, but also the instantaneous cognitive, emotional, and physical reactions without which he could not survive.

When a man's mind is in active focus, the goal or purpose he has set determines what material, out of the total content of his knowledge, will be fed to him from the subconscious. If, for instance, a man is thinking about a problem in physics, then it is the material relevant to that particular problem which will normally flow into his conscious mind. Focal awareness controls the subconscious process by setting the appropriate goal(s)—by grasping the requirements of the situation and, in effect, issuing the appropriate orders to the subconscious.

The subconscious is regulated, not only by the orders it receives in any immediate moment, but by the "standing orders" it has received—i.e., by a man's long-term interests, values, and concerns. These affect how material is retained and classified, under what conditions it is reactivated and what kind of subconscious connections—in response to new stimuli or data—are formed.

This is very evident in the case of creative thinking. Creative thinking rests on the establishment of a standing order to perceive and integrate everything possibly relevant to a given subject of interest. The problem with which he is concerned may not occupy a thinker's mind day and night; at times he will focus on other issues; but his subconscious holds the standing order to maintain a state of constant readiness, and to signal for the attention of the conscious mind should any significant data appear. The phenomenon of the sudden "inspiration" or "flash of insight" is made possible by a final, split-second integration which rests on innumerable earlier observations and connections retained in the subconscious and held in waiting for the final connection that will sum them up and give them meaning.

Now let us turn to the psychology of repression.

Repression, mechanically, is simply one of the many instances of the principle of automatization. Repression entails an automatized standing order exactly opposite to the one involved in creative thinking: it entails an order *forbidding* integration.

The simplest type of repression is the blocking from conscious awareness of painful or frightening memories. In this case, some event that was painful or frightening when it occurred *and would be painful or frightening if recalled,* is inhibited from entering conscious awareness.

The phenomenon of forgetting as such, is not, of course, pathological; memory, like awareness, is necessarily selective; one normally remembers that to which one attaches importance. But in cases of repression, memories do not simply "fade away"; they are actively blocked.

Consider the following example. A twelve-year-old boy succumbs to the temptation to steal money from a friend's locker in school. Afterward, the boy is tremblingly fearful that he will be found out; he feels humiliated and guilty. Time passes and his act is not discovered. But whenever the memory of his theft comes back to him, he re-experiences the painful humiliation and guilt; he strives to banish the memory, he hastily turns his attention elsewhere, telling himself, in effect, "I don't want to remember. I wish it would go away and leave me alone!" After a while, *it does.*

He no longer has to eject the memory from conscious awareness; it is inhibited from entering. It is repressed. The act of banishing the memory has become automatized.

Should the memory ever begin to float toward the surface of awareness, it is blocked before it can reach him. A kind of psychological alarm-signal is set off and the memory is again submerged.

Twenty years later, he may encounter the friend from whom he stole the money and greet him cheerfully; he remembers nothing of his crime. Or he may feel vaguely uncomfortable in his friend's presence and disinclined to renew the acquaintance—but with no idea of the reason.

Repressed memories are not always as localized and specific as in this example. Repression has a tendency to "spread out," to include other events associated with the disturbing one—so that memories of entire areas or periods of a man's life can be affected by the repressive mechanism.

People with traumatically painful childhoods sometimes exhibit something close to amnesia concerning their early years. They do not simply repress individual incidents; they feel that they want to forget the events of an entire decade, and they often succeed to a remarkable extent. If any questions about their childhood are raised, they may feel a heavy wave of pain or depression, with very meager, if any, ideational content to account for it.

Thoughts and evaluations, like memories, may be barred from awareness because of the pain they would invoke.

A religious person, for example, might be appalled to find himself entertaining doubts about his professed beliefs; he condemns himself as sinful and, in effect, tells these doubts, "Get thee behind me, Satan"—and the doubts retreat from his field of awareness. A first, he evades these doubts; later, it is not necessary: he has repressed them. He may then proceed to reinforce the repression by intensified expressions of religious fervor, which will help to divert his attention from any lingering uneasiness he cannot fully dispel.

Or consider the case of a neurotically dependent woman who is married to a cruel, tyrannical man. She dares not let any criticism of him enter her awareness—because she has surrendered her life to him, and the thought that her owner and master is irrational and malevolent would be terrifying to her. She observes his behavior, her mind carefully kept empty, her judgment suspended. She has automatized a standing order forbidding evaluation. Somewhere within her is the knowledge of how she would judge her husband's behavior if it were exhibited by any other man—but this knowledge is not allowed to be integrated with the behavior she is observing in her husband. Her repression is reinforced and maintained by considerable evasion; but her blindness is not caused *only* by evasion; to an important extent, she has *programmed* herself to be blind.

Not uncommonly, one can see a similar pattern of repression among children whose parents are frighteningly irrational. Children often repress negative evaluations of their parents, finding it more bearable to reproach themselves in the case of a clash, than to consider the possibility that their parents are monsters. One can observe this same phenomenon among the citizens of a dictatorship, in their attitude toward the rulers.

Perhaps the most complex instances of repression are those involving the attempt to negate emotions and desires.

An emotion can be attacked through the repressive mechanism in two ways: the repression can occur *before* the emotion is experienced, by inhibiting the evaluation that would produce it— or it can occur *during* and/or *after* the emotional experience, in which case the repression is directed at a man's knowledge of his own emotional state.

(As was noted earlier, emotions as such cannot be repressed; whenever I refer to "emotional repression," I mean it in the sense of the above paragraph.)

A man seeks to repress an emotion because in some form he regards it as threatening. The threat involved may be simply pain, or a sense of loss of control, or a blow to his self-esteem.

Consider the case of a mild, amiable woman, who tends to be imposed upon and exploited by her friends. One day, she experiences a violent fit of rage against them—and she is shocked and made anxious by her own feeling. She is frightened for three reasons: she believes that only a very immoral person could experience such rage; she is afraid of what the rage might drive her to do; and she is apprehensive lest her friends learn of her feeling and abandon her. She tells herself fiercely, in effect, "Do not judge their actions—above all, do not judge their behavior toward you— be agreeable to everything." When this order is automatized on the subconscious level, it acts to paralyze her evaluative mechanism; she no longer feels rage—at the price of no longer feeling much of anything. She does not know what any events really mean to her. She then proceeds to compound her repression by instigating an additional block to prevent her from recognizing her own emotional emptiness; she assures herself that she feels all the emotions she believes it appropriate to feel.

Or: A man finds himself spending more and more time with a married couple who are his friends. He does not note the fact that he is far more cheerful when the wife is present than when he and the husband are alone. He does not know that he is in love with her. If he knew it, it would be a blow to his sense of personal worth—first, because he would see it as disloyalty to the husband; second, because he would see it as a reflection on his realism and "hard-headedness," since the love is hopeless. If brief flashes of love or desire enter his awareness, he does not pause on them or appraise their meaning; their significance does not register; the normal process of integration has been sabotaged. He no longer remembers when the first dim thoughts of love rose to disturb him, and his mind slammed tightly closed before they reached full awareness, and a violent "No!" without object or explanation took their place in his consciousness. Nor does he know why, when he leaves his friends' home, his life suddenly seems unaccountably, desolately arid.

Or: A man who has never made much of himself is resentful and envious of his talented, ambitious younger brother. But the man has always professed affection for him. When his brother is drafted into the army, there is one brief moment when the man feels triumphant pleasure. Then, in the next moment, the knowledge of the nature of his emotion is evaded—and then repressed— and he jokes with his brother about the army "making a man of him." Later, when he receives the news that his brother has been killed in action, he does not know why all he can feel is a heavy numbness and a diffuse, objectless guilt; he tells himself that his grief is too profound for tears; and he drags himself around, strangely exhausted, not knowing that all of his energy is engaged in never letting himself identify the repressed wish which some enemy bullet has fulfilled.

Or: A woman sacrifices her desire for a career to her husband's desire for children and for a wife who has no interests apart from the family. Then, after a while, she feels an occasional spurt of hatred for her children, which horrifies her. She repressed such feelings and is not aware of them again—except that sometimes she is inexplicably and uncharacteristically careless of her children's physical safety. Then she is horrified to discover feelings of contempt for her husband. She represses them, she throws herself with renewed fervor into the role of devoted wife—except that sexual relations with her husband become empty and boring. She takes great pains to present to their friends the picture of a cheerful, "well-adjusted" wife and mother—except that she begins to drink when she is alone.

Or: Since childhood, a man has regarded the emotion of fear as a reflection on his strength, and has struggled never to let himself know when he is afraid. He has instituted a block against recognizing the emotion when it appears. His manner is superficially calm, but he tends to be somewhat stiff and monosyllabic; he backs away from any sort of personal involvement. No values seem to arouse any response in him. An enormous amount of his energy goes into simply maintaining the illusion of inner equilibrium— into keeping his face pleasantly inscrutable and his mind cautiously empty. He feels safest when social conversation involves "small talk"—or some neutral subject where no moral judgments are expected of him or are expressed by anyone else. At home, he practices body-building stolidly and earnestly, and admires the emptiness of his face in the mirror, and feels manly—except that he tends to avoid women because he is close to being impotent.

There are two particularly disastrous errors that can drive a person to repression.

1. Many people believe that the fact of experiencing certain emotions is a moral reflection on them.

But a man's moral worth is not to be judged by the content of his emotions; it is to be judged by the degree of his rationality: only the latter is directly in his volitional control (Chapters Seven and Twelve).

A man may make errors, honestly or otherwise, that result in emotions he recognizes as wrong and undesirable; it may be the case that some of these inappropriate emotions are the result of *past* errors or irrationality. But what determines his moral stature in the *present* is the policy he adopts toward such emotions.

If he proceeds to defy his reasons and his conscious judgment and to follow his emotions blindly, acting on them while knowing they are wrong, he will have good grounds to condemn himself. If, on the other hand, he refuses to act on them and sincerely strives to understand and correct his underlying errors, then, in the present, he is following the policy of a man of integrity, whatever his past mistakes.

If a man takes the content of his emotions as the criterion of his moral worth, repression is virtually inevitable. For example, the Bible declares that a man's sexual desire for his neighbor's wife is the moral equivalent of his committing adultery with her; if a man accepts such a doctrine, he would feel compelled to repress his desire, even if he never intended to act on it.

All of the foregoing applies equally to the repression of "immoral" thoughts.

Freudian psychoanalysts teach that irrational and immoral desires are inherent in man's nature (i.e., contained in man's alleged "id"), and that man cannot escape them; he can only repress them and sublimate them into "socially acceptable" forms. The Freudians teach that repression is a necessity of life. Their secularized version of the doctrine of Original Sin compels them to do so. Since they do not recognize that a man's emotions and desires are the product of acquired (not innate) value-premises which, when necessary, can be altered and corrected—since they regard certain immoral and destructive desires as inherent in human nature at birth—they can have no solution to offer man except repression.

To quote from psychoanalyst A. A. Brill's *Lectures on Psychoanalytic Psychiatry:*

Please note that it is not repression, but the *failure* of it, which produces the (neurotic) symptom. People constantly misinterpret

Freud as having said that one gets sick because of repression, and, *ergo*, they deduce that the best way to remain healthy is never to repress. Now only a complete fool could believe or say such a thing. No one—not even an animal—can do just what he pleases; and certainly Freud and his school never advocated such nonsense.[3]

This leads us to the second major error that prompts men to repress:

2. Many people believe that if one feels an emotion or desire, one will and must act on it.

This premise is implicit in the above quotation from Brill. Note the alternative he sets up: either a man represses certain desires, i.e., makes himself unconscious of them—or else he does "just what he pleases," i.e., surrenders to any impulse he happens to experience. This is absurd.

A rational man neither represses his feelings nor acts on them blindly. One of the strongest protections *against* repression is a man's conviction that he will not act on an emotion merely because he feels it; this allows him to identify his emotions calmly and to determine their justifiability without fear or guilt.

It is an interesting paradox that repression and emotional self-indulgence are often two sides of the same coin. The man who is afraid of his emotions and represses them, sentences himself to be pushed by subconscious motivation—which means, to be ruled by feelings whose existence he dares not identify. And the man who indulges his emotions blindly, has the best reason to be afraid of them—and, at least to some extent, is driven to repress out of self-preservation.

If, then, a man is to avoid repression, he must be prepared to face any thought and any emotion, and to consider them rationally, secure in the conviction that he will not act without knowing what he is doing and why.

Ignorance is not bliss, not in any area of man's life, and certainly not with regard to the contents of his own mind. Repressed material does not cease to exist; it is merely driven underground, to affect a man in ways he does not know, causing reactions he is helpless to account for, and, sometimes, exploding into neurotic symptoms.

There are occasions in man's life when it is necessary for him to *suppress* thoughts and feelings. But suppression and repression are different processes. Suppression is a conscious, deliberate, nonevasive expelling of certain thoughts or feelings from focal awareness, in order to turn one's attention elsewhere. Suppression does not involve a denial of any facts, or a pretense that they do not exist; it involves the implicit premise that one will focus on the suppressed material later, when appropriate.

For example, if a student is studying for an examination, he may have to suppress his thoughts and feelings about an eagerly awaited vacation; he is not evading or repressing; but he recognizes that at present his attention is required elsewhere, and he acts accordingly. Or: a man finds himself becoming angry in the midst of a discussion; he suppresses the anger, he does not deny its existence—in order to think more clearly and to address his mind exclusively to the issues that need to be resolved.

Sometimes, however, there is a certain danger in suppression: a man may suppress thoughts or feelings when there are still unresolved conflicts involved that require further attention and analysis. He may do so with no intent of dishonesty. But a suppression that is repeated consistently can turn into a repression; in effect, the suppression becomes automatized.

Although repression is often preceded and reinforced by evasion, evasion is not a necessary and intrinsic part of the repressive process. A person may mistakenly (but not necessarily dishonestly) believe that he can (and should) *order* undesirable or painful emotions out of existence; such orders, repeated often enough, can result in an automatized block.

However, the more a man practices evasion, i.e., the more firmly he establishes in his mind the principle that the unpleasant or disturbing need not be looked at—the more susceptible he becomes to the instantaneous repression of negatively charged material. In such a case, the policy of repression becomes generalized—it becomes a characteristic, automatic response.

Emotions and Repression: The Repression of Positives

The Freudian view of human nature has caused the concept of repression to be associated primarily with negatives, i.e., with the repression of the irrational and immoral. But there are many tragic instances of men who repress thoughts and feelings which are rational and desirable.

When a person represses certain of his thoughts, feelings, or memories, he does so because he regards them as threatening to him in some way. When, specifically, a person represses certain of his emotions or desires, he does so because he regards them as *wrong*, as unworthy of him, or inappropriate, or immoral, or unrealistic, or indicative of some irrationality on his part—and as *dangerous*, because of the actions to which they might impel him.

Repression, as we have discussed, is not a rational solution to the problem of disturbing or undesirable mental contents. But it is particularly unfortunate when the repressed ideas or feelings are, in fact, *good*, right, normal, and healthy.

A person may judge himself by a mistaken standard, he may condemn emotions and desires which are entirely valid—and if he does so, it is not vices he will attempt to drive underground, but virtues and legitimate needs.

As an example of this error, consider the psychology of a man who represses his desire to find rationality and consistency in people, and who represses his pain and frustration at their absence—under the influence of the fallacious belief that a placid, uncondemning expectation and acceptance of irrationality in people is a requirement of maturity and "realism."

The encounter with human irrationality, in childhood, is one of the earliest psychological traumas in the lives of many people, and one of the earliest occasions of repression. At a time when a young mind is struggling to acquire a firm grasp of reality, it is often confronted—through the actions of parents and other adults—with what appears to be an incomprehensible universe. It is not inanimate objects that appear incomprehensible, but people. It is not nature that appears threatening, but human beings. And, more often than not, the problem is submerged by him, repressed, ignored, never dealt with, never understood, never conquered.

In the case of the man we are considering, the irrationality to which he was exposed as a child was not the expression of intentional cruelty or ill-will. It was simply the "normal" manner of functioning, on the part of his parents, which most adults take for granted.

It consisted of such things as: making promises capriciously, and breaking them capriciously—oversolicitude when the parent was in one mood, and callous remoteness when the parent was in another—answering questions pleasantly one day, and irritably dismissing them the next—sudden expressions of love followed by sudden explosions of resentment—arbitrary unexplained rules and arbitrary, unexplained exceptions—unexpected rewards and unprovoked punishments—subtle pressures, gentle sarcasms, smiling lies, masquerading as affection and parental devotion—switching, irreconcilable commandments—vagueness and ambiguity and impatience and coldness and hysteria and indulgence and reproaches and anxious tenderness.

It was not the trauma of a single moment or episode, but a long accumulation of blows delivered to a victim who was not yet able to know he was a victim, or of what. He could not understand his elders' behavior; he knew only that he felt trapped in a world that was unintelligible and menacing.

As he grew older, this impression was confirmed and reinforced by many other people he encountered, by the irrational behavior of playmates, teachers, etc.

The process of repressing his feelings began early. His bewilderment and dread were painful and he did not like to experience them. He could not understand his feelings; he could not yet conceptualize the factors involved. He could not yet be fully confident of his ability to judge his parents and other people correctly; his judgments lacked the conviction of certainty. At times, he experienced his feeling of horror as overwhelming and paralyzing. And so, to reduce his anguish and to maintain a sense of control, he strove to deny the reality of the problem. This meant: when faced with dishonesty, hypocrisy, inconsistency, evasiveness, to feel nothing—to be an emotional blank. *This* meant: to inactivate his capacity to pass moral judgments.

Now, as an adult, he has learned to "accept" human irrationality. "Acceptance," in this context, does not mean the knowledge that a great many men behave irrationally and that he must be prepared to meet this problem; it means he accepts irrationality as the *normal* and *natural*, he ceases to regard it as an aberration, he does not condemn it.

If a friend whom he had every reason to trust commits some act of betrayal, and he cannot escape feeling hurt and shocked, he *reproaches himself* for his reaction: he feels that he is naïve and out of touch with reality.

To the extent that he cannot fully extinguish his frustrated, anguished desire for rationality, he feels *guilty*. Such is the corruption that repression has worked on his thinking.

Now consider another case: a man who represses his *idealism*, i.e., his aspiration to any values above the level of the commonplace.

When he was a boy, no one understood or shared his feelings about the books he read or the things he liked; no one shared or understood his feeling that a man's life should be important, that he should achieve something difficult and great. What he heard from people was: "Oh, don't take yourself so seriously. You're impractical." He did not strive to conceptualize his own desires and values, to weigh the issue consciously and rationally; he was hurt by people's attitude; he felt like an outcast; he did not want to feel that way; so he gave up. If he saw a romantic movie about some man's heroic achievement, he would remark to his friends, indifferently: "Not bad. But pretty corny, wasn't it?"—and repress the memory of what he had felt in the theatre for two hours, protected by darkness. Now, as a middle-aged Babbitt, he listens with empty eyes and an emptier soul while his own soul speaks of the great things he wants to do when he grows up, and he tells his son to go mow the lawn, and then, sitting alone, why, he wonders, why should I be crying?

Or: The man who, in adolescence, had been desperately lonely. He had found no one whom he could like or admire, no one to whom he could talk. The one girl he cared for had deserted him for another boy. He came to believe that his loneliness was a weakness; that the pain of his frustrated longing for a person he could value was a flaw which he must conquer in himself; that a truly strong, independent man could have no such longing. He became progressively more repressed emotionally. His public manner became more remote and more cheerful. Now, at the age of thirty, he meets a woman with whom he falls desperately in love. But a subconscious block forbids him to know how much he loves her: to know it would unlock the pain of his past and expose him to new pain, should his love not be reciprocated. Since his repression seals off the knowledge of her meaning to him, he cannot communicate it to her. He sees her frequently, but assumes a manner of detached, amused affection: he feels that this manner expresses strength. At first, she responds to him. But eventually she withdraws, alienated by a passionless remoteness which she perceives as weak and unmasculine.

Or: The man who represses his desire for an appreciation and admiration he has earned, because, mistakenly, he views his desire as a failure of independence—and does not understand the feelings of loneliness and a strange, unwanted bitterness that hit him at times.

Or: The woman who represses her sexual passion, because she is afraid of shocking her timid, conventional husband—and does not understand the apathy that invades more and more areas of her life.

Or: The woman who represses her femininity, because she has accepted the popular notion that femininity and intellectuality are incompatible—and who does not understand her subsequent tension and hostility in the realm of sex. (Or: The woman who represses her intellectuality, because she has accepted the same dichotomy, and is left with the same bitterness.)

Or: The man of authentic self-esteem who represses the strength of his impulse to self-assertiveness, out of consideration for the neurotic sensibilities of people who are less secure psychologically—and does not understand his periodic explosions of rebellious, seemingly unprovoked anger.

When a person represses, his intention is to gain an increased sense of control over his life; invariably and inevitably, he achieves the opposite. Observe that in every one of the above cases, repression leads to increased frustration and suffering, not to their amelioration. Whether a person's motive is noble or ignoble, facts cannot be wiped out by self-made blindness; the person who attempts it merely succeeds in sabotaging his own consciousness.

Repression devastates more than a man's emotions; it has disastrous effects on the clarity and efficiency of his thinking. When a man tries to consider any problem in an area touched by his repression, he finds that his mind tends to be unwieldy and his thinking distorted. His mind is straightjacketed; it is not free to consider all possibly relevant facts; it is denied access to crucial information. As a consequence, he feels helpless to arrive at conclusions, or the conclusion she reaches are unreliable.

This does not mean that, once a man has repressed certain thoughts or feelings, he is permanently incapacitated: with sustained effort, it is possible for him, to *de*-repress. Since the represser's mind is only *partially* disabled by blocks, the unobstructed area of his mind retains the capacity to work at removing them.

Repressed material does not vanish completely; it reveals itself in countless indirect ways. The two broadest categories of clues by which repressed material can be traced are: (1) the presence of emotions and desires that appear causeless and incomprehensible in terms of one's conscious convictions; (2) the presence of contradictions in one's responses—contradictions between one's desires, or between one's emotions and one's actions. A concern with detecting such contradictions is the necessary precondition of successful de-repression; it is the starting point of one's introspective efforts to remove mental blocks.

The details of the process of de-repression are outside the scope of this discussion. It must be noted, however, that the process can be extremely difficult. Sometimes, such complexities are involved that a man may require the aid of a competent psychotherapist.

In order to avoid repression—or in order to *de*-repress—it is imperative that a man adopt the policy of *being aware* of his emotions: that he take note of and *conceptualize* his emotional reactions and that he identify their reasons. This policy, practiced consistently, makes repression almost impossible; the chief reason why it is often so easy for men to repress is their policy of unconcern with, and obliviousness to, their own mental states and processes.

If his emotions are to be a source of pleasure to man, not a source of pain, he must learn to *think* about them. Rational awareness is not the "cold hand" that kills; it is the power that liberates.

Chapter Six

Mental Health

The Standard of Mental Health

One of the prime tasks of the science of psychology is to provide definitions of mental health and mental illness.

Psychological disorders are recognized to be the foremost health problem in the nation. These disorders far surpass any group of physical diseases (such as heart or cancer) with regard to number of victims, economic costs, and general devastation of lives. More than half of the hospital beds in this country are occupied by the mentally ill. More than half of the physical complaints for which patients consult physicians are judged to be of psychological origin. It is estimated that one out of twelve persons in the population will spend some part of his life in a mental institution. (Some estimates are one out of ten.) The percentage of persons who turn for psychological help to therapists in private practice, is many times higher.

But there is no general agreement among psychologists and psychiatrists about the nature of mental health or illness—no generally accepted definitions, no basic standard by which to gauge one psychological state or the other.

Many writers declare that no objective definitions and standards can be established—that a basic, universally applicable concept of mental health is impossible. They assert that, since behavior which is regarded as healthy or normal in one culture may be regarded as neurotic or aberrated in another, all criteria are a matter of "cultural bias."

The theorists who maintain this position usually insist that the closest one can come to a definition of mental health is: conformity to cultural norms. Thus, they declare that a man is psychologically healthy to the extent that he is "well-adjusted" to his culture.

Whether or not the speakers are avowed cultural relativists, the theme of "social adaptability" is perhaps the most common one encountered in discussions of mental health. We are never told *why* social adaptability is the definition and standard of mental health; we are not given any rational or scientific justification, we are merely given the *assertion*.

The obvious questions that such a definition raises, are: What if the values and norms of a given society are *irrational*? Can mental health consist of being well-adjusted to the irrational? What about Nazi Germany, for instance? Is a cheerful servant of the Nazi state—who feels serenely and happily at home in his social environment—an exponent of mental health?

The extreme cultural relativists generally prefer to ignore such questions. But if pressed, they are obliged to answer: *Yes*—such a man *is* mentally healthy; it is only from the standpoint of our own cultural biases that he seems aberrated. The moderates, less willing to sever their ties to reality so unreservedly, answer differently. Such a man is *not* mentally healthy, they declare, because he is not *really* happy; he *cannot* be; no one could be well-adjusted to so monstrously irrational a society. Their answer is undeniably true—but observe that it implies a concept of mental health *other than* mere social adaptability; it implies a standard which the speakers are not acknowledging explicitly.

The irrational arbitrariness of equating mental health with social adaptability—and the absurdities to which such an equation leads—have been noted by a number of writers. Seeking more tenable definitions, different psychologists and psychiatrists have proposed a variety of criteria for judging mental health.

The mentally healthy person is said, for example, to have an obstructed capacity for "growth, development and self-actualization"; to "know who he is," i.e., to have a firm sense of identity; to have insight into his own motivation; to have a high tolerance for stress; to be "self-accepting"; to be unencumbered by paralyzing conflicts; to have an integrated personality; etc.

Such descriptions may be valid, but they are not *definitions* of mental health—and their precise meaning is not always clear. One can agree with the above characterizations, in a general way; but they are not adequate to the problem. What must be provided is a *fundamental principle,* an identification of the *essence* of mental health. Such characteristics as the above are effects or consequences. But what is their cause?

The key to the problem of defining the concepts of health and disease, as they pertain to man's mind, consists of placing the issue in a biological context—of remembering that man is a living organism, and that the concepts of health and disease are inextricably linked to the basic alternative confronting all organisms: the issue of life and death.

In the sphere of *physical* health and disease, this fact is clearly recognized. A healthy body is one whose organs function efficiently in maintaining the life of the organism; a diseased body is one whose organs do not. The health or disease of any part of man's body is judged by the standard of how well or poorly it performs its survival-function. *Life* is the standard of judgment.

No other rational standard is possible. It is only the alternative of life or death that makes the concept of health or of disease meaningful or possible. An inanimate object can be neither well nor ill; the concepts are not applicable. Without life as the standard, the concepts of health and disease are not intelligible.

Just as medical science evaluates a man's body by the standard of whether or not his body is functioning as man's life requires, so the science of psychology must employ the same standard in appraising the health or disease of a man's mind. The health of a man's mind must be judged by how well that mind performs its biological function.

What is the biological function of mind? Cognition—evaluation—and the regulation of action.

The basic function of man's consciousness is *cognition,* i.e., awareness and knowledge of the facts of reality. Since man must act, his survival requires that he *apprehend* reality, so that he may regulate his behavior accordingly.

The crucial connecting link between cognition and the regulation of action is *evaluation.* Evaluation is the process of identifying the beneficial or harmful relationship of some aspect of reality to oneself. Evaluations underlie and generate desires, emotions, and goals. His judgments of what is for him or against him determine the ends a man sets himself, as well as the means by which he seeks to achieve them.

If a man's values and goals are in conflict with the facts of reality and with his own needs as a living organism, then he unwittingly moves toward self-destruction. Thus, man's survival requires that the evaluative function of consciousness be ruled by the cognitive function—i.e., that his values and goals be chosen in the full context of his rational knowledge and understanding.

Man is not infallible, and mental health does not require never making an error of knowledge or judgment. The concept of mental health pertains to *the method by which a mind functions*. It pertains to the principles by which a mind operates in dealing with the material of reality. It pertains to a man's "psycho-epistemology."[1]

The concept of "psycho-epistemology" is crucially important, not only to the problem of mental health, but to the entire subject-matter of this book. Let us, therefore, consider the meaning of this concept.

Psycho-Epistemology

As a field of scientific study, psycho-epistemology should be classified as a branch of psychology. It may be described as the psychology of thinking (or of cognition).

Epistemology, of course, is a branch of philosophy; it is the science that studies the nature and means of human knowledge. Its primary purpose is to establish the *criteria* of knowledge, to define principles of evidence and proof, to enable man to distinguish between that which he may and may not regard as knowledge. Epistemology assumes, or takes as its "given," a normal (i.e., healthy) consciousness; it assumes an intact mind intent on knowing the facts of reality. Insofar as it is concerned with the internal operations of mind, it is concerned from one standpoint exclusively: the standpoint of relevance to establishing the *criteria of knowledge*. Its basic concern is with the relationship of ideas to reality—not with mental processes *as such*.

The study of mental processes as such is the province of psychology—most particularly, of psycho-epistemology.

The concept of "psycho-epistemology" is introduced in order to designate the study of mental operations on the conscious and subconscious levels of man's mind. The subject is an extremely broad one, and involves many issues that are beyond the scope of this discussion. I shall confine myself in the present context, to those essentials which have a direct bearing on the question of mental health.

Mental processes may be conscious or subconscious, and volitional or automatic. In any act of thinking, there is constant interaction between conscious, volitional operations and subconscious, automatic ones. For example, the goal of solving a certain problem is chosen consciously, and knowledge retained on a subconscious level is instantly activated and made an integral part of the thinking that ensues. On the conscious level, the mind sets goals, breaks problems into sub-problems, monitors the thinking process for consistency, relevance, etc.; on the subconscious level, the mind's vast integrative machinery, utilizing previously acquired knowledge, memories, observations, associations, etc., works to provide the material which will lead to the achievement of those chosen goals.

This interaction between the conscious, volitional operations of man's mind and the subconscious, automatic operations, is characteristic of all goal-directed mental activity—whether the goal be to achieve knowledge, or to evoke a memory, or to imagine some event, etc.

Psycho-epistemology is the study of the nature of, and the relationship between, the conscious, goal-setting, self-regulatory operations of the mind, and the subconscious, automatic operations.

This branch of psychology is concerned with all the possible types of mental operations (normal and pathological) of which man's mind is capable; and with individual differences among men in their manner of cognitive functioning.

I have stressed the fact that man is a self-programmer whose conclusions, values, and standing orders direct the automatic integrative mechanism of his subconscious (Chapter Five). As a person develops, he acquires a characteristic manner of cognitive functioning—a characteristic method of dealing with problems, thinking about issues, "processing" the data of reality, etc. He may acquire the habit of seeking the highest possible level of mental clarity with regard to any issue he is considering; or he may come to accept as "normal" some level of *un*clarity or confusion. He may adopt the policy of always seeking to understand issues in terms of principles; or he may attempt to deal with problems in terms of the concretes of a given situation, with no effort to isolate the essential from the nonessential or to relate his observations to wider abstractions. His thinking may be flexible, in the sense of being open to new facts, new considerations, new evidence; or it may be rigid, inhibited, dogmatic. He may learn to differentiate clearly between his thinking and his emotions; or he may tend to treat his emotions as tools of cognition. He may consistently exercise his own first-hand judgment in any matter he chooses to consider; or he may acquire the habit of relying on the judgments of others. He may learn to identify his emotions and desires conceptually; or he may automatize a policy of repression in any case of conflict, uncertainty, or self-doubt.

The mental habits a person acquires, and the standing orders he establishes, constitute his characteristic psycho-epistemology, his self-programmed method of mental functioning. These habits and standing orders play a crucial role in directing the mind's subconscious, automatic operations—in determining the integrations that will or will not be made, the material that will or will not flow into conscious awareness, the implications a mind will or will not grasp, the ease, speed, and productiveness of a given thinking process, etc.

It is clear from the foregoing that a person's characteristic psycho-epistemology may or may not be appropriate to the task of properly apprehending reality; or may be appropriate to a greater or lesser degree. This brings us to the relationship of psycho-epistemology to the issue of mental health and illness.

The Meaning of Mental Health

A man's psycho-epistemological processes may be directed (or predominantly directed) by the goal of awareness, of cognition, i.e., they may be reality-oriented in their operation. Or his psycho-epistemology may be ruled (or predominantly ruled) by goals that entail reality-avoidance operations, i.e., goals that entail the subversion of his cognitive apparatus.

This is the alternative at the root of the issue of mental health. If no such alternative in the operation of man's mind were possible, no such question as a mind's health or disease could arise.

Mental health is the unobstructed capacity for reality-bound cognitive functioning—and the exercise of this capacity. Mental illness is the sustained impairment of this capacity.

The justification of this definition lies, as we have seen, in the biological function of consciousness.

Thus, a man is mentally healthy to the extent that his psycho-epistemological processes are controlled by and fulfill the requirements of cognition, i.e., of awareness of and contact with reality. A man is mentally unhealthy to the extent that his psycho-epistemological processes are incompatible with the requirements of cognition, and subvert his cognitive efficacy.

Cognition is the primary function of consciousness—the function that, properly, controls the other mental functions—and, therefore, any operations or practices that are inimical to this basic task, are agents or causes of psychological illness.

Biologically, life is a state and process of integration: the physical integrity of an organism, and the integration of its actions in the direction of life-serving goals, are the precondition and essence of biological well-being—of an organism's success at the task of survival. Any forces that work against integration, work against life; disintegration is motion toward death.

Integration is basic to the cognitive process and to mental health. Disintegration and conflict are the hallmark of mental illness.

Reality-avoidance practices—evasion, repression, rationalization, and their various derivatives—are disintegrative by their very nature and intention. Their effect is to sabotage cognition. They are prime instigators of psychological disorders.

An unobstructed, integrated consciousness, a consciousness in unbreached cognitive contact with reality, is *healthy*. A blocked, disintegrated consciousness, a consciousness incapacitated by fear or immobilized by depression, a consciousness corrupted in its function by reality-avoidance mechanisms, a consciousness dissociated from reality—is *unhealthy*.

Mental illness is, fundamentally, psycho-epistemological; a mental disorder is a *thinking* disorder.

This is fairly obvious in cases where the patient's predominant symptoms are hallucinations, delusions, "word-salads," neologisms, time-space disorientations, etc. But it is equally true in cases where the patient's symptoms are less obviously cognitive or psycho-epistemological in origin—such as pathological anxiety, depression, hypochondriasis, conversion reactions, sado-masochism, etc. (Chapter Nine).

Neurotic and psychotic manifestations, such as inappropriate emotional responses or aberrant behavior, are the *symptoms* and *consequences* of a mind's malfunctioning. But the root problem is always: the mind's alienation from reality (in some form, to a greater or lesser extent).

Consider, for example, a case of pathological depression. A secretary is asked by her employer to make certain that she finishes some office reports by the end of the day; she hears this request as a declaration of her incompetence and worthlessness—and she collapses in acute depression. It is misleading to say that she suffers from "an *emotional* disorder." She suffers from a psycho-epistemological disorder. Her problem lies in the mental processes by which she *interprets* the things she perceives and hears. Her problem lies in the mental processes *generating* her emotions.

Once such disturbed emotions are generated, they tend to have a negative effect on the person's thinking—which then leads to further disturbed emotions, and so on. This is one of the ways in which harmful psycho-epistemological policies are self-reinforcing and self-perpetuating. But disturbed emotions do not create the initial problem; the initial problem creates the disturbed emotions.

Emotions reflect evaluations and interpretations; inappropriate or disturbed emotions proceed from inappropriate or disturbed judgments; these proceed from inadequate or disturbed thinking.

The same principle applies to behavior. If a man is dishonest, parasitical and exploitative in his human relationships, it is not his *behavior* that constitutes his mental illness, but the psycho-epistemological policies behind his behavior.

Irrational beliefs, emotions, and actions are the symptoms by which we detect the presence of mental illness. They are aids to diagnosis. But they must not be confused with their psychological causes or roots. The tendency to such a confusion underlies the arguments of those cultural relativists who observe that beliefs, emotional responses, and behavior considered healthy in one culture may be regarded as neurotic in another.

Such observations have no bearing on the *nature* of mental health. For example: if a primitive man spoke to trees, believing they were inhabited by conscious spirits, this would not necessarily indicate mental illness; whereas a modern man who acted in this manner would almost certainly be psychotic. In appraising the psychological significance of a man's behavior, it is necessary to take cognizance of his context, of the knowledge available to him. We cannot necessarily know, from an observation of behavior taken out of context, whether or not it reflects an aberration in a mind's thinking processes. This is an important point for the diagnostician to remember—but it has nothing to do with the question of what constitutes mental health.

It should be noted that mental illness is not indicated by a man's *momentary* loss of cognitive contact with reality, such as might occur under the impact of a violent emotion. Mental illness implies the presence of *enduring* obstructions to a mind's cognitive efficacy. Mental illness implies the presence of automatized (or partially automatized) obstructions to conceptual integration.

Even in cases where the causes of mental illness are physical (genetic, biochemical, etc.), the patient's condition is designated as a *mental* illness only because there is a breakdown in his cognitive function. In the absence of this breakdown, the condition is not mental illness.

A man whose cognitive contact with reality is unbreached, whose perceptions, judgments, and evaluations are free of blocks and distortions—a man who is willing and able to look at any fact relevant to his life, whose integrative powers are unimpaired—does not exhibit symptoms such as pathological anxiety, depersonalization, obsessive-compulsive reactions, conversion hysteria, or delusions of persecution.

It is difficult to escape the conclusion that in most (and perhaps all) instances of mental illness whose cause is psychological, there is some degree of complicity on the part of the victim. He did not will his illness directly; but he volitionally initiated reality-avoiding policies which brought him to that end. The small evasions, the indulgences in irrational wishes, the surrenders to surmountable fears, the willful acts of self-blindness—such are the means by which the infection is started, and is subsequently reinforced as the condition worsens across the years. In some cases, it must be said the factor of evasion appears to be largely or entirely absent; the "complicity" may be devoid of any element of dishonesty, but may simply entail a policy of repression that nonetheless leads to very harmful consequences.

An irrational environment can and often does play a devastating *contributory* role in the development of psychological disorders. Instead of encouraging the child's healthy cognitive development, many parents do a great deal to stifle it. But they seldom, if ever, succeed without the victim's cooperation.

There are children who resist such pressures by persevering in their will to understand to achieve cognitive clarity. They do not destroy the health of their minds in order to "adjust" to an insane background.

The notion that mental health is to be equated with social adaptability is worse than false; it is actively dangerous; it *encourages* the development of mental illness.

When a child or an adult is confronted by irrationality and injustice on the part of those around him, his mental health can depend on his identifying the facts of the situation consciously and clearly. If he represses his judgment, if he represses his horror or disapproval—in order to alleviate his suffering or to achieve "social harmony"—the corruption of his consciousness is the price he pays for his "adjustment."

There are many adults who have not resolved this conflict one way or the other: they are caught between their desire to "belong"—and their still-struggling critical judgment which tells them that the values, beliefs, and way of life of other people are *wrong*, are not to be accepted. The fact that they are in conflict, that they have not surrendered, is a sign of unextinguished health. But these people are often the victims of the "health-as-adjustment" school. They are pushed by their psychotherapists over the abyss of intellectual self-abnegation into a swamp of conformity.

Mental health is unobstructed cognitive efficacy. Unobstructed cognitive efficacy requires and entails intellectual independence. A doctrine that is subversive of intellectual independence is subversive of mental health.

Psychological Maturity

Closely related to the concept of mental health is that of psychological maturity.

"Maturity," in the broadest sense, is the state of being fully grown or developed. A living organism is mature when its normal process of development is completed, and it functions on the "adult" level appropriate to its species. "*Psychological* maturity," then, is a concept pertaining to the successful development of man's consciousness, to the attainment of a level of functioning appropriate to man *qua* man.

Man is a rational being; to be guided in action by a conceptual form of consciousness, is his distinctive characteristic among living species. His psychological maturity is an issue of the proper growth and development of his conceptual faculty; it is a psycho-epistemological matter.

At first, a child knows only perceptual concretes; he does not know abstractions or principles. His world is only the immediate *now;* he cannot think, plan, or act long-range; the future is largely unreal to him. At this stage, he is a dependent, necessarily: his method of functioning (although biologically inevitable at this period of his life) is inadequate to the requirements of survival as an independent entity.

As the child grows, his intellectual field widens: he learns language, he begins to grasp abstractions, he generalizes, he makes increasingly subtle discriminations, he looks for principles, he acquires the ability to project a distant and more distant future—he rises from the sensory-perceptual level of consciousness to the conceptual level. His power to deal independently with the world around him, with the facts of reality, rises accordingly—in step with his increasing knowledge and increasing proficiency at conceptual mental functioning.

The first and basic index of psychological maturity is *the ability to think in principles*.

More broadly, the basic index of successfully achieved adulthood is the policy of conceptualizing. This means: "an actively sustained process of identifying one's impressions in conceptual terms, of integrating every event and every observation into a conceptual context, of grasping relationships, differences, similarities in one's perceptual material and of abstracting them into new concepts, of drawing inferences, of making deductions, of reaching conclusions, of asking new questions and discovering new answers and expanding one's knowledge into an ever-growing sum."[2]

It must be stressed that this policy constitutes evidence of maturity only when it is practiced in all areas of a person's life and not exclusively in the area of his professional work. There are men who are brilliant at conceptualizing and thinking in principles when their focus is on higher mathematics or some distant galaxy or some business activity—but who become helplessly insecure, concrete-bound children, blind to abstractions and principles, seeing nothing but the immediate moment, when their focus is on, say, current politics or a problem in their personal life. Maturity is evidenced by the ability to think in principles *about oneself.*

All other aspects of psychological maturity are derivatives and consequences of developing one's conceptual faculty. The most important of these aspects are the following:

1. A man who deals with the facts of reality on the conceptual level of consciousness has accepted the responsibility of a *human* manner of existence—which entails his acceptance of responsibility for his own life and actions.

A child cannot accept such responsibility; he is still in the process of acquiring the knowledge and skills necessary for independence. But an adult who expects others to take care of him—and/or who habitually cries, when the consequences of his actions catch up with him, "I couldn't help it!"—is a case of self-arrested development, a person who has defaulted on the process of human maturation.

2. The acceptance of responsibility for one's own life requires a policy of planning and acting long-range, so that one's actions are integrated to one another and one's present to one's future. A child, in large measure, "lives for the moment." A healthy adult plans and acts in terms of a lifespan.

This policy entails a corollary: the willingness to defer immediate pleasure or rewards, when and if necessary, and to tolerate unavoidable frustration.

An infant's typical reaction to frustration is crying. If a child learns that he cannot go to the circus on the day he had expected to, he may, understandably, feel crushed; next week, to him, seems like an infinite time away. But a healthy adult does not view his life and goals in this manner. He does not repress his frustrations; if he can find a way to overcome them, he does: if he cannot, he moves on; he is not paralyzed by them.

3. A cardinal characteristic of maturity is emotional stability. This trait is the consequence of one particular aspect of the policy of conceptual functioning: the ability to preserve the full context of one's knowledge under conditions of stress—frustration, disappointment, fear, anguish, shock. It is the ability, under the pressure of such emotions, to preserve one's capacity to think. The opposite of this state is described as "going to pieces."

One of the unmistakable signs of *im*maturity is the characteristic of being habitually swamped, mentally, by the concrete problem of the moment, so that one loses one's abstract or long-range perspective, one loses the wider context of one's knowledge, and one is taken over by feelings of anger or panic or despair that paralyze thought.

A young person's hold on an abstract perspective, under conditions of stress, is, at best, tenuous; that perspective is still in the process of being formed and of growing firm. But a properly developed adult's perspective has hardened and does not normally crack under pressure.

(This kind of emotional stability must be distinguished sharply from that counterfeit form of stability which is achieved by emotional repression. The repressor, who is so fearful of losing control that he dares not let himself know what he feels, is not an exponent of maturity.)

4. Finally, there is an aspect of psychological maturity that is profoundly important and that few adults fully achieve. It pertains to one's attitude toward the unknown—not toward knowledge which has not yet been discovered by anyone, but toward knowledge which is available but which one does not possess.

To a child, the world around him is—necessarily—an immense unknown. He is aware that adults possess knowledge far in excess of his own and that there are many things he is not yet able to understand. He knows that he does not yet know the wider context of his life and actions. He tells himself in effect: "I will have to wait until I grow up. There are many things I cannot understand now. They are known to other people, but they are beyond me at present."

This is not the attitude of a genuinely mature adult. An adult, too, of course, may recognize (and, indeed, must often be prepared to recognize) that there are things he does not yet know and needs to learn. But he does not entertain such a category as that which is known to others but *unknowable* to him—unknowable in principle. This does not mean that his goal is to possess encyclopedic knowledge. It means that, within the sphere of his first-hand concerns, of his own actions and goals, he regards himself as competent to know that which he needs to know and to acquire whatever knowledge his interests and purposes demand. It means that he does not resign himself to the permanently unknown, when and if the knowledge is available and is relevant to his activities. It means that he does not regard himself as a second-class citizen psycho-epistemologically. It is this attitude, consistently maintained, that marks a man's entry into full adulthood, i.e., into full self-responsibility.

Part Two

The Psychology of Self-Esteem

Chapter Seven

The Nature and Source of Self-Esteem

The Meaning of Self-Esteem

There is no value-judgment more important to man—no factor more decisive in his psychological development and motivation—than the estimate he passes on himself.

This estimate is ordinarily experienced by him, not in the form of a conscious, verbalized judgment, but in the form of a feeling, a feeling that can be hard to isolate and identify because he experiences it constantly: it is part of every other feeling, it is involved in his every emotional response.

An emotion is the product of an evaluation; it reflects an appraisal of the beneficial or harmful relationship of some aspect of reality to oneself. Thus, a man's view of himself is necessarily implicit in all his value-responses. Any judgment entailing the issue, "Is this for me or against me?"—entails a view of the "*me*" involved. His self-evaluation is an omnipresent factor in man's psychology.

The nature of his self-evaluation has profound effects on a man's thinking process, emotions, desires, values, and goals. It is the single most significant key to his behavior. To understand a man psychologically, one must understand the nature and degree of his self-esteem, and the standards by which he judges himself.

Man experiences his desire for self-esteem as an urgent imperative, as a basic need. Whether he identifies the issue explicitly or not, he cannot escape the feeling that his estimate of himself is of life-and-death importance. No one can be indifferent to the question of how he judges himself; his nature does not allow man that option.

So intensely does a man feel the need of a positive view of himself, that he may evade, repress, distort his judgment, disintegrate his mind—in order to avoid coming face to face with facts that would affect his self-appraisal adversely. A man who has chosen or accepted irrational standards by which to judge himself, can be driven all his life to pursue flagrantly self-destructive goals—in order to assure himself that he possesses a self-esteem which in fact he does not have (Chapter Eight).

If and to the extent that men lack self-esteem, they feel driven to *fake* it, to create the *illusion* of self-esteem—condemning themselves to chronic psychological fraud—moved by the desperate sense that to face the universe without self-esteem is to stand naked, disarmed, delivered to destruction.

Self-esteem has two interrelated aspects: it entails a sense of personal efficacy and a sense of personal worth. It is the integrated sum of self-confidence and self-respect. It is the conviction that one is *competent* to live and *worthy* of living.[1]

Man's need of self-esteem is inherent in his nature. But he is not born with the knowledge of what will satisfy that need, or of the standard by which self-esteem is to be gauged; he must discover it.

Why does man need self-esteem? (The fact that men *desire* it, does not constitute proof that it is a need.) How does it relate to man's survival? What are the conditions of its attainment? What is the cause of its profound motivational power? These are the questions we must consider.

There are two facts about man's nature which hold the key to the answer. The first is the fact that reason is man's basic means of survival. The second is the fact that the exercise of his rational faculty is volitional—that, in the conceptual realm, man is a being of volitional consciousness.

Most men do not identify the role and importance of reason in their lives. But from the time that a child acquires the power of self-consciousness, he becomes inescapably aware, if only implicitly, that his consciousness is his basic tool for dealing with reality, that no manner of existence is possible to him without it, and that his well-being depends on the efficacy of his mental operations. There is a primitive level on which no one can avoid grasping the importance of reason. Observe, for instance, that if a person were to think himself "stupid" or "insane," he would necessarily regard this as a devastating reflection on his ability to deal with reality.

From the time that a child acquires the capacity for conceptual functioning, he becomes increasingly aware—implicitly and sub-verbally—of his responsibility for regulating his mind's activity. To maintain the conceptual level of awareness, he must generate *directed* mental effort. He acquires the ability to discriminate between a state of mental focus and a state of mental fog—and to choose one state or the other.

Now let us consider the relevance of these facts to man's need of self-esteem.

Self-Confidence: The Sense of Efficacy

Since reality confronts him with constant alternatives, since man must *choose* his goals and actions, his life and happiness require that he be *right*—right in the conclusions he draws and the choices he makes. But he cannot step outside the possibilities of his nature: he cannot demand or expect omniscience or infallibility. What he needs is that which *is* within his power: the conviction that his *method* of choosing and of making decisions—i.e., his characteristic manner of using his consciousness (his psycho-epistemology)—is right, right *in principle,* appropriate to reality.

An organism whose consciousness functions automatically, faces no such problem: it cannot question the validity of its own mental operations. But for man, whose consciousness is volitional, there can be no more urgent concern.

Man is the only living species able to reject, sabotage, and betray his own means of survival, his mind. He is the only living species who must make himself competent to live—by the proper exercise of his rational faculty. It is his primary responsibility as a living organism. How a man chooses to deal with this issue is, psychologically, the most significant fact about him—because it lies at the very core of his being as a biological entity.

To the extent that a man is committed to cognition—to the extent that the primary goal regulating the functioning of his consciousness is awareness, i.e., understanding—the mental operations activated by his choice lead in the direction of cognitive *efficacy*. To the extent that he fails or refuses to make awareness the regulating goal of his consciousness—to the extent that he evades the effort of thought and the responsibility of reason—the result is cognitive *in*efficacy.

To think or not to think, to focus his mind or to suspend it, is man's basic act of choice, the one act *directly* within his volitional power. This choice is involved in three fundamental psycho-epistemological alternatives—alternatives in his basic pattern of cognitive functioning. They reflect the status that reason, understanding, and reality occupy in a man's mind.

1. A man can activate and sustain a sharp mental focus, seeking to bring his understanding to an optimal level of precision and clarity—or he can keep his focus to the level of blurred approximation, in a state of passive, undiscriminating, goalless mental drifting.

2. A man can differentiate between knowledge and feelings, letting his judgment be directed by his intellect, not his emotions—or he can suspend his intellect under the pressure of strong feelings (desires or fears), and deliver himself to the direction of impulses whose validity he does not care to consider.

3. A man can perform an independent act of analysis, in weighing the truth or falsehood of any claim, or the right or wrong of any issue—or he can accept, in uncritical passivity, the opinions and assertions of others, substituting their judgment for his own.

To the extent that a man characteristically makes the right choices in these issues, he experiences a sense of control over his existence—the control of a mind in proper relationship to reality. Self-confidence is confidence in one's mind—in its reliability as a tool of cognition.

Such confidence is not the conviction that one can never make an error. It is the conviction that one is competent to think, to judge, to know (and to correct one's errors)—that one is competent *in principle*—that one is unreservedly committed to being in unbreached contact with reality to the fullest extent of one's volitional power. It is the confidence of knowing that one places no value or consideration higher than reality, no devotion or concern higher than one's respect for facts.

This basic type of confidence must be distinguished from other, more superficial and localized types of self-confidence, which reflect a person's sense of efficacy at particular tasks or in particular areas. This basic self-confidence is not a judgment passed on one's knowledge or special skills; it is a judgment passed on that which acquires knowledge and skills. It is psycho-epistemological self-confidence; it is a judgment (an implicit judgment, not necessarily conscious) passed on one's characteristic manner of facing and dealing with the facts of reality.

Man *needs* such self-confidence, because to doubt the efficacy of his tool of survival is to be stopped, paralyzed, condemned to anxiety and helplessness—rendered unfit to live.

Self-Respect: The Sense of Worthiness

A man's *character* is the sum of the principles and values that guide his actions in the face of moral choices.

Very early in his development, as a child becomes aware of his power to choose his actions, as he acquires the sense of being a *person,* he experiences the need to feel that he is *right* as a person, right in his characteristic manner of acting—that he is *good.* He is not aware of this question in relation to the issue of life or death; he is aware of it only in relation to the alternative of joy or suffering. To be right as a person is to be fit for happiness; to be wrong is to be threatened by pain.

As I have stressed, no other living species faces such questions as: What kind of entity should I seek to become? By what moral principles should I guide my life? But there is no way for man to escape these questions.

Man cannot exempt himself from the realm of values and value-judgments. Whether the values by which he judges himself are conscious or subconscious, rational or irrational, consistent or contradictory, life-serving or life-negating—every human being judges himself by *some* standard; and to the extent that he fails to satisfy that standard, his sense of personal worth, his self-respect, suffers accordingly.

Man *needs* self-respect because he has to act to achieve values— and in order to act, he needs to value the *beneficiary* of his action.

In order to seek values, man must consider himself worthy of enjoying them. In order to fight for his happiness, he must consider himself worthy of happiness.

The two aspects of self-esteem—self-confidence and self-respect—can be isolated conceptually, but they are inseparable in a man's psychology. Man makes himself *worthy* of living by making himself *competent* to live: by dedicating his mind to the task of discovering what is true and what is right, and by governing his actions accordingly. If a man defaults on the responsibility of thought and reason, thus undercutting his competence to live, he will not retain his sense of worthiness. If he betrays his moral convictions, thus undercutting his sense of worthiness, he does so by evasion, he commits treason to his own (correct or mistaken) judgment, and thus will not retain his sense of competence. The root of *both* aspects of self-esteem is psycho-epistemological.

Such are the nature and causes of man's need of self-esteem.

It must be remembered that self-esteem is a moral appraisal, and morality pertains only to the volitional, to that which is open to man's choice. An unbreached *rationality*—i.e., an unbreached determination to use one's mind to the fullest extent of one's ability, and a refusal ever to evade one's knowledge or act against it— is the only valid criterion of virtue (Chapter Twelve) and the only possible basis of authentic self-esteem.

The Basic Conditions of Self-Esteem

If man is to achieve and maintain self-esteem, the first and fundamental requirement is that he preserve an indomitable *will to understand*. The desire for clarity, for intelligibility, for comprehension of that which falls within the range of his awareness, is the guardian of man's mental health and the motor of his intellectual growth.

The potential range of a man's awareness depends on the extent of his intelligence, i.e., on the breadth of his abstract capacity. But the principle of the will to understand remains the same on all levels of intelligence: it requires the identification and integration, to the best of a man's knowledge and ability, of that which comes into his mental field.

Unfortunately, this attitude is usually relinquished or breached very early in a person's life—and the person "adjusts" to the sense of living in an unintelligible, bewildering, and frightening universe, in which cognitive self-confidence is impossible. Sometimes, the cause is a volitional default on the part of the child—a disinclination to generate the energy of thought, an attitude of irresponsible passivity and dependence. Sometimes, the cause is the child's desire to indulge in wishes or actions he knows to be irrational, which requires that a policy of evasion be instituted—which requires that the will to understand be suspended.

Often, however, the causes are more complex—as, for instance, in the case of a child who comes up against human irrationality with which he does not know how to cope. A child may find the world around him, the world of his parents and other adults, incomprehensible and threatening; many of the actions, emotions, ideas, expectations, and demands of the adults appear senseless, contradictory, oppressive, and bewilderingly inimical to him. After a number of unsuccessful attempts to understand their policies and behavior, the child gives up—*and takes the blame for his feeling of helplessness.* He may react with anger or hostility or anxiety or depression or withdrawal, but, consciously or subconsciously, he takes his failure to understand as a reflection on himself; he accepts an unearned guilt; he concludes that there is something wrong with him, that he is intellectually or morally deficient in some nameless way. Gradually, he gives up the expectation that he will ever be able to make sense of the world around him; he resigns himself to living with the permanently unknowable.

A child is vulnerable, because he is not yet able to recognize clearly and unequivocally that his elders *are* irrational—particularly when some of the time they are not, but are reasonable, thoughtful, fair, and affectionate. He cannot grasp their motives, he knows they know more than he does, but he senses, miserably, desperately, and inarticulately, that there is something terribly wrong— with them, or with himself, or with *something.* What he feels is: I'll never understand people, I'll never be able to do what they expect of me, I don't know what's right or wrong—and I'm never going to know.

So long as a child continues to struggle, so long as he does not give up the will to understand, he is psychologically safe, no matter what his anguish or bewilderment: he keeps his mind and his desire for efficacy intact. When he surrenders the expectation of achieving efficacy, he surrenders the possibility of achieving full self-esteem.

Every child realizes that there are things he cannot expect to know until he grows older; that is not his problem. The problem lies in the things he feels he will *never* know, yet *needs* to know if he is to function successfully. This makes him regard himself, in effect, as an outcast in that foreign land: reality.

A child who clings tenaciously to the will to understand may suffer enormously in his early years, if he is caught in an irrational environment—but he will survive psychologically; he will continue struggling to find his way to the rational view of life that should have been exemplified by his elders, but wasn't; he will doubtless feel alienated from many of the people around him—and legitimately so; but he will not feel alienated from reality. He will not feel that it is *he* who is incompetent to live.

There are other ways in which a young person can resign himself to the unknowable, and thus do harm to his self-esteem. For instance, in his school years, a student may encounter certain subjects with which he has great difficulty. The cause may be that he is not really interested in the subjects, sees no reason to learn them, is poorly taught, or experiences some form of mental block in those areas; perhaps the cause is simply that he has not applied himself. But a young person is in danger psychologically if he concludes, in effect, that the trouble is "just me—I can't understand certain things—that's my nature."

He is *not* in danger if he identifies the causes of his difficulty; he may or may not choose to overcome them, depending on other factors in his personal context. But he subverts his cognitive self-confidence if he merely resigns himself to the notion that some aspects of reality are incomprehensibly closed to him. Once this premise is established, it spreads very easily, extending to more and more issues and problems.

Man controls his mind's activity and growth by the goals he sets—in effect, by the assignments he gives to his consciousness. If he holds to the will to understand, if he regards cognitive efficacy as an absolute, not to be surrendered or relinquished, he thereby activates a process of growth and development which continually raises his mind's power. If he abandons the will to understand, his mind reacts accordingly: it does not continue to rise to higher levels of cognitive efficiency.

If, as a young person matures, he maintains the will to understand, he will be led, necessarily, to the policy of conceptualizing—of looking for and thinking in terms of principles—at the indispensable means of cognitive clarity. Without a process of integration, understanding is impossible—and without concepts and principles, integration is impossible.

The policy of conceptualizing—of thinking in principles—is the basic characteristic of psychological maturity. It is an invariable concomitant of a fully achieved self-esteem.

Such, then, is the basic condition necessary for the achievement of self-esteem: the preservation of the will to understand, in every aspect of one's life.

Now let us consider another condition necessary for the achievement of self-esteem.

In the course of a human being's development, he encounters a problem which—according to how he chooses to deal with it—has profound repercussions on his self-esteem. First encountered in childhood, it is a problem that every person faces on some occasions in his life. There are times when a man's mind and emotions are not instantly and perfectly synchronized: he experiences desires or fears that clash within his rational understanding, and he must choose to follow either his rational understanding or his emotions.

One of the most important things a child must learn is that emotions are not adequate guides to action. The fact that he desires to perform some action is not proof that he should perform it; the fact that he fears to perform some action is not proof that he should avoid performing it. Emotions are not tools of cognition nor criteria of judgment. The ability to distinguish between knowledge and feelings is an essential element in the process of a mind's healthy maturation. It is vital for the achievement and preservation of self-esteem.

Self-esteem requires and entails *cognitive self-assertiveness*, which is expressed through the policy of thinking, of judging, and of governing action accordingly. To subvert the authority of one's rational understanding—to sacrifice one's mind in favor of feelings one cannot justify or defend—is to subvert one's self-esteem.

Reason is the active, initiating element in man—the process that he must generate volitionally; emotions are the passive, reactive element—the automatic product of subconscious integrations, which, in a given case, may or may not be appropriate to reality. To judge the appropriateness or validity of his emotional responses is one of the proper tasks of man's reason. If the authority of his reason is abnegated, if a man permits himself to be carried along passively by feelings he does not judge, he loses the sense of control over his existence: he loses the sense of self-regulation that is essential to self-esteem.

Healthy self-regulation does not consist of or entail repression; nor does it consist of dismissing one's emotions as unimportant. It consists of recognizing that emotions are *effects*—consequences of value-judgments—and of being concerned to know the nature of those judgments and the degree of their validity in a given context.

Significantly, it is the policy of rational self-regulation that is most conducive to healthy emotional spontaneity—in contexts where spontaneity is appropriate (which only reason can judge); whereas a policy of unbridled emotionalism necessarily leads a man to disasters, and ends by causing him to *fear* his emotions as sources of danger and guilt (Chapter Five).

A child, at first, is not aware of such a concept or dichotomy as valid desires versus invalid desires; this distinction rests on knowledge yet to be acquired. He comes to learn, from his experiences and from the teachings of his parents, that some of the things he desires are good for him and others are not; later, he learns another, subtler distinction: he is entitled to some of the things that he desires, but not to others. Thus, he comes to learn that the validity of his desires must be judged.

Consider the case of a child who, at an age when he is old enough to know the meaning of theft, is tempted to steal the toy of a friend. He hesitates to commit the theft, because he knows that he has no right to the toy and that he would be indignant if his friend were to steal one of *his* toys. But he *wants* this particular toy. So he evades his knowledge and commits the theft.

Within a few months, he forgets about the incident. But its consequences are not ended. Wordlessly registered in his mind is a certain principle that was implied and entailed by his action: the principle that it is permissible, at times, to ignore knowledge and facts in order to indulge a desire. This is the legacy of this theft—this, plus a residue of vague, nameless guilt, the sense of some inner uncleanliness, the state of a mind learning to distrust itself.

He is free, subsequently, to repudiate this principle consciously and expunge it from his psychology. But if he fails to do so, if, instead, he reinforces it by repeated acts of evasion and irrational emotional indulgence, he undermines his self-esteem still further. How badly his self-esteem is damaged will depend on the frequency of his evasions, the extent of the knowledge he evades and the nature of the desires he indulges.

If a person develops healthily, if he acquires an integrated set of values, his mind and emotions achieve harmony: he is not chronically torn by conflicts between his desires and his knowledge. But, no matter how well integrated a person may be, the process of holding and applying correctly the full, long-range context of his knowledge is not automatic; the subconscious integrations that generate his emotions are not infallible. Thus, a man always has the responsibility of monitoring and appraising his desires; it is never appropriate for him to regard them as self-justifying primaries.

The majority of men, as adults, suffer from a significant deficit of self-esteem. The senseless tragedy of their lives is that most of them betrayed their mind, not for the sake of gratifying some violent if irrational passion, but for the sake of indulging meaningless or senseless whims that they can no longer remember, for the sake of being free to act on the impulse or spur of the moment, without the responsibility of awareness or thought.

If it is psychologically disastrous to reject one's mind under the pressure of irrational desires, there is another practice which is, perhaps, more disastrous still: rejecting one's mind under the pressure of *fear.* The pursuit of irrational desires might still represent some twisted, neurotic form of self-assertiveness, a groping for pleasure or enjoyment—but the sacrifice of one's mind to fear is undiluted self-abnegation.

The experience of fear per se is not, of course, abnormal or pathological. In many instances, fear has a definite value: it can activate man to cope with some danger. What is crucial for man's psychological well-being is his *attitude* toward fear, his method of dealing with it.

For instance, it is very common for young children to have the experience of being frightened by a barking dog. But children can react to this experience in different ways. One child may be careful to avoid the dog, as a practical, precautionary measure, and cease to feel any further concern; later, he may learn that the dog is not harmful but playful, and may make himself approach the dog and pat him, until all fear is gone. Another child may avoid the dog, after the first encounter, but continue to whimper and whine whenever he sees or hears the dog, even at a great distance; no amount of evidence that the dog is friendly alters his attitude.

The difference in their reactions reflects the different attitudes they adopt toward their fear. The first child, even though afraid, remains in cognitive control; he does not permit the fear to swamp and overwhelm his consciousness; consequently, he does not regard the fear and his avoidance of the dog as a reflection on himself, on his personal worth; he is able to grasp, when the evidence presents itself, that the dog is not in fact a danger to him, and his policy toward the dog changes accordingly. But the second child is swamped and overwhelmed by fear—swamped and overwhelmed psycho-epistemologically; his self-awareness is reduced to a sense of all-encompassing helplessness: nothing is real to him, nothing matters, except that he is afraid; that is why his avoidance of the dog is experienced as humiliating; and that is why his mind is not open to evidence that could change his policy toward the dog. (It goes without saying that intelligent parents can make a major contribution to their child's healthy development by teaching him to handle his fears properly.)

In the life of a young child, a certain amount of fear is to be expected, since the child knows so little and the world around him is unfamiliar and strange. Normally and healthily, with the growth of his knowledge and abilities, these fears are overcome and left behind, so that, with the transition to adulthood, fewer and fewer things have the power to invoke fear in him. The extent to which a child follows this course to full maturity depends on the policy he adopts for dealing with his fears.

The process of growth presents many challenges to a child; every day presents him with new opportunities to expand his knowledge and skills, to explore the world around him, and gain greater proficiency in dealing with it. In the face of certain challenges, a child may experience a measure of apprehension—doubt of his ability to cope with them, fear of failure—for example, when confronted by the challenge of mastering some new subject or skill.

Here, again, children can react to their own apprehension in different ways. One child's chief concern is with the value of succeeding, of expanding his powers; he ignores the fear and marches forward—and the fear dissolves. Another child is primarily concerned with the fear; it is of far more importance to him than the opportunity to grow and to master the unfamiliar; so he retreats—and the fear masters him, instead. (I am speaking here of challenges that are within the child's range of accomplishment, not of challenges that are, in fact, beyond the child's ability to cope with.)

Now consider the following example. A young person ventures some opinion that seems entirely reasonable to him (and, perhaps, *is* reasonable); his father reacts to it with shock and violent rage. The child feels apprehension; perhaps his father will strike him, as he has done in the past. The fear is understandable and natural. But there is more than one way the child can proceed to react, psychologically.

He can retain the awareness that his father has not answered him, has not given reason to support his disagreement, but has merely shouted abuse and shaken his fist; he can remain conscious and judging, even though he is afraid and recognizes that to argue with his father is futile; he can preserve the will to understand, even though he is bewildered and distressed. Or he can let himself be mentally swamped by the fear, so that nothing else matters to him, neither truth nor understanding; he can begin to doubt the validity of the view he expressed; he can decide that he must be wrong, and surrender to a single desire: to escape this frightening situation and to avoid its recurrence—and be willing to suspend his independent judgment in order to achieve this aim.

If, in such situations, a child struggles to preserve the clarity of his mind, he will find, as he grows older, that his susceptibility to fear diminishes radically; what he will often feel, in its place, is a thoroughly appropriate contempt. If, however, he characteristically surrenders to fear—surrenders psycho-epistemologically—then fear gains a greater and greater power over him, and each subsequent surrender feels more and more inevitable. His sense of personal efficacy is affected accordingly.

The same principles apply on an adult level. If, for example, a man remains silent and passively unprotesting when things which he values are being attacked, through fear of not "belonging" or not being "accepted"; or if a man retreats from the challenges of life and buries himself in the "safety" of the routine, the familiar, the undemanding, through fear of failure or of making mistakes; or if a man is compulsively driven to the pursuit of meaningless sexual adventures, through fear of being regarded (or of regarding himself) as "unmasculine"; or if a woman conceals and represses her desire for a career, through fear of being considered "unfeminine"; or if a woman blinds herself to any defect in her husband, through fear of damaging their relationship—the result, necessarily, is a profound sense of humiliation, of self-abasement, of self-renunciation, which means: a profound loss of self-esteem.

Sometimes, of course, a fear-experience can be so intense that the capacity for thought is momentarily wiped out. But such panic reactions pertain to short-term, emergency situations, and are necessarily short-lived. In such cases, a person's attitude and policy toward fear is manifested through what he does when the panic dies down. Does he then proceed to think about the experience, to assimilate it and to prepare himself for future, similar situations—in other words, does he seek to *reassert* mastery and control over his life? Or does he merely shudder at the memory of the fear, struggle to evade the issue, and hope he will not encounter such problems again, resigning himself to the belief that, should such problems recur, helplessness is all that is possible to him?

The policy a man adopts in dealing with fear depends on whether he preserves the *will to efficacy;* it depends on whether he preserves the value of self-confidence as a goal not to be relinquished, and, consequently, regards a state of fear as the temporary and abnormal, as that which he must overcome—or whether he gives up the expectation of achieving efficacy, resigns himself to a sense of impotence, and accepts fear as a basic, unalterable "given" of his existence, to be endured, not to be defeated. Just as the will to understand requires that man never resign himself to accepting the unknowable as an inherent part of his life—so the will to efficacy requires that he never resign himself to living with uncontested fear.

It must be stressed that the concept of surrender to fear pertains to a psycho-epistemological process; the subversion of one's consciousness, of one's faculty of awareness, in order to avoid or minimize a fear experience. This practice is entirely different from the rational avoidance of real and practical dangers to which there is no reason to expose oneself. In fact, *opposite* principles are at work in these two cases: in the first case, one is *fleeing* from reality; in the second, one is taking proper cognizance of it.

The preservation of the will to understand, and of the supremacy of one's rational judgment, entails the same fundamental principle: that of a profound *respect for facts*—a profound sense of reality and objectivity—a recognition that existence exists, that A is A, that reality is an absolute not to be evaded or escaped, and that the primary responsibility of consciousness is to perceive it.

This principle is at issue in a decision that is crucial to a man's self-esteem: the choice between judging what is true or false, right or wrong, by the independent exercise of his own mind—or passing to others the responsibility of cognition and evaluation, and uncritically accepting their verdicts.

Here, again, the basic choice involved is: to think or not to think.

A man cannot think through the mind of another. One man can learn from another, but knowledge entails understanding, not mere repetition or imitation; in order for it to be *his* knowledge, a process of independent thought is required. The necessity of intellectual independence is implicit in the will to understand. "Understanding" is a concept that pertains only to an individual mind.

Since the basic sense of control over one's existence, which lies at the heart of self-esteem, is psycho-epistemological—since it pertains to the efficacy of one's consciousness—to relinquish the responsibility of independent thought is necessarily to relinquish self-esteem.

"What are the facts of reality?" and "What do people *say* or *believe* or *feel* are the facts of reality?" are two radically different questions, and reflect two radically different psychologies and methods of psycho-epistemological functioning.

Implicit in the choice to think or not to think, is the choice to accept or to rebel against man's nature as a rational being who must survive by the use of his mind. Since thinking requires an effort, and since man is not infallible, a man may respond with fear to the responsibility of thought and intellectual self-reliance; and, surrendering to that fear, he may attempt to transfer to others the cognitive burden of his existence. But if he does so, the result is a sense of alienation from reality—a sense of being "a stranger and afraid, in a world I never made" (Chapter Ten).

Self-Esteem, Pride, and Unearned Guilt

The policies by which a man determines the state of his self-esteem are formed gradually across time; they are not the product of the choices of a single moment or issue. The collapse of self-esteem is not reached in a day, a week, or a month: it is the cumulative result of a long succession of defaults, evasions, and irrationalities—a long succession of failures to use one's mind properly. Self-esteem (or the lack of it) is the reputation a man acquires with himself.

In the process of his psychological growth and development, a human being creates his own character; he does not do so self-consciously or by explicit intention; he does so by means of the volitional choices he makes day by day. The nature and implications of these choices are summed up subconsciously—with his brain functioning, in effect, as an electronic computer; and the sum is his character and his sense of himself.

A child does not commit himself to the will to understand, in explicit terms. But in issue after issue that falls within the range of his awareness, he strives to achieve the fullest clarity and intelligibility possible to him—and thus acquires a mental habit, a policy of dealing with reality, which can be identified conceptually as the will to understand. It is a policy that he must reaffirm volitionally in each new issue he encounters, for as long as he lives; it always remains a matter of choice.

Similarly, a child does not *decide,* as a matter of principle to relinquish the will to efficacy and abnegate the authority of his mind under the pressure of fear. But in a long series of individual situations, faced with the alternative of struggling for mental clarity and control or letting his mind be filled and overcome by a fear he had the power to surmount, he defaults on the responsibility of thought and concedes supremacy to his emotions—and, as a consequence, builds into his psychology a sense of helplessness, which becomes more and more "natural" and is experienced as "just me."

The choices a human being makes, with regard to the operation of his consciousness, do not vanish, leaving no trace behind them. These choices have long-term psychological consequences. The way a man chooses to deal with reality registers in his mind, for good or for bad: either it confirms and strengthens his self-esteem or it undermines and depletes it. The fact that man cannot escape from the judgment of his own ego, is entailed by his power of self-consciousness—by the fact that he is the one species able to appraise and regulate his own mental processes.

The concept of self-esteem must be distinguished from the concept of pride. The two are related, but there are significant differences in their meaning. Self-esteem pertains to a man's conviction of his fundamental efficacy and worth. Pride pertains to the pleasure a man takes in himself on the basis of and in response to *specific* achievements or actions. Self-esteem is confidence in one's capacity to achieve values. Pride is the consequence of having achieved some particular value(s). Self-esteem is "I can." Pride is "I have." A man can take pride in his actions in reality, i.e., in his existential achievements, and in the qualities he has achieved in his own character. The deepest pride a man can experience is that which results from his achievement of self-esteem: since self-esteem is a value that has to be earned, the man who does so feels proud of his attainment.

If, in spite of his best efforts, a man fails in a particular undertaking, he does not experience the same emotion of pride that he would feel if he had succeeded; but, if he is rational, *his self-esteem is unaffected and unimpaired.* His self-esteem is not—or should not be—dependent on *particular* successes or failures, since these are not necessarily in a man's direct, volitional control and/or not in his exclusive control.

The failure to understand this principle causes an incalculable amount of unnecessary anguish and self-doubt. If a man judges himself by criteria that entail factors outside his volitional control, the result, unavoidably, is a precarious self-esteem that is in chronic jeopardy.

For example, a man finds himself in a situation where it would be highly desirable for him to possess certain knowledge; but he does not possess it—not because of evasion or irresponsibility, but because he had seen no reason to acquire it, or had not known how to acquire it, or because the means to acquire it were not available to him. In reason, such a man has no grounds to reproach himself for inadequacy or moral failure. Yet he does so, telling himself that "somehow" he should know the things he does not know—and his self-esteem suffers accordingly.

Or: a man is struggling to solve a certain problem, and he is thinking about it to the best of his honest ability. He fails; he cannot solve it—or he cannot solve it in a given period of time. He reproaches himself morally, feeling that he should have been able to do it "somehow," even though he has no clue as to how—and his self-esteem suffers accordingly.

Or: after thinking about an issue as carefully and conscientiously as he can, a man makes an error of judgment—and harmful consequences follow. The man feels guilty, on the premise that he should have avoided the error "somehow," even though he does not know what he could have done differently, given his knowledge at the time of the decision—and his self-esteem suffers accordingly.

It would be superficial and false to conclude, as many psychologists today would conclude, that these men's error consists of being "perfectionists." The error of men who make impossible, unrealistic demands on themselves, is not that of "perfectionism," but of judging themselves by a mistaken and irrational *standard* of perfection, a standard that is incompatible with man's nature. A rational standard of moral perfection demands that a man use his mind to the fullest extent of his ability, that he practice an unbreached rationality; it does not demand omniscience, omnipotence, or infallibility (Chapter Twelve).

One of the worst wrongs a man can do to himself is to accept an unearned guilt on the premise of a "somehow"—"Somehow I should know," "Somehow I should be able to do it"—when there is no cognitive content to that "somehow," only an empty, undefined charge supported by nothing.

There is, however, one reason in particular why many men are susceptible to this error. Although a man may be blameless in the present situation, previous irrationalities and failures to think may have led to a general sense of self-distrust, so that he never feels fully certain of his moral status. The solution to this problem lies in recognizing this form of uncertainty for what it is, identifying it as a symptom and striving to be objective and factual in one's self-appraisal. The struggle to achieve a rational policy in dealing with guilt will—in itself—contribute to the regaining of self-esteem.

Self-Esteem and Productive Work

In analyzing the psychology of self-esteem, one of the most important aspects to consider is the relationship of self-esteem to productive work and, more broadly, to the growth and exercise of a
man's mental abilities.

When I discussed earlier the concept of efficacy, I was speaking of what may be termed *metaphysical* efficacy, i.e., the kind of efficacy which pertains to a man's basic relationship to reality and
which reflects the reality-oriented nature of his thinking processes.
But there is another sense in which the concept of efficacy may be
used: it may refer to a man's effectiveness in specific areas of
endeavor, resulting from particular knowledge and skills he has
acquired. I shall designate this latter type as *particularized* efficacy.

A man may possess a variety of practical skills, feel confident of
his abilities in a number of delimited areas—thus exhibiting a
degree of particularized efficacy—and yet be profoundly lacking
in that sense of fundamental efficacy which pertains to self-esteem.
For example, a man may be confident at his job, but terrified by
any wider need for independent thinking, fearing to step outside
the frame of reference established by his "significant others." In
basic attitude and orientation, he is a profoundly dependent
person—dependent, not in the financial, but in the psycho-
epistemological sense.

On the other hand, a man may possess a profound self-esteem,
a profound sense of metaphysical efficacy; but, being highly spe-
cialized in his interests, he may lack many of the practical skills that
most men take for granted, such as, for instance, the knowledge of
how to drive an automobile or to perform some simple task of
home repair. He does not experience fear of such tasks and feels
confident of his ability to acquire the requisite skills, should he
need to do so: a sense of metaphysical efficacy entails confidence
in one's ability, *in principle,* to learn that which one has a valid reason to learn.

The kinds of particularized efficacy men acquire, the specific
skills they attain, vary according to their interests, values, context,
knowledge, etc. Metaphysical efficacy is necessarily expressed
through some forms of particularized efficacy, since the exercise
of one's rational faculty entails dealing with some *specific* aspect of

reality. But metaphysical efficacy is not confined, in its expression, to any particular form of activity: it is applicable to, and expressible in, every form of rational endeavor.

Self-esteem (or metaphysical efficacy) is not a value which, once achieved, is maintained effortlessly and automatically thereafter. As in the case of every value of a living organism, action is necessary not only to gain it, but also to keep it. Just as the breathing a man does today will not keep him alive tomorrow, so the thinking a man does today will not preserve his self-esteem tomorrow, if he then chooses to evade, to stagnate mentally, to arrest and subvert his rational faculty.

Man maintains his metaphysical efficacy by continuing to expand his particularized efficacy throughout his life—i.e., to expand his knowledge, understanding, and ability. Continual intellectual growth is a necessity of self-esteem—as it is a necessity of man's life.

"Life is a process of self-sustaining and self-generated action."[2] The nature and range of the actions possible to man far exceed those of any other living species—and so does his capacity for growth and self-development. The capacity for development possessed by an animal ends at physical maturity; thereafter, its life consists of the actions necessary to maintain itself at a fixed level; after reaching maturity, it does not continue to grow *in efficacy* to any significant extent, i.e., it does not increase its ability to cope with its environment. But man's capacity for growth does *not* end at physical maturity; his capacity is virtually limitless. His mind is man's basic means of survival—and his ability to think, to learn, to discover new and better ways of dealing with existence, to expand the range of his powers, *to grow intellectually,* is an open door to inexhaustible possibilities.

Man survives, not by adjusting himself to his physical environment in the manner of an animal, but by transforming his environment through *productive work.* If life is a process of self-sustaining action, then to think, to produce, to meet the challenges of existence by a never-ending effort and inventiveness, is the distinctively *human* mode of action and survival.

When man discovered how to make fire to keep himself warm, his need of thought and effort was not ended; when he discovered how to fashion a bow and arrow, his need of thought and effort was not ended; when he discovered how to build a shelter out of stone, then out of brick, then out of glass and steel, his need of thought and effort was not ended; when he moved his life expectancy from nineteen to thirty to forty to sixty to seventy, his need of thought and effort was not ended; so long as he lives, *his need of thought and effort is never ended.*

Every achievement of man is a value in itself, but it is also a stepping-stone to greater achievement and values. Life is growth; not to move forward, is to fall backward; life remains life, only so long as it advances. Every step upward opens to man a wider range of action and achievement, and creates the *need* for that action and achievement. There is no final, permanent "plateau." The problem of survival is never "solved," once and for all, with no further thought or motion required. More precisely, the problem of survival *is* solved, by the recognition that survival demands constant growth and creativeness.

The desire to grow in knowledge and skills, in understanding and control, is the expression of a man's commitment to the life process—and to the state of being human. If and when a man decides that, in effect, he has "thought enough," that no further learning is necessary, that he has nowhere to go and nothing to achieve—he has decided, *in fact,* that he has "lived enough." Stagnant passivity and self-esteem are incompatible.

The foregoing should not be taken to mean that, for the psychologically healthy man, life consists exclusively of problem-solving, productive work, and the pursuit of long-range goals. Leisure, recreation, love, human companionship are vital elements in human existence. But productive work is the process through which a man achieves that sense of control over his life which is the precondition of his being able fully to enjoy the other values possible to him. The man whose life lacks direction or purpose, the man who has no productive aim, necessarily feels helpless and out of control; the man who feels helpless and out of control, feels inadequate to and unfit for existence; and the man who feels unfit for existence is incapable of enjoying it. A productive purpose is a psychological *need*—a requirement of psychological well-being.

Observe that the earliest, self-generated pleasure of a human being's life is the pleasure of gaining a sense of control, a sense of efficacy. As the child learns to move his body, to crawl, to walk, to bang a spoon against a table and produce a sound, to build a structure of blocks, to pronounce words, the enjoyment he exhibits is that of a living being gaining power over its own existence. It is profoundly significant, psychologically and morally, that a child begins his life by experiencing the sense of virtue and the sense of efficacy as a single, indivisible emotion; pride is inextricably tied to achievement.

It is this form of pleasure that a psychologically healthy man never loses; it remains a central motive of his life. This attitude accounts for the phenomenon of the mentally active man who is young at ninety—just as the absence of this attitude accounts for the phenomenon of the mentally passive man who is old at thirty.

It should be stressed that all of the above considerations apply to women no less than to men. It is beyond the scope of this analysis to discuss the incalculable damage that has been wrought by the conventional view that the pursuit of a productive career is an exclusively masculine prerogative, and that women should not aspire to any role or function other than that of wife and mother. A woman's psychological well-being requires that she be engaged in a long-range career; she is not some sort of second-class citizen, metaphysically, for whom mental passivity and dependence are a natural condition.[3]

The scope of a person's productive ambition reflects, not only the range of his intelligence, but, most crucially, the degree of his self-esteem. The higher the level of a man's self-esteem, the higher the goals he sets for himself and the more demanding the challenges he tends to seek. (This refers, of course, to healthy, *rational* forms of ambition—not to the pretentious aspirations of a self-doubting individual who is struggling to evade and deny his own deficiencies.) On any level of intelligence or ability, one of the characteristics of self-esteem is a man's eagerness for the new and the challenging, for that which will allow him to use his capacities to the fullest extent—just as a fondness for the familiar, the routine, the unexacting, and a fear of the new and the difficult, is a virtually unmistakable indication of a self-esteem deficiency. In the realm of his work, the primary desire of a man of self-confidence is to face challenges, to achieve and to grow; the primary desire of the man lacking in self-confidence is to be "safe."

It must be emphasized that productive achievement is a consequence and an expression of healthy self-esteem, *not* its cause. The cause of authentic self-esteem is psycho-epistemological: the rational, reality-directed character of a mind's thinking processes. The causal sequence is as follows: a rational psycho-epistemology leads to the attainment of self-esteem; the two together lead (under normal conditions) to achievements; achievements lead to pride. Metaphysical efficacy leads to particularized efficacy.

Failing to understand this causal sequence, many men make the disastrous error of attempting to base their self-esteem on their existential achievements—the error of gauging their personal worth by how well they succeed in achieving particular productive goals. As mentioned earlier, success of this kind is not necessarily in a man's direct, volitional control and/or not in his exclusive control. Since man is neither omniscient nor infallible, and since, in many productive endeavors, the participation of other men is involved—it is profoundly dangerous to a man's self-esteem, and therefore to his psychological well-being, to let his sense of personal worth depend on factors beyond his control.

Sometimes, this error is made innocently, through an honest failure of understanding. Sometimes, however, it is neurotically motivated: a man who is brilliantly talented and successful at his work, but who is flagrantly irrational in the conduct of his private life, may desperately *want* to believe that the sole criterion of virtue is productive performance, that nothing else matters, that no other sphere of action has moral significance. Such a man may bury himself in his work, in order to evade feelings of shame and guilt stemming from other areas of his life—so that productive work becomes, not a healthy passion, but a neurotic escape, a refuge from reality and from the judgment of his own ego.

Self-Esteem and Pleasure

Pleasure, for man, is not a luxury, but a profound psychological need.

Pleasure (in the widest sense of the term) is a metaphysical concomitant of life, the reward and consequence of successful action—just as pain is the insignia of failure, destruction, death.

Through the state of enjoyment, man experiences the value of life, the sense that life is worth living, worth struggling to maintain.

In order to live, man must act to achieve values. Pleasure or enjoyment is at once an emotional payment for successful action and an incentive to continue acting.

Further, because of the metaphysical meaning of pleasure to man, the state of enjoyment gives him a direct experience of his own efficacy, of his competence to deal with reality, to achieve his values, to live. Implicitly contained in the experience of pleasure is the feeling: "I am in control of my existence"—just as implicitly contained in the experience of pain is the feeling: "I am helpless." As pleasure entails a sense of efficacy, so pain entails a sense of impotence.

Thus, in letting man experience, in his own person, the sense that *life* is a value and that *he* is a value, pleasure serves as the emotional fuel of his existence.

As we have discussed (Chapter Five), it is a person's *values* that determine what he seeks for pleasure—not necessarily his conscious, professed values, but the actual values of his inner life.

If a man makes an error in his choice of values, his emotional mechanism will not correct him: it has no will of its own. If a man's values are such that he desires things which, in reality, lead to his destruction, his emotional mechanism will not save him, but will, instead, urge him on toward destruction: he will have set it in reverse, against himself and against reality, against his own life. Man's emotional mechanism is like an electronic computer: man has the power to program it, but no power to change its nature—so that if he sets the wrong programming, he will not be able to escape the fact that the most self-destructive desires will have, for him, the emotional intensity and urgency of life-saving actions. He has, of course, the power to change the programming—but only by changing his values.

A man's basic values reflect his conscious or subconscious view of himself and of existence. They are the expression of (a) the degree and nature of his self-esteem or lack of it, and (b) the extent to which he regards the universe as open to his understanding and action or closed—i.e., the extent to which he holds what may be called a "benevolent" or "malevolent" view of existence. Thus, the things which a man seeks for pleasure or enjoyment are profoundly revealing psychologically: they are the index of his character and soul. (By "soul," I mean: a man's consciousness and his basic motivating values.)

There are, broadly, five (interconnected) areas that allow man to experience the enjoyment of life: productive work, human relationships, recreation, art, sex.

Productive work is the fundamental area; productive work is essential to man's sense of efficacy—and thus is essential to his ability fully to enjoy the other values of his existence.

I have said that one of the chief characteristics of a person of self-esteem, who regards the universe as open to his effort, is the profound pleasure he experiences in the productive work of his mind—the pleasure he experiences in *using* his intellectual and creative powers. A different kind of soul is revealed by the person who, predominantly, takes pleasure in working only at the routine and familiar, who is inclined to enjoy working in a semi-daze, who sees happiness in freedom from challenge or struggle or effort: the soul of a person profoundly deficient in self-esteem, to whom the universe appears as unknowable and vaguely threatening, a soul whose central motivating impulse is a longing for safety, not the safety that is won by efficacy, but the safety of a world in which efficacy is not demanded.

Still a different kind of soul is revealed by the person who finds it inconceivable that work—*any* form of work—can be enjoyable, who regards the effort of earning a living as a necessary evil, who dreams only of the pleasures that begin when the workday ends, the pleasure of drowning his brain in alcohol or television or billiards or women, *the pleasure of not being conscious:* the soul of a person with scarcely a shred of self-esteem, who never expected the universe to be comprehensible and takes his lethargic dread of it for granted, and whose only form of relief and only notion of enjoyment is the dim flicker of undemanding sensations.

Still another kind of soul is revealed by the person who takes pleasure, not in achievement, but in destruction, whose action is aimed, not at attaining efficacy, but at *ruling* those who have attained it: the soul of a person so abjectly lacking in self-value, and so overwhelmed by terror of existence, that his sole form of self-fulfillment is to unleash his resentment and hatred against those who do not share his state, those who are *able* to live—as if, by destroying the confident, the strong, and the healthy, he could convert impotence into efficacy.

A rational, self-confident man is motivated by a love of values and by a desire to achieve them. A neurotic (to the extent that he is neurotic) is motivated by fear and by a desire to escape it. This difference in motivation is reflected, not only in the things each type will seek for pleasure, but in the nature of the pleasure he will experience.

The emotional quality of the pleasure experienced by the four men described above, for instance, is not the same. The quality of any pleasure depends on the mental processes that give rise to and attend it, and on the nature of the values involved. The pleasure of using one's consciousness properly, and the "pleasure" of being unconscious, are not the same—just as the pleasure of achieving real values, of gaining an authentic sense of efficacy, and the "pleasure" of temporarily diminishing one's sense of fear and helplessness, are not the same. The man of self-esteem experiences the pure, unadulterated enjoyment of using his faculties properly and of achieving actual values in reality—a pleasure of which the other three men can have no inkling, just as he has no inkling of the dim, murky state which *they* call pleasure.

This principle applies to all forms of enjoyment. Thus, in the realm of human relationships, a different form of pleasure is experienced, a different sort of motivation is involved, and a different kind of character is revealed, by the person who seeks for enjoyment the company of men of intelligence, integrity, and self-esteem, who share his exacting standards—and by the person who is able to enjoy himself only with men who have no standards whatever and with whom, therefore, he feels free to be himself; or by the person who finds pleasure only in the company of people he despises, to whom he can compare himself favorably; or by the person who finds pleasure only among people he can deceive and manipulate, from whom he derives the lowest neurotic substitute for a sense of genuine efficacy: a sense of power.

For the rational, psychologically healthy man, the desire for pleasure is the desire to celebrate his control over his existence. For the neurotic, the desire for pleasure is the desire to escape reality.

Now consider the sphere of recreation—for instance, a party. A rational man enjoys a party as an emotional reward for achievement, and he can enjoy it only if *in fact* it involves activities that are enjoyable, such as seeing people whom he likes, meeting new people whom he finds interesting, engaging in conversations in which something worth saying and hearing is being said and heard. But a neurotic can "enjoy" a party for reasons unrelated to the real activities taking place; he may hate or despise or fear all the people present, he may act like a noisy fool and feel secretly ashamed of it—but he will feel that he is enjoying it, because people are emitting the vibrations of approval, or because it is a social distinction to have been invited to this party, or because *other* people appear to be gay, or because the party has spared him, for the length of the evening, the terror of being alone.

The "pleasure" of being drunk is obviously the pleasure of escaping from the responsibility of consciousness. And so are the kind of social gatherings, held for no other purpose than the expression of hysterical chaos, where the guests wander around in an alcoholic stupor, prattling noisily and senselessly, and enjoying the illusion of a universe where one is not burdened with purpose, logic, reality, or awareness.

Observe, in this connection, the modern "youthniks" (if I may coin a term)—for instance, their manner of dancing. What one too often sees is not smiles of authentic enjoyment, but the vacant, staring eyes, the jerky, disorganized movements of what looks like decentralized bodies, all working very hard—with a kind of flat-footed hysteria—at projecting an air of the purposeless, the senseless, the mindless. *This* is the "pleasure" of unconsciousness.

Or consider the *quieter* kind of "pleasures" that fill many people's lives: family picnics, ladies' teaparties or "coffee klatches," charity bazaars, vegetative kinds of vacation—most of them occasions of quiet boredom for all concerned, in which the *boredom* is the value. Boredom, to such people, means safety, the known, the usual, the routine—the absence of the new, the exciting, the unfamiliar, the *demanding*.

What is a *demanding* pleasure? A pleasure that demands the use of one's mind; not in the sense of problem-solving but in the sense of exercising discrimination, judgment, awareness.

One of the cardinal pleasures of life is offered to man by works of art. Art, at its highest potential, as the projection of things "as they might be and ought to be," can provide man with an invaluable emotional fuel. But, again, the kind of art work one responds to, depends on one's deepest values and premises.

A man can seek the projection of the heroic, the intelligent, the efficacious, the dramatic, the purposeful, the stylized, the ingenious, the challenging; he can seek the pleasure of *admiration,* of looking up to great values. Or he can seek the satisfaction of contemplating gossip-column variants of the folks next door, with nothing demanded of him, neither in thought nor in value-standards; he can feel himself pleasantly warmed by projections of the known and familiar, seeking to feel a little less of "a stranger and afraid in a world [he] never made." Or his soul can vibrate affirmatively to projections of horror and human degradation; he can feel gratified by the thought that he's not as bad as the dope-addicted dwarf or the crippled lesbian he's reading about; he can relish an art which tells him that man is evil, that reality is unknowable, that existence is unendurable, that no one can help anything, that his secret terror is *normal.*

All art projects an implicit view of existence—and it is one's *own* view of existence that plays a central role in determining the kind of art one will respond to. The soul of the man whose favorite play is *Cyrano de Bergerac* is radically different from the soul of the man whose favorite play is *Waiting for Godot.*[4]

Of the various pleasures that man can achieve, one of the greatest is *pride*—the pleasure he takes in his own achievements and in the creation of his own character. The pleasure he takes in the character and achievements of another human being is that of *admiration.* The highest expression of the most intense union of these two responses—pride and admiration—is romantic love. Its celebration is sex.

We will discuss the psychology of sex and romantic love—and their relationship to self-esteem—in greater detail in Chapter Eleven. But for the moment, to complete our analysis here, a few general observations are in order.

It is in this sphere above all—in a man's romantic-sexual responses—that his view of himself and of existence stands eloquently revealed. A man falls in love with and sexually desires the woman who reflects his own deepest values.

There are two crucial respects in which a man's romantic-sexual responses are psychologically revealing: in his choice of partner—and in the *meaning,* to him, of the sexual act.

A man of self-esteem, a man in love with himself and with life, feels an intense need to find human beings he can admire—to find a spiritual equal whom he can love. The quality that will attract him most is self-esteem—self-esteem and an unclouded sense of the value of existence. To such a man, sex is an act of celebration, its meaning is a tribute to himself and to the woman he has chosen, the ultimate form of experiencing concretely and in his own person the value and joy of being alive.

The need for such an experience is inherent in man's nature. But if a man lacks the self-esteem to earn it, he attempts to *fake* it—and he chooses his partner (subconsciously) by the standard of her ability to help him fake it, to give him the illusion of a self-value he does not possess and of a happiness he does not feel.

Thus, if a man is attracted to a woman of intelligence, confidence, and strength, if he is attracted to a heroine, he reveals one kind of soul; if, instead, he is attracted to an irresponsible, helpless scatterbrain, whose weakness enables him to feel masculine, he reveals another kind of soul; if he is attracted to a frightened slut, whose lack of judgment and standards allows him to feel free of reproach, he reveals another kind of soul.

This same principle, of course, applies to a woman's romantic-sexual choices.

The sexual act has a different meaning for the person whose desire is fed by pride and admiration, to whom the pleasurable self-experience it affords is an end in itself—and for the person who seeks in sex the proof of masculinity (or femininity), or the amelioration of despair, or a defense against anxiety, or an escape from boredom.

Paradoxically, it is the so-called pleasure-chasers—the men who seemingly live for nothing but the sensation of the moment, and are concerned only with having a "good time"—who are psychologically incapable of enjoying pleasure as an end in itself. The neurotic pleasure-chaser imagines that, by going through the motions of a celebration, he will be able to make himself feel that he has something to celebrate.

One of the hallmarks of the man who lacks self-esteem—and the real punishment for his psychological default—is the fact that most of his pleasures are pleasures of escape from the two pursuers whom he has betrayed and from whom there is no escape: reality and his own mind.

Since the function of pleasure is to afford man a sense of his own efficacy, the neurotic is caught in a deadly conflict: he is compelled, by his nature as man, to feel a desperate need for pleasure, as a confirmation and expression of his control over reality—but for the most part, he can find pleasure only in an *escape* from reality. That is the reason why his pleasures do not work, why they bring him not a sense of pride, fulfillment, inspiration, but a sense of guilt, frustration, hopelessness, shame. The effect of pleasure on a man of self-esteem is that of a reward and a confirmation. The effect of pleasure on a man who lacks self-esteem is that of a threat—the threat of anxiety, the shaking of the precarious foundation of his *pseudo*-self-value, the sharpening of the ever-present fear that the structure will collapse and he will find himself face to face with a stern, absolute, unknown, and unforgiving reality.

One of the commonest complaints of patients who seek psychotherapy is that nothing has the power to give them pleasure, that authentic enjoyment seems impossible to them. This is the inevitable dead end of the policy of pleasure-as-escape.

To preserve an unclouded capacity for the enjoyment of life, is an unusual moral and psychological achievement. Contrary to popular belief, it is not the prerogative of mindlessness, but the exact opposite: it is the reward of self-esteem.

Chapter Eight

Pseudo-Self-Esteem

Fear Versus Thought

The possession of self-esteem does not provide a man with automatic immunity to errors—errors about life, about other men, about the appropriate course of action to pursue—that may have painful emotional consequences. Rationality does not guarantee infallibility.

But a healthy self-esteem gives man an inestimable weapon in dealing with errors: since his own value and the efficacy of his mind are not in doubt, since he does not feel that reality is his enemy, he is free to bring the full of his intellectual powers and knowledge to the task of identifying facts and of dealing with problems. The *foundation* of his consciousness is secure, so to speak.

Conversely, one of the most disastrous consequences of an impaired or deficient self-esteem is that it tends to hamper and undercut the efficiency of a man's thinking processes—depriving him of the full strength and benefit of his own intelligence.

To the extent that a man lacks self-esteem, his consciousness is ruled by fear: fear of reality, to which he feels inadequate; fear of the facts about himself which he has evaded or repressed. Fear is the antithesis of thought. If a man believes that crucial aspects of reality, with which he must deal, are hopelessly closed to his understanding, if he faces the key problems of his life with a basic sense of helplessness, if he feels that he dare not pursue certain lines of thought because of the unworthy features of his own character that would be brought to light—if he feels, in any sense whatever, that reality is the enemy of his self-esteem (or his pretense at self-esteem)—these fears act as the saboteurs of his psycho-epistemological efficacy.

There are many ways in which a deficiency in self-esteem can adversely affect a man's thinking processes.

A man who faces the basic problems of life with an attitude of "Who am I to know? Who am I to judge? Who am I to decide?"—is undercut intellectually at the outset. A mind does not struggle for that which it regards as impossible: if a man feels that his thinking is doomed to failure, he does not think—or does not think very persistently.

If a man sees himself as helpless and ineffectual, his actions will tend to confirm and reinforce his negative self-image—thus setting up a vicious circle. By the same principle, a man who is confident of his efficacy will tend to function efficaciously. A man's self-appraisal has profound motivational consequences, for good or for bad. Its most immediate impact is felt in the quality and ambitiousness of his thinking.

The nature of a man's self-esteem and self-image does not *determine* his thinking, but it affects his emotional incentives, so that his feelings *tend* to encourage or discourage thinking, to draw him toward reality or away from it, toward efficacy or away from it.

Many men become, in effect, the psychological prisoners of their own negative self-image. They define themselves as weak or mediocre or unmasculine or cowardly or ineffectual, and their subsequent performance is affected accordingly. The process by which this occurs is subconscious; most men do not hold their self-image in conceptual form, nor do they identify its consequences conceptually.

While men are capable of acting contrary to their negative self-image—and many men do so, at least on some occasions—the factor that tends to prevent them from breaking free is their attitude of resignation toward their own state. They succumb to a destructive sense of determinism about themselves, the feeling that to be weak or mediocre or unmasculine, etc., is their "nature," not to be changed. This is a particularly tragic error which can hit men of great, unactualized potential, causing them to function at a fraction of their capacity.

If a man with a self-esteem problem attempts to identify the motives of his behavior in some area or issue, a generalized sense of guilt or unworthiness can significantly distort his introspection. He may be drawn, not to the most logical explanation of his behavior, but to the most *damaging*, to that which puts him in the worst light morally. Or, if he is confronted with the unjust accusations of others, he may feel disarmed and incapable of confuting their claims; he may accept their charges as true, paralyzed and exhausted by a heavy feeling of "How can I know?"

It is illuminating to remember, in this connection, that one of the common strategies employed in "brain-washing" is that of inculcating or provoking some form of guilt in the victim—on the premise that a guilt-ridden mind is less inclined to critical, independent judgment, and is more susceptible to indoctrination and intellectual manipulation. Guilt subdues self-assertiveness.

The principle involved is not a new discovery. Religion has been utilizing it for many, many centuries (Chapter Twelve).

When a man suffers from low self-esteem and institutes various irrational defenses to protect himself from the knowledge of his deficiency, he necessarily introduces distortions into his thinking. His mental processes are regulated, not by the goal of apprehending reality correctly, but (at best) by the goal of gaining only such knowledge as is compatible with the maintenance of his irrational defenses, the defenses erected to support a tolerable form of self-appraisal.

In attempting to counterfeit a self-esteem he does not possess, he makes his perception of reality conditional; he establishes, as a principle of his mind's functioning, that certain considerations supersede reality, facts, and truth in their importance to him. Thereafter, his consciousness is pulled, to a significant and dangerous extent, by the strings of his wishes and fears (above all, his fears); *they* become his masters; it is to *them*, not to reality, that he has to adjust.

Thus he is led to perpetuate and strengthen the same kind of antirational, self-defeating policies which occasioned his loss of self-esteem in the first place.

Consider, for example, the case of a man who, lacking authentic self-esteem, attempts to gain a sense of personal value from the near-delusional image of himself as a "big operator" in business, a daring and shrewd "go-getter" who is just one deal away from a fortune. He keeps losing money and suffering defeat in one "get-rich-quick" scheme after another—always blind to the evidence that his plans are impractical, always brushing aside unpleasant facts, always boasting extravagantly, his eyes on nothing but the hypnotically dazzling image of himself as a brilliantly skillful businessman. In order to protect a view of himself that the facts of reality cannot sustain, he severs cognitive contact with reality—and moves from one disaster to another, his sight turned inward, dreading to discover that the vision of himself which feels like a life belt is, in fact, a noose choking him to death.

Or consider the case of a middle-aged woman whose sense of personal value is crucially dependent on the image of herself as a glamorous, youthful beauty—who perceives every wrinkle on her face as a metaphysical threat to her identity—and who, to preserve that identity, plunges into a series of romantic relationships with men more than twenty years her junior. Rationalizing each relationship as a grand passion, evading the characters and motives of the young men involved, repressing the humiliation she feels in the company of her friends, she affects an ever more frantic gaiety—dreading to be alone, constantly needing the reassurance of fresh admiration, running faster and faster from the haunting, relentless pursuer which is her own emptiness.

Pretense, self-deception, "role-playing" are so much an uncontested part of most men's lives that they have virtually lost (if they ever possessed) the knowledge of what it means to have an unreserved respect for the facts of reality—i.e., what it means *to take reality seriously*. They spend most of their lives in a subjective world of their own neurotic creation, then wonder why they feel anxiety and helplessness in the real world.

There is no way to preserve the clarity of one's thinking so long as there are considerations in one's mind that take precedence over the facts of reality. There is no way to preserve the unbreached power of one's intelligence so long as one is implicitly committed to the premise that the maintenance of one's self-esteem requires that certain facts not be faced.

The misery, the frustration, the terror that characterize the psychological state of most men, testify to two facts: that self-esteem is a basic need without which man cannot live the life proper to him—and that self-esteem, the conviction that he is competent to deal with reality, can be achieved only by the consistent exercise of the one faculty that permits man to apprehend reality: his reason.

Self-Esteem Versus Pseudo-Self-Esteem

To the extent that a person fails to attain self-esteem, the consequence is a feeling of anxiety, insecurity, self-doubt, the sense of being unfit for reality, inadequate to existence. Anxiety is a psychological alarm-signal, warning of danger to the organism (Chapter Nine).

In varying degrees of intensity, the experience of such anxiety is the fate of most human beings.

Most men never identify the importance of reason to their existence, they do not judge themselves by the standard of devotion to rationality, and they are not aware of the issue of self-esteem in the terms discussed here. They are aware only of a desperate desire to feel confident and in control, and to feel that they are *good*, good in some basic way which they cannot name. But the cause of that formless fear and guilt which haunts their lives is a failure which is psycho-epistemological, i.e., a failure in the proper use of their consciousness—a default on the responsibility of reason. The anxiety they experience is part of the price they pay for that default.

Since self-esteem is a fundamental need of man's consciousness, since it is a need that cannot be bypassed, men who fail to achieve self-esteem, or who fail to a significant degree, strive to *fake* it—to evade its lack and to seek protection from their state of inner dread behind the barricade of a *pseudo*-self-esteem.

Pseudo-self-esteem, an irrational pretense at self-value, is a nonrational, self-protective device to diminish anxiety and to provide a spurious sense of security—to assuage a need of authentic self-esteem while allowing the real causes of its lack to be evaded.

A man's pseudo-self-esteem is maintained by two means, essentially: by evading, repression, rationalizing, and otherwise denying ideas and feelings that could affect his self-appraisal adversely; and by seeking to derive his sense of efficacy and worth from something *other than* rationality, some *alternative* value or virtue which he experiences as less demanding or more easily attainable, such as "doing one's duty," or being stoical or altruistic or financially successful or sexually attractive.

This complex process of self-deception, on which the neurotic builds so much of his life, holds the key to his motivation, to his values and goals. To understand the nature and form of a particular man's pseudo-self-esteem, is to understand the mainspring of his actions, to know "what makes him tick."

In the psychology of a man of authentic self-value, there is no clash between his recognition of the facts of reality and the preservation of his self-esteem—since he *bases* his self-esteem on his determination to know and to act in accordance with the facts of reality as he understands them. But to the man of pseudo-self-esteem, reality appears as a threat, as an enemy; he feels, in effect, that it's reality *or* his self-esteem—since his pretense at self-esteem is purchased at the price of evasion, of entrenched areas of blindness, of cognitive self-censorship. This is why a man may be perfectly rational and lucid in an area that does not touch on or threaten his pseudo-self-esteem, and be flagrantly irrational, evasive, defensive, and *stupid* in an area which *is* threatening to his self-appraisal. His characteristic response to any potential assault on his pseudo-self-esteem is the suspension of consciousness. The anxiety triggered off by such an assault acts as a psycho-epistemological disintegrator. Thus, he perpetuates the very process of psycho-epistemological self-sabotaging by which he caused his initial failure of self-esteem.

In this phenomenon, one may see the lead to one index of mental health and illness: A man is psychologically healthy to the extent that there is no clash in him between perceiving reality and preserving his self-esteem; the degree to which such a clash exists, is the degree of his mental illness.

The process of evasion, repression, etc., is not sufficient to provide a neurotic with the illusion of self-esteem; that process is only part of the self-deception he perpetrates. The other part consists of the values he chooses as the means of achieving a sense of personal worth. In the process of choosing values, there is a fundamental difference in principle between the motivation of a man of self-esteem and a man of pseudo-self-esteem.

An individual who develops healthily derives intense pleasure and pride from the work of his mind, and from the achievements which that work makes possible. Feeling confident of his ability to deal with the facts of reality, he will want a challenging, effortful, *creative* existence. Creativeness will be his highest love, whatever his level of intelligence. Feeling confident of his own value, he will be drawn to self-esteem in others; what he will desire most in human relationships is the opportunity to feel *admiration;* he will want to find men and achievements he can respect, that will give him the pleasure which his own character and achievements can offer others. In the sphere both of work and of human relationships, his base and motor is a firm sense of confidence, of efficacy—and, as a consequence, a love for existence, for the fact of being alive. What he seeks are means to *express* and *objectify* his self-esteem (Chapter Eleven).

The base and motor of the man without self-esteem is not confidence, but fear. Not to live, but to escape his terror of life, is his fundamental goal. Not creativeness, but *safety,* is his ruling desire. And what he seeks from others is not the chance to experience admiration, but an escape from moral values, an escape from moral judgment, a promise to be forgiven, to be accepted, *to be taken care of*—to be taken care of *metaphysically*—to be comforted and protected in a terrifying universe. His values are not the *expression* of his self-esteem, but the confession of its lack.

A man's self-esteem or pseudo-self-esteem determines his *abstract* values, not the *specific* goals he will seek; the latter proceed from a number of factors, such as a man's intelligence, knowledge, premises, and personal context. For instance, a man of high self-esteem will desire intellectually challenging work; but whether he chooses to enter business or science or art depends on narrower, less fundamental considerations. Similarly, a man of pseudo-self-esteem will desire that others protect him from reality; but a variety of factors determine whether he feels more at home among the country club set or the academic set or the underworld set.

The principle that distinguishes the basic motivation of a man of self-esteem from that of a man of pseudo-self-esteem, is the principle of *motivation by love* versus *motivation by fear.* Love of self and of existence—versus the fear that one's self is *unfit* for existence. Motivation by *confidence*—versus motivation by terror.

Here, then, is another index of mental health and illness: A man is psychologically healthy to the extent that he functions on the principle of motivation by confidence; the degree of his motivation by fear is the degree of his mental illness.

To the extent that a man lacks self-esteem, he lives *negatively* and *defensively.* When he chooses his particular values and goals, his primary motive is, not to afford himself a positive enjoyment of existence, but to defend himself against anxiety, against painful feelings of inadequacy, self-doubt, and guilt.

If a man's life is in physical danger, say, if he suffers from some major disease, his primary concern in such an emergency situation is not the pursuit of enjoyment but the removal of the danger, i.e., regaining his health, re-establishing the context in which the pursuit of enjoyment will again be possible and appropriate. But to the man devoid of self-esteem, life is, in effect, a *chronic* emergency; he is *always* in danger—psychologically. He never reaches normality, he never feels free for the enjoyment of life, because his method combating the danger consists, not of dealing with it rationally, not of working to remove it, but of *seeking to persuade himself that it does not exist.* Since A is A, since facts are facts and are not to be wiped out by self-made blindness, he can never succeed; but most of his evasions, repressions, and self-defeating actions are aimed at this goal.

Fear is the ruling element in such a man's psychology. Just as fear rules him *psycho-epistemologically,* undercutting the clarity of his perception, distorting his judgments, restricting his cognitive ambition, and driving him to ever-wider evasions—so fear rules him *motivationally,* subverting his normal value-development, sabotaging his proper growth, leading him toward goals that promise to support his pretense at efficacy, driving him to passive conformity or hostile aggressiveness or autistic withdrawal, to *any* path that will protect his pseudo-self-esteem against reality.

Values chosen in this manner may be termed *"defense-values."* A defense-value is one motivated by fear and aimed at supporting a pseudo-self-esteem. It is experienced, in effect, as a means of survival, as a substitute for rationality. It is an *anti-anxiety* device.

Such a value is unhealthy, not necessarily by virtue of its nature, but by virtue of the motivation for choosing it. The value itself may not be irrational; what is irrational is the reason for its selection. Productive work, for instance, is a rational value; but escaping into work as a means of evading one's flaws, shortcomings, and con-flicts, is *not* rational. Often, however, defense-values are irrational in *both* respects—as in the case of a man who seeks to escape anxi-ety and fake a sense of efficacy by acquiring power over others.

The extent to which a man lacks self-esteem is the extent to which defense-values constitute the building-blocks of his soul. The following example illustrates the process by which defense-values and pseudo-self-esteem develop, and the psychological crisis to which they can lead.

Consider the case of a person who, as a child, is characteristi-cally antipathetic to exerting mental effort: who rebels against the responsibility of thinking, who resents the necessity of judgment, who prefers an undemanding state of mental fog, and drifts at the mercy of unexamined emotions. Whenever feelings of inadequacy or anxiety penetrate his chronic lethargy, warning him of the dan-ger of his course, he seeks to evade them as best he can. He clings to the guidance and authority of those around him, in order to obtain a sense of security and protection.

As a result of his policy of unquestioning obedience, his par-ents praise him as a "good" boy.

At school, his work is mediocre; and he feels an unadmitted resentment against the brighter boys in his class. He is pleased whenever they show signs of unruliness and are chastised by the teacher; this proves, he feels, that they are *not* "good" boys and that, notwithstanding his intellectual weakness, he is their moral superior.

He enjoys going to church, where he is informed that it is not the head that matters, but the heart—and that "the meek shall inherit the earth."

As he grows to adulthood, he is seldom conscious of the steps by which he selects his values and goals. But, moving like a som-nambulist under the direction of subconscious orders, he is guided through all his crucial decisions by his unacknowledged sense of impotence, his fear of independence, his longing for safety and his antipathy to thought. These lead him unerringly to choose friends of undistinguished intelligence, to accept a job in his uncle's hard-ware store, to join the same political party as his father, and to marry the girl next door whom he has known all his life.

Whenever he feels vaguely guilty over his inertia, or whenever his wife reproaches him for his lack of ambition and nags him to demand a raise, he responds by summoning the thought that he is a "decent citizen," a "good provider," a "devoted, faithful husband," a "God-fearing man," and that he has done all the things "one is supposed to do." Whenever he feels a surge of envy or hostility toward those men around him who have made more of their lives than he has, he tells himself that *his* cardinal virtue is *humility*—and that people are at fault in not recognizing this and giving him the respect he deserves. It is thus that he makes his existence tolerable psychologically.

At the hardware store, he performs the routine tasks he has been taught, initiating nothing, learning nothing, thinking nothing. But occasionally he dreams of the higher income and enhanced prestige he will enjoy when his uncle dies and leaves him the business; if the moral implications of his wish rise to trouble them, he promptly unfocuses his mind and thus eludes them.

However, when the longed-for event finally happens, he does not experience the elation he had imagined. A day after his uncle's funeral, he awakens in the middle of the night, his heart pounding frantically, in a state of acute dread. He does not know how to account for it; he knows only that he feels overwhelmed by a sense of impending disaster.

The evasion and self-deception which have been habitual since childhood, now forbid him to know the meaning of his anxiety. For years, he had been shrinking his perception—and the dimensions of the world with which he had to deal—in order to avoid coming face to face with his moral and psychological default, and to escape any potential threat to his precarious inner "security." He has crawled through his life, accepting, nodding, agreeing, obeying, seeking to bypass the effort and responsibility of thought by making *humility* his *means of survival,* seeking to establish for himself a world in which this would be possible. But now reality has demolished the walls of that world, he has been thrown into a situation where *intellectual responsibility* will be demanded of him, where he will have to exercise *judgment.* Two thoughts have collided within him: "I've *got* to know what to do!" and "I *can't!*" In response to this collision, the chronic fear he had always evaded explodes into terror—the terror of the knowledge that his defense-values are now inadequate to protect him and that there is no longer any place to run.

Just as a psychologically healthy man bases his self-esteem on the use of his mind, and gains an ever-increasing sense of control over his existence by choosing values that demand constant intellectual growth—so this man based his pseudo-self-esteem on his humility, counting on *others* to solve the problem of his survival, and chose values appropriate to this manner of existence, values intended to reassure him of the validity and safety of his course. The terror he feels when he assumes ownership of the hardware store is the terror of a man suddenly divested of his means of survival, who must act and function in reality without weapons.

A significant characteristic of defense-values is the unreasoning compulsiveness with which they are usually held. Men of pseudo-self-esteem cling to these values with blind tenacity and fanatical devotion—as they would cling to a life-preserver in a stormy sea. Man's greatest fear is not of dying, but of feeling unfit to live. And to escape the agony of that feeling, men will pay any price: they will defy logic, they will sacrifice their practical self-interest, sometimes they will even forfeit their life.

With rare exceptions, they will pay any price except the one that could save them: they will not acknowledge the fraudulence of their defenses, and work to achieve an *authentic* self-esteem; they will not accept the responsibility of living as rational beings.

The number of different defense-values which men can adopt, is virtually limitless. Most of these values, however, fall into one broad category: they are values generally held in high regard by the culture or subculture in which a person lives.

The following examples illustrate common defense-values of this category:

—The man who is obsessed with being popular, who feels driven to win the approval of every person he meets, who clings to the image of himself as "likeable," who, in effect, regards his appealing personality as his means of survival and the proof of his personal worth;

—The woman who has no sense of personal identity and who seeks to lose her inner emptiness in the role of a sacrificial martyr for her children, demanding in exchange only that her children adore her, that their adoration fill the vacuum of the ego she does not possess;

—The man who never forms independent judgments about anything, but who seeks to compensate by making himself authoritatively knowledgeable concerning *other* men's opinions about everything;

—The man who works at being aggressively "masculine," whose other concerns are entirely subordinated to his role as woman-chaser, and who derives less pleasure from the act of sex than from the act of reporting his adventures to the men in the locker room;

—The woman whose chief standard of self-appraisal is the "prestige" of her husband, and whose pseudo-self-esteem rises or falls according to the number of men who court her husband's favor;

—The man who feels guilt over having inherited a fortune, who has no idea of what to do with it and proceeds frantically to give it away, clinging to the "ideal" of altruism and to the vision of himself as a humanitarian, keeping his pseudo-self-esteem afloat by the belief that charity is a moral substitute for competence and courage;

—The man who has always been afraid of life and who tells himself that the reason is his superior "sensitivity," who chooses his clothes, his furniture, his books, and his bodily posture by the standard of what will make him appear "idealistic."

Among defense-values, those of a religious nature figure prominently. In such cases, obedience to some religious injunction(s) is made the basis of pseudo-self-esteem. Faith in God, asceticism and systematic self-abnegation, adherence to religious rituals, are devices commonly employed to allay anxiety and purchase a sense of worthiness.

Still another type of defense-value may be observed in the person who rationalizes behavior of which he feels guilty by telling himself that such behavior "does not represent the *real* me," that "the real me is my *aspirations*." Such a person supports his pseudo-self-esteem by the vision of himself as an *aspirer*—an aspirer who is prevented from acting in accordance with his professed ideals by reasons beyond his control, such as the evil of "the system," the malevolence of the universe, the tragedy of some unspecified "circumstances," "human infirmity," "I never got a break," "I'm too honest and decent for this world," etc. The concept of a "real me," which bears little relation to anything one says or does in reality, is an especially prevalent anti-anxiety device, and often coexists with other defense-values.

Defense-values and pseudo-self-esteem do not always or necessarily break down in a violent and dramatic form, as in the case of the man discussed above, who collapsed into acute anxiety. Often, the process of psychological erosion and disintegration is quieter, more insidious; the person involved is not brought to a moment of unmistakable crisis; rather, his energy is slowly drained, he becomes increasingly more subject to fatigue, depression, and, perhaps, a variety of minor somatic complaints, his pretense at self-value becomes progressively more frayed and worn—and his life peters out in desolate, meaningless misery, without climaxes, without explosions, with only an occasional, lethargic wonder, wearily evaded, as to what failure could have so impoverished his existence.

No evasion, no defense-values, no strategy of self-deception can ever provide a man with a substitute for authentic self-esteem. The sense of efficacy and virtue men long for, cannot be purchased by any of the self-frauds men perpetrate. Man needs the conviction that he is *right* for reality, right *in principle*—and only a policy of rationality can achieve it.

Let a man tell himself that self-esteem is to be earned, not by the fullest exercise of his intellect, but by its abandonment in submission to faith; let him hold that efficacy is attained, not by thinking, but by conformity to the beliefs of others; let him hold that efficacy consists of *gaining* love; let him believe that his basic worth is to be measured by the number of women he sleeps with; or by the number of women he *doesn't* sleep with; or by the people he can manipulate; or by the nobility of his dreams; or by the money he gives away; or by the sacrifices he makes; let him renounce the world; let him lie on a bed of nails—but whatever he may expect to achieve, be it a moment's self-forgetfulness or a temporary illusion of virtue or a temporary amelioration of guilt, he will *not* achieve self-esteem.

The tragedy of most men's lives comes from their attempts to escape this fact.

Self-esteem is the key to man's motivation—by virtue either of its presence or of its absence. And perhaps the most eloquent testimony to the urgency of man's need of self-esteem, is the terror that haunts the lives of those who fail to achieve it, the twisted paths along which that terror drives them—and the inevitable wreckage at the end.

Chapter Nine

Pathological Anxiety: A Crisis of Self-Esteem

The Problem of Anxiety

There is no object of fear more terrifying to man than fear itself—and no fear more terrifying than that for which he knows no object.

Yet to live with such fear as a haunting constant of their existence is the fate of countless millions of men and women: it has been the fate of most of the human race. I do not speak of that fear which few men today can escape: the fear of dictatorship, of concentration camps, of war, of enslavement, of economic collapse, of arbitrary, unpredictable violence—of all the insignia of a world such as the present, in which reason has so largely been abandoned and open force is everywhere in the ascendency. Such fear can be natural and rational, a realistically appropriate response to concrete and tangible dangers. The fear of which I speak occurs without the existence of any such clearly apparent perils. Its unique characteristic is that it appears to be causeless. Its victims know only that it has struck them; but they do not know why.

Project the kind of terror a man would feel while hanging by a frayed rope over an abyss—then omit the rope and the abyss, and conceive of a person victimized by such an emotion, not while suspended precariously in space, but while safely at home in his living room, or at his office, or walking down the street. *This* is pathological anxiety—in its acute stage.

Pathological anxiety is a state of dread experienced in the absence of any actual or impending, objectively perceivable threat.

Pathological anxiety differs, not only from those rationally warranted fears afflicting the world at large, but from the ordinary fears of everyday life: ordinary fear is a proportionate and localized reaction to a concrete, external, and immediate danger, such as fear of standing in the path of an oncoming car. It differs, also, from *objective* or *normal* anxiety: normal anxiety is a feeling of apprehension and helplessness directed, like fear, toward a specific source, but the danger is less immediate than in the case of fear and the emotion is more anticipatory, such as the feeling that might overcome a person confronted with signs of some serious illness, or might strike parents whose child is in the hands of kidnappers. Fear and objective anxiety vanish when the danger is removed; they are not, in effect, a personality attribute of their possessor. But pathological anxiety is.

Pathological or *subjective* anxiety does not always appear in an intense or violent form. Many of its victims know it, not as an acute attack of panic or as a chronic sense of dread, but only as an occasional uneasiness, a diffuse sense of nervousness and apprehension, coming and going unpredictably, pursuing some incomprehensible pattern of its own. It can exist on a continuum from faint discomfort to an experience of such agony that many who have known it have sworn they would sooner die than undergo it a second time.

The common denominators linking the mildest form of this anxiety to the most extreme, are: the sufferer can give no identity to that which he fears, he feels afraid of nothing in particular and of everything in general; if he *tries* to offer some rationalized explanation for his feeling, if he grasps at some sign in the external world to prove he *is* in danger, his explanations are transparently illogical; and he acts as though that which he fears is not any specific concrete, but reality as such.

One of the most graphic descriptions of the onset of an anxiety attack is given in an autobiographical passage by Henry James, Sr., the father of philosopher-psychologist William James. The elder James describes his traumatic experience as follows:

> One day . . . towards the close of May, having eaten a comfortable dinner, I remained sitting at the table after the family had dispersed, idly gazing at the embers in the grate, thinking of nothing,

and feeling only the exhilaration incident to a good digestion, when suddenly—in a lightning-flash as it were—"fear came upon me, and trembling, which made all my bones to shake." To all appearance it was a perfectly insane and abject terror, without ostensible cause, and only to be accounted for, to my perplexed imagination, by some damned shape squatting invisible to me within the precincts of the room and raying out from his fetid personality influences fatal to life. The thing had not lasted ten seconds before I felt myself a wreck; that is, reduced from a state of firm, vigorous, joyful manhood to one of almost helpless infancy. The only self-control I was capable of exerting was to keep my seat. I felt the greatest desire to run incontinently to the foot of the stairs and shout for help to my wife,—to run to the roadside even, and appeal to the public to protect me; but by an immense effort I controlled these frenzied impulses, and determined not to budge from my chair till I had recovered my lost self-possession. This purpose I held to for a good long hour, as I reckoned time, beat upon meanwhile by an ever-growing tempest of doubt, anxiety, and despair, with absolutely no relief from any truth I had ever encountered save a most pale and distant glimmer of the divine existence, when I resolved to abandon the vain struggle, and communicate without more ado what seemed my sudden burden of inmost, implacable unrest to my wife.

Now, to make a long story short, this ghastly condition of mind continued with me, with gradually lengthening intervals of relief, for two years, and even longer.[1]

The percentage of people in the world who suffer from an acute form of mental or emotional disturbance is high. Yet such persons constitute only a very small percentage of the total number of men and women who suffer from pathological anxiety throughout most of their lives, but whose disorder never reaches a sufficiently alarming degree of intensity to command the attention of a psychotherapist or to gain recognition in any statistical survey. These individuals would, in most cases, be regarded by those around them as quite normal and would not themselves think of questioning their psychological health merely because they are prey to fits of inexplicable, objectless apprehension.

These are the persons who, for instance, cannot bear to be alone; who cannot live without sleeping pills; who jump at every unexpected sound; who drink too much to calm a nervousness that comes too often; who feel a constantly pressing need to be amusing and to entertain; who flee to too many movies they have no desire to see and to too many gatherings they have no desire to attend; who sacrifice any vestige of independent self-confidence to an obsessive concern with what others think of them; who long to be emotional dependents or to be depended upon; who succumb to periodic spells of unaccountable depression; who submerge their existence in the dreary passivity of unchosen routines and unchallenged duties and, as they watch their years slip by, wonder, in occasional spurts of frustrated anguish, what has robbed them of their chance to live; who run from one meaningless sexual affair to another; who seek membership in the kind of collective movements that dissolve personal identity and obviate personal responsibility—a vast, anonymous assemblage of men and women who have accepted fear as a built-in, not-to-be-wondered-about fixture of their soul, dreading even to identify that what they feel is fear or to inquire into the nature of what which they seek to escape.

It is generally recognized by clinical psychologists and psychiatrists that pathological anxiety is the central and basic problem with which they must deal in psychotherapy—the symptom underlying the patient's other symptoms. Sometimes, the other symptoms represent direct physical *consequences* of anxiety, such as headaches, choking sensations, heart palpitations, intestinal ailments, dizziness, trembling, nausea, excessive perspiration, insomnia, painful bodily tensions, and chronic fatigue. Sometimes, they represent *defenses* against anxiety, such as hysterical paralyses, obsessions, compulsions, and passive depression. But in all cases anxiety is the motor of neurosis.

The neurotic's essential attribute, his chronic response to the universe, is uncertainty and fear. Not every neurotic is the victim of obsessive thoughts or compulsive actions; not every neurotic dreads heights or open spaces; not every neurotic develops somatic ailments for which there is no somatic cause. But every neurotic is afraid. A cheerful neurotic, confident of his ability to deal successfully with life, is a contradiction in terms.

What is the nature and cause of pathological anxiety?

To answer this question, one should begin by noting a conspicuous and significant attribute of this anxiety: its *metaphysical* character. The fear seems to be directed at the universe at large, at existence as such—as thought implying that to be, is to be in mortal danger.

The anxious person feels, as an intrinsic component of the anxiety experience, a profound sense of helplessness, of impotence. He feels a sense of shapeless but impending disaster. And—often—he feels a unique, nameless sense of guilt. The guilt, too, has a metaphysical quality: he feels wrong, wrong *as a person,* wrong in some fundamental way that is wider than any particular fault or defect he can identify. (Sometimes, the guilt is in the forefront of his consciousness; sometimes, it is unidentified, undiscriminated, in effect, subconscious.)

When a person suffers from this metaphysical kind of dread, the cause does not lie in the external world; it lies within himself. It is not something that reality has done to him; it is something he has done to himself. He carries the threat and danger within his own consciousness.

Confidence in oneself, as a basic attitude, is confidence in the efficacy of one's consciousness. Pathological anxiety is the antipode of this state. It is nature's alarm signal, warning a man that he is in an improper psychological condition, that his relationship to reality is wrong; it is his mind's cry of inefficacy and loss of control. It is a crisis of self-esteem.

If self-esteem is the conviction that one's mind is competent to grasp and judge the facts of reality, and that one's person is worthy of happiness—pathological anxiety is the torment of a person who is crippled or devastated in this realm, who feels cut off from reality, alienated, powerless.

Behind a fear which is experienced as metaphysical lies a disaster which is psycho-epistemological—a failure or default in the proper functioning of a man's consciousness.

Whenever a man feels fear, any kind of fear, his response reflects an estimate of some danger to him, i.e., some threat to his values. What is the value being threatened in the case of pathological anxiety? It is the sufferer's *ego.*

A man's ego is his mind, his faculty of awareness, his ability to think—the faculty that perceives reality, preserves the inner continuity of his own existence, and generates his sense of personal identity. "Ego" and "mind" denote the same act of reality, the same attribute of man; the difference in the use of these terms pertains to an issue of perspective: I use the term "ego" to designate man's power of awareness *as he experiences it.*

Any threat to a man's ego—anything which he experiences as a danger to his mind's efficacy and control—is a potential source of pathological anxiety. The pain of this anxiety is the most terrible that man can know—because the value at stake is, necessarily, the most crucial of all his values.

As a being of volitional consciousness, man is capable of undercutting and betraying his basic means of survival, his mind. He can subvert the clarity and integrity of his own mental processes by evasion, repression, rationalization, etc.—thus alienating himself from reality, and condemning himself to a state where to be *is* to be in mortal danger.

Now let us consider the means by which a man can sabotage the perceiving-integrating function of his consciousness, and bring himself to a state of pathological anxiety.

In order to deal with existence successfully, to achieve the values and goals his life and well-being require, man needs to strive for an unobstructed cognitive contact with reality. This means that he must maintain a full mental focus, must seek the clearest possible awareness with regard to his actions and concerns and everything which bears upon them.

If a man defaults on the responsibility of this task, the consequences are not merely the failures and defeats he suffers existentially: the deadlier penalty is the consequence for his ego, for his sense of himself. He is sentenced to the feeling that his mind is not a reliable instrument. Whatever a man may have the power to fake, he has no way to fake an efficacy his ego does not possess; if his mind is out of control, it is out of control; no rationalizations, no denials, can wipe this fact out of existence—or extinguish its psychological consequence: self-distrust.

If, motivated by lethargy or fear, a man refuses to give thought to issues which he knows (clearly or dimly) require his attention, he may evade the fact of his evasion, but the contradiction between his knowledge and his performance is a fact that cannot be escaped; the fact does not vanish; it is registered in his subconscious—along with the knowledge that the evaded issues have not vanished, either. The result is self-distrust.

If a man adopts a policy of throwing his mind out of focus, and retreating into the comfort of autistic dreams when confronted by any painful aspect of existence, he may gain a momentary relief, but the betrayal of his cognitive development remains real—as sternly, as unforgivingly real as the unchanging reality beyond his closed eyelids. The result is self-distrust.

If, under the guidance of his emotions, a man takes actions that are contrary to his convictions, contrary to that which he believes to be right, he may disintegrate his conscious mind in order to escape the implications of his actions and of the psycho-epistemological policy behind them—but the implications do not cease to exist and a merciless computer within his brain sums them up. He is left with the implicit knowledge that, in the event of a clash between his reason and his emotions, it is his reason that he will sacrifice; under pressure, it is his mind, his conscious judgment, that becomes expendable. The result is self-distrust.

If, in order to escape emotions and desires which he experiences as threatening to his self-esteem or equilibrium, a man resorts to repression, if he institutes mental blocks that forbid him to know the nature of his own feelings, he does not solve his problem; he merely creates a worse one. He subverts his power of introspection and his ability to think about his problems. And he is left with the sense that somewhere within him he harbors a dangerous enemy whom he can neither face nor escape—an enemy whom he has sought to defeat by blinding *himself.*

If, by the implications of his psycho-epistemological policies, a man establishes within his consciousness the principle that it is permissible to act with his mind unfocused, that he need not know what he is doing or why, that the difficult need not be thought about, the painful need not be faced, the undesirable need not be acknowledged—if the ruling principle of his mental activity is not "know the truth," but "avoid effort" and/or "escape pain"—then *this* is the secret knowledge about its method of functioning that a man's ego cannot escape; *this* is the root of self-distrust, self-doubt, and guilt.

When one considers the amount of reckless irrationality that most men permit themselves and regard as *normal,* one does not have to be astonished at their psychological state, or at the plague-like prevalence of "causeless" fear. If men feel anxiously uncertain of their ability to deal with the facts of existence, they have given themselves ample grounds for their feeling.

But pathological anxiety, it must be remembered, *is* pathological, i.e., is symptomatic of an abnormal and unhealthy condition.

The writings of Existentialists and certain religionists, who suggest the contrary, necessitate this emphasis. A state of chronic dread is *not* man's natural condition. The fact that man is neither omniscient nor omnipotent nor infallible nor immortal, does not constitute grounds for his ego to feel overwhelmed by a sense of inefficacy. A rational man does not set his standard of efficacy in opposition to his own nature and to the nature of reality. Neither is man born with any sort of Original Sin; if a man feels guilty, it is not because he is guilty by nature; sin is not "original," it is *originated*. The problem of anxiety is psychological, not metaphysical.

The Nature of Anxiety Conflicts

To the extent that a person indulges in irrational mind-subverting psycho-epistemological policies, he sentences himself to a chronic anticipation of disaster.

If he fails to do the thinking his life and concerns require, he cannot escape the awareness that the range of his action exceeds the range of his thought, that challenges and demands will confront him to which he is inadequate; he feels afraid because of the thinking he failed to do, and guilty because of the knowledge that he should have done it.

If he acts contrary to his convictions, if he takes actions which he regards as wrong and/or fails to take actions which he regards as right, he comes to experience the feeling, not merely that his *actions* are wrong, but that *he* is wrong, wrong as a person—since a person's deepest sense of himself has its base and origin in his method of psycho-epistemological functioning, in the processes by which his mind deals with reality.

Even if the moral precepts he accepts are mistaken or irrational, so long as they represent his actual beliefs, he cannot act against them with psychological impunity; he will be left with the feeling that he has betrayed his own consciousness, and thereby rendered himself unfit for reality. (This is one of the reasons why the psychological and existential results for his life are so devastating, if he accepts a code of values that, in fact, is inimical to his nature and needs—as we shall discuss in Chapter Twelve.)

There is another, related reason why a man who acts against his own moral convictions will suffer a sense of impending disaster. Whether the moral values a man accepts are rational or irrational, man cannot escape the knowledge that, in order to deal with reality successfully, in order to live, he needs *some* sort of moral principles to guide him; he cannot escape his nature as a conceptual being. And, implicit in this knowledge, is the awareness (however dim, however confused by the other-worldly teachings of mystics) that ethical principles are a *practical* necessity of his life on earth. A corollary of this awareness is his expectation that moral and immoral actions *have consequences,* even if he cannot always predict them. If he takes actions which he regards as good, he expects to benefit, existentially or psychologically; if he takes actions which he regards as bad, he expects to suffer, existentially or psychologically—although this expectation is often evaded and repressed. Thus, what he is left with, if and when he betrays his own standards, is the sense of some unknown danger, some unknown retribution, waiting for him ahead.

It would be a gross error to interpret this attitude as merely a consequence of the influence of religion. The issue is much wider and deeper. It arises—to repeat—from man's *implicit* awareness that he cannot live successfully without *some* long-range principles to guide his actions. (As to religion, it merely represents, among other things, a misguided and irrational attempt to satisfy this need—or to cash in on it.)

The experience of pathological anxiety always involves and reflects conflict. Not all conflicts, however, result in pathological anxiety. Conflicts *per se* are not pathological. A particular kind of conflict is involved in neurotic anxiety—and the acute anxiety attack is occasioned by the ego's confrontation with that conflict.

Let us consider three different instances of an anxiety attack, in order to observe in what manner this occurs and to grasp the nature of the conflict involved.

1. A mild, undistinguished clerk has held the same position for twenty years. He feels embarrassed and humiliated by the number of times he has been passed by for promotion. He does not complain to his superiors; but he complains to his wife and talks endlessly about how much better he would run things if he were given a position with more responsibility and authority.

He is a man who never wanted to think, has done the minimum amount of thinking possible, and secretly wants nothing more demanding than his present position, which offers him security and protection for his mediocrity. He evades and represses this fact.

Then, one day, he is informed that he is to be given a major promotion. He receives the news with apparent gratitude and delight. But that evening he begins to complain of queer sensations in his head and a painful tightness in his chest. During the night, he awakens in a state of violent anxiety.

In the days that follow, he begins to express worry and concern about his children's school grades, then he begins to moan that the house is under-insured, finally he begins to cry that he is going insane. But the issue of his promotion does not enter his conscious mind.

What triggered his anxiety? It was the collision of two absolutes: "I must know what to do" (meaning: I must know how to handle the responsibilities of my new position)—and "I don't (and can't)." The conflict is not conscious; it is repressed; but it is real and devastating, nonetheless. The effect of the conflict is to demolish the man's pretense at control over his life, and thus to precipitate his anxiety.

In this case, the conflict is brought about by an outside event: the news of the promotion. But the foundation for such a conflict, and for many other similar conflicts, is in the man's psychoepistemological policies.

Observe the nature of the conflict: it is a clash between a value-imperative, engaging the man's sense of personal worth, his self-esteem (or pretense at it)—and a failure or flaw or inadequacy that the man experiences as a breach of that imperative. Thus, he experiences *a crisis of self-esteem.*

2. A young woman is raised in a severely religious home where, from her earliest days, she is taught that she is sinful by nature. She is urged to search her conscience each night for moral infractions of which she might have been guilty during the day. In her upbringing, particular stress is placed by her mother on the inviolate sacredness of family life and the depravity of sex outside of marriage.

The girl does not question or challenge her parents' teachings; it is not her policy to think out moral issues for herself.

However, as she grows older, she discovers that her contemporaries do not share her parents' views—and, in college, she affects a more "liberal" attitude toward sex, in order to "belong," i.e., to be accepted by her "peer group." After a few experimental excursions into romance, none of which are consummated sexually, she finally plunges into an affair—with a married man. She is able, to some extent, to control her guilt over the affair by the thought that she is desperately in love.

But the religious beliefs she had absorbed in childhood are still operative, even though partially repressed. One night, when she is returning home after a date with her lover, a host of long-evaded thoughts and long-denied fears burst into her conscious awareness for one brief moment—and she faints on her parents' doorstep. When she regains consciousness, the memory of that brief moment is swept away, and she finds herself in the midst of an acute, "causeless" anxiety attack.

The two absolutes that have collided within her are: "I must not (have this affair)"—and "I am (and will continue to)."

The clash is between a value-imperative, engaging her sense of personal worth, her self-esteem (or pretense at it)—and her actions which contradict that imperative. Thus, she experiences *a crisis of self-esteem.*

3. A man who has been married for ten years falls in love with another woman. For a long time, he has resisted identifying his marital dissatisfaction, as well as his feeling for the other woman. But gradually the repression breaks down and he finds himself daydreaming about the other woman more and more frequently.

He does not think the issue out consciously; his thinking has been reserved for his work; in the conduct of his personal life, he has acted under the guidance of his feelings. So he does not reach any reasoned decision; he merely lets himself and the problem drift, in the hope that "somehow" a solution will come to him.

One night, accidental circumstances bring him and the other woman together; and he begins an affair with her. He did not intend to begin an affair; his emotions made the decision for him. He feels guilty and represses the guilt and continues to drift, evading the other woman's questions about their future; he is still waiting for the solution to come from somewhere.

His wife decides to take a trip to visit her parents. As he stands at the airport, watching her plane depart, the thought comes to him—and it is as much a *desire* as a thought—that if the plane crashed, he would be free and would have no further problems.

But the wish is savagely thrust from his mind—along with a sudden burst of hostility toward his wife which he would never have admitted himself capable of experiencing.

Driving home, he suddenly finds that he has difficulty distinguishing the colors of the signal lights, everything in his field of vision seems to be swimming, and terrible pains appear to be coming from his heart. He feels that he is going to die of a heart attack. But what he is suffering from—the anxiety that has exploded within him—is a self-esteem attack.

The collision is: "I must not"—and "I did, and do, and will (wish for my wife's death)."

The clash is between a value-imperative, engaging his sense of personal worth, his self-esteem (or pretense at it)—and an emotion, a *desire* which contradicts that imperative. Thus, he experiences *a crisis of self-esteem.*

In every instance of pathological anxiety, there is a conflict in some such form as: "I must (or should have)"—and "I cannot (or did not)"; or "I must not"—and "I do (or did or will)." There is always a conflict between some value-imperative that is tied, in a crucial and profound way, to the person's self-appraisal and inner equilibrium—and some failure or inadequacy or action or emotion or desire that the person regards as a breach of that imperative, a breach that the person believes expresses or reflects a basic and unalterable fact of his "nature."

The mechanics of the anxiety process have been described in a variety of ways by psychologists and psychiatrists of different theoretical orientations. But if one studies the case histories they themselves report—or any of the case histories pertaining to anxiety in the many textbooks available today—one can discern very clearly the basic pattern described above, however the particular cases may differ in details.

One of the commonest errors made by theorists in their interpretations of the anxiety process, is to mistake a particular instance of pathological anxiety for the abstract prototype of all pathological anxiety—in other words, to make unwarranted generalizations.

Freud, for instance, in the final version of his theory of anxiety, maintained that anxiety is triggered by forbidden sexual desires that break through the barrier of repression and cause the ego to feel threatened and overwhelmed. Karen Horney countered with the declaration that this may have been true in the Victorian age, but in our day the source of anxiety is the emergence of *hostile* impulses.

In fact, the basic principle involved is demonstrably wider than either of these explanations. Pathological anxiety is—to repeat— a crisis of self-esteem, and the possible sources of anxiety are as numerous as the rational or irrational values on which a person's self-appraisal may be based.

There are certain facts about the nature of these anxiety-producing conflicts that must be noted. 1. The value-imperative involved in the conflict may be rational or irrational; it may be consonant with the facts of reality and with man's nature, or it may be contrary to both. 2. The value-imperative entails a standard, expectation, demand, or claim which, rightly or mistakenly, the person believes should be within his volitional power to satisfy. This belief may not be held consciously; but it is implicit in the fact that what is involved is a *value-imperative,* and that the person holds himself morally at fault if he fails that imperative. 3. The person implicitly experiences his moral breach as deterministically indicative of his "real" self. 4. The conflict, *qua* conflict, is typically subconscious; either half of it, however, may be conscious or partially conscious.

This last does *not* mean that if and when the conflict becomes entirely conscious, the anxiety automatically disappears; the anxiety is often maintained by the vast psycho-epistemological chaos that underlies the conflict and prevents it from being resolved. Furthermore, the unblocking of one repressed conflict often tends to stir up and release other repressed conflicts, which are anxiety provoking.

There are cases, however, when the anxiety does disappear, once the central conflict is de-repressed—particularly when the conflict is seen to be readily solvable.

Guilt

One of the most significant aspects of the anxiety experience, whether chronic or acute, is the factor of *guilt.* The degree of consciously experienced guilt does not necessarily correspond to the degree of consciously experienced anxiety. The awareness of guilt may be repressed. But there is another reason why the intensity of the guilt may not correspond to the intensity of the anxiety.

The lowest level of guilt appears to be experienced by those persons who—although they have failed to do the thinking and achieve the psycho-epistemological clarity their life requires—have not knowingly violated their moral convictions, have not attempted to cheat reality and get away with the irrational.

A heavier guilt is suffered by those who do act against their moral convictions—and the severity of the guilt usually reflects the severity of the breach and/or the degree of harm that results from their actions. But, here, a major distinction must be made.

There are the people who do achieve and maintain a substantial degree of independence in their value-judgments; if they violate their own principles, they experience guilt as well as anxiety, but they do not, in effect, "feel guilty all the way down." Their guilt is localized and delimited; they do not feel worthless. They are protected by their own psychological sovereignty—by the fact that their moral concern is authentic and first-hand. If a man feels, in effect, "It was unworthy of me to fail my own standards in this manner"—he is still preserving a major hold on self-esteem.

Then there are the persons who are *basically* lacking in intellectual sovereignty. The worst guilt is reserved for this psychological type, i.e., those whose approach to moral judgments is authoritarian. In such cases, the force of their moral beliefs derives, not from rational understanding, but from the say-so of "significant others." And when the authorities' rules are breached, there is no healthy core of inner sovereignty to protect the transgressors from feelings of *metaphysical* worthlessness. To themselves, they are *nothing but* their bad actions. This is one of the reasons why pathological anxiety is so often experienced as fear of the disapproval of others. "Others" are perceived as the voice of objective reality—calling them to judgment. It is among such persons that guilt is most often a conscious part of the anxiety experience. Also, it is among such persons that the anxiety itself is likely to be most severe.

Anxiety and Depression

One of the worst consequences of pathological anxiety is its destructive impact on the objectivity and clarity of a man's thinking. This is one of the ways in which harmful psycho-epistemological practices tend to be self-perpetuating. The anxiety engendered by such policies encourages evasion and repression as defenses against it— as well as the elaboration of more complex systems of neurotic defense, which require psycho-epistemological self-sabotaging in order to be maintained (Chapter Eight).

Pathological anxiety is both a consequence of self-doubt and a cause of further self-doubt. Anxiety disintegrates the neurotic's precarious sense of personal identity and undercuts whatever precarious confidence in his mind he may have possessed. When that confidence is undermined, so are the firmness and objectivity of his cognitive frame of reference. The result is a pronounced tendency to lose the distinction between the subjective and the objective, between that which pertains to consciousness and that which pertains to existence, so that consciousness *is given primacy over existence*—thus generating the cognitive distortions so characteristic of neurosis.

When a man doubts the efficacy of his mind, his tendency is to surrender to the guidance of his emotions—since they appear to possess a certainty and authority that his intellect lacks. This is the form in which a man experiences the process of subordinating the objective to the subjective. His emotions are not a substitute for rational cognition at any time, but they are never a less reliable guide than in the midst of an anxiety state.

Because the experience of anxiety is so intrinsically painful, neurotics adopt a vast variety of devices and techniques in order to defend themselves against it. Evasion, repression, and rationalization are basic and underlie most, if not all, of such defenses.

The neurotic can blank out the reality of his objectionable actions; he can repress his resolved conflicts; he can disown his guilt feelings; he can deny or rationalize his fear; he can seek to distract himself by the frenzied pursuit of various activities; he can shrink the sphere of his concerns and commitments so as to avoid the challenges of the unfamiliar; he can elaborate a fantasized self-image to protect him from a self-evaluation he dreads to acknowledge.

Often, the repression of the anxiety problem, and of the conflicts underlying it, results in the formation of other neurotic symptoms. One of these symptoms is particularly worthy of attention in the present context: neurotic depression. (I do not wish to imply that all depression is necessarily a defense against anxiety; but I am concerned with depression here only insofar as it is such a defense.)

Depression, like anxiety, can be normal or pathological. Anxiety is a response to the *threatened* destruction or loss of a value; depression is a response to the *accomplished* destruction or loss of a value. Anxiety is anticipatory, it is directed to the future; depression is directed to the past.

Depression is regarded as pathological when it is unrelated to any object loss, or when its intensity and duration are grossly disproportionate to the loss.

Neurotic depression is characterized by despair, passivity, a feeling that action and effort are futile, that nothing is worth doing—and by feelings of self-rejection and self-condemnation.

Now, in what manner can depression relate to anxiety?

A person is made anxious because of urgent demands, claims, or self-expectations which he feels unable to satisfy; for example, the imperative that he possess certain knowledge and be able to cope with certain responsibilities; or that he act in a certain manner; or that he respond emotionally in a certain manner; or that he live up to certain standards and ideals. He is caught in a conflict. Suppose that he attempts to deal with it, and to minimize his anxiety, by repressing both the conflict and the related guilt. In its place, on the conscious level of his awareness, he experiences a sense of passivity, futility, and general worthlessness.

If one listens closely to his declarations that he is hopeless, that life is hopeless, that he is "no good," one can discern another message to be read in his words: *Expect nothing of me—demand nothing of me.* Since he is incurably worthless, he is outside the realm of moral expectations; for him, there can be no "I must." In this manner he "resolves" the conflict that threatens him with anxiety.

In other words, he seeks to anticipate the worst and make it a *fait accompli*—without coming to grips with his actual problem. Under the guise of renouncing his self-esteem, he is still secretly trying to protect it by neurotic means.

This is one of the ways in which depression can be a subconsciously elected alternative to anxiety. But it is not the only pattern. Here is another.

This pattern is related to the foregoing, but is more indirect in its workings. It is the by-product of repression. Suppose that a man, rightly or wrongly, accepts certain moral standards or value-imperatives as essential criteria of his personal worth—and yet, in some crucial respect, feels unable to comply with them; or suppose he desires something desperately which he regards as immoral and, therefore, impossible to assert or pursue. The conflict is repressed. Since it is repressed, it cannot be resolved; he can either recheck his standards and discover whether he has made an error—nor can he form any rational policy in regard to the failure(s) or action(s) or desire(s) that is in conflict with his self-expectations.

He is left with the oppressive, enervating sense of some nameless, unalterable, irremediable burden, which he is sentenced to carry and live with to the end of his days. He has lost or minimized his anxiety. He may be comparatively free of conscious guilt. But what he experiences, instead, is *despair*—an exhausting despair that paralyzes the will to act.

He has relinquished the possibility of achieving self-esteem or happiness. But these are a man's motive power.

If, in the context of psychotherapy, the basic question to ask in regard to a patient's anxiety is: "What is your crime?"—the basic question to ask in regard to a patient's depression, is often: "What do you desire that you consider immoral and unattainable?"

To regain his mental health, the depressed person *must be willing to experience anxiety*—must be willing to relinquish the "comfort" of despair and to confront his anxiety-provoking conflicts, in order to resolve them and move forward.

Consider the situation of a man lost in some vast, icy, northern terrain, with snow stretching desolately and endlessly around him. He knows that there is a camp somewhere far ahead and he must reach it, that his life depends on reaching it. But he is exhausted and bitterly cold, and his passionate desire is only to lie down and rest. Yet if he does, he knows that he will fall asleep and die. To move is torture; but stillness is the end of hope.

The person suspended between anxiety and depression is like that man. He must resist the illusory comfort of despair and be willing to endure anxiety, to drive himself forward, to keep searching and moving, in order to reach safety, efficacy, and health.

Anxiety is still a sign of life—of conflict and struggle—therefore, of possible victory. But depression is resignation to defeat.

Now a concluding word about the biological utility of anxiety and guilt. Anxiety and guilt are painful, and disruptive of clear, objective thinking; and the psychotherapist strives to free his patient of their grip—just as the physician strives to free his patient of physical pain. But just as physical pain has a crucial survival-value, warning a man that his body is in danger—so anxiety and guilt have the same survival-value, and perform the same function, for man's mind and person.

The harmful, existential consequences of a man's irrational psycho-epistemological policies are not always immediate or direct. If a man had no advance warnings of danger, no advance signals of disaster, he could pursue a course of self-destruction with nothing to restrain him or to indicate that he needed to re-examine his method of functioning—until it was hopelessly too late.

Man is free to ignore the warning-signals of danger, but the warning is there, in the form of a penalty he cannot escape. Thus, paradoxically, pathological anxiety is at once man's protector and his nemesis. If a man defaults on the responsibility of reason, then his self-betrayed ego becomes its own avenger.

A man need not have solved his every psychological problem before he can be free of anxiety and guilt. But it is necessary that he correct the base of his problems: the policy of permitting some other considerations to take precedence over his perception of the facts of reality. The determination to face his problems, to look at reality—to restore his ego to its proper function as a tool of cognition—is the essential first step in the process by which a man sets himself free of fear and guilt. If and to the extent that this determination is maintained and implemented, psychological liberation will follow.

| Social Metaphysics

The Nature and Source of Social Metaphysics

Entailed by the process of achieving self-esteem is a corollary process: that of forming a strong, positive sense of personal identity—the sense of being a clearly defined psychological entity.

A man's "I," his ego, his deepest self, is his faculty of awareness, his capacity to think. Across his lifetime, a man's knowledge grows, his convictions may change, his emotions come and go; but that which knows, judges, and feels—*that* is the changeless constant within him.

To choose to think, to identify the facts of reality—to assume the responsibility of judging what is true or false, right or wrong—is man's basic form of *self-assertiveness*. It is his acceptance of his own nature as a rational being, his acceptance of the responsibility of intellectual independence, his commitment to the efficacy of his own mind.

The essence of *selflessness* is the suspension of one's consciousness. When and to the extent that a man chooses to evade the effort and responsibility of thinking, of seeking knowledge, of passing judgment, his action is one of *self-abdication*. To relinquish thought is to relinquish one's ego—and to pronounce oneself unfit for existence, incompetent to deal with the facts of reality.

The hallmark of healthy self-assertiveness in a child is his visible delight in the action of his mind, his desire for the new, the unexplored, the challenging, his refusal to accept on faith the platitudes of his elders and his insistent use of the word "why?", his boredom with routine, his indifference toward the undemanding, his obsession with questions, his hunger for that which will invoke and necessitate the fullest exercise of his powers and thus allow him to achieve and experience the growing pride of self-esteem.

Above all, as he grows and develops, such a child is the originator of his own goals. He does not look to others to tell him what will give him enjoyment; he does not expect and does not wish to be told what to do with his time, what to admire, what to pursue— and, years later, what career to select. He desires and needs the help of his elders in providing him with rational guidance and education, but *not* in providing him with ready-made goals and values. In the selection of values, he is a *self-generator*—and he welcomes, he is not frightened by, the responsibility.

It is this policy, this attitude toward life and toward oneself, that results in the formation of a strong, positive sense of personal identity.

A strong sense of personal identity is the product of two things: a policy of independent thinking—and the possession of an integrated set of values. Since it is his values that determine a man's emotions and goals, and give direction and meaning to his life, a man experiences his values as an extension of himself, as an integral part of his identity, as crucial to that which makes him himself.

The process of healthy growth to psychological maturity rests on a person's acceptance of intellectual responsibility for his own existence. As a human being grows to adulthood, reality confronts him with increasingly more complex challenges at each succeeding stage of his development: the range of thought, knowledge, judgment, and decision-making required of him at the age of twelve is greater than that required at the age of five; the range required at twenty is greater than that required at twelve. At each stage, the responsibility demanded of him involves both cognition and evaluation; he has to acquire a knowledge of facts and he has to pass value-judgments and choose goals. The acceptance of full responsibility for this task is not automatic; the decision to function as an intellectually independent, self-responsible entity is not "wired in" to his brain by nature. It is a challenge to which he responds—positively or negatively, with acceptance or rejection— volitionally, i.e., by choice.

The consequence of responding positively is the self-confident state of a sovereign consciousness. The consequence of responding negatively is a state of psycho-epistemological dependency.

There are at least four factors that can motivate (*not* necessitate) a person's default on the responsibility of independence and cognitive self-reliance.

1. Thinking requires an effort; thinking is mental *work*.

2. A policy of thinking, practiced consistently as a way of life, forbids one the possibility of indulging desires or emotions that clash with one's understanding and convictions.

3. Man's mind is fallible; he can make an error at any step of the thinking process—and, if he acts on his error, he may suffer pain or defeat or destruction.

4. His independent thinking may bring a person into conflict with the opinions and judgments of others, thus provoking disapproval or animosity.

Since the default under discussion does not consist of a single choice or a single moment, but of a long succession of choices in a long succession of situations, different factors may be operative on different occasions. Sometimes, one of these factors will tend to predominate in the case of a given individual.

By far the most commonly operative factor is fear associated with the issue of fallibility—fear of being wrong, fear of failure, fear of the risks of acting on one's own fallible judgment; which logically implies: fear of a universe in which success is not automatically guaranteed. This fear tends to make one susceptible to the other three factors. It is through a successive series of surrenders to such fear—through successive retreats from the challenges of life—that a person relinquishes the intellectual self-assertiveness which is the base of psychological sovereignty.

There are children who, when first presented with blocks or other construction toys, respond with timidity and apprehension; they see the situation, not as a pleasurable challenge, not as an opportunity to expand their skills, but as a threat to their "security," as an enemy which invokes feelings of helplessness by demanding that they cope with the new. If they characteristically surrender to fear in situations of this kind, if they back away from challenges rather than learn to master them, the effect on their psychological development is devastating: they institute a basic sense of impotence which tends to remain with them—and to be continually reinforced—throughout their life. They abort their own maturational development. The same principle applies to a human being's conceptual maturation. The problem is far, far commoner in this realm and far less recognized.

Without ever confronting the issue in fully identified terms, the overwhelming majority of men begin retreating, very early in life, from the challenges of proper conceptual growth—and they die, never having actualized more than a small fraction of their potential intelligence. The self-esteem deficiency expressed in the feeling of "Who am I to know? Who am I to judge? Who am I to decide?" is the consequence of too many retreats from the responsibility of thought and judgment in situations where the person did not have to retreat, where an effort could and should have been made but was not, where the disvalue of fear and uncertainty took precedence over the value of efficacy and knowledge.

Often, this policy of self-abdication is wittingly or unwittingly encouraged by parents and other elders who act in such a way as to penalize intellectual independence and initiative on the part of the child and/or to create an impression of such bewildering irrationality that the child gives up the effort to understand, his incentives undercut by the feeling that human beings are hopelessly unintelligible. By the same token, parents make a positive contribution to the child's proper development to the extent that they encourage and reward independence and self-responsibility, and act in a consistent, predictable, intelligible manner which supports and/or implants in the child the conviction that he is living in a knowable world.

A person's retreat from the responsibility of intellectual growth and his default on the process of proper conceptual maturation, affects adversely both the cognitive and the evaluative sphere of his mental activity. The worst devastation, however, is wrought in the evaluative sphere. Many persons—who are not basically anti-effort and may actively enjoy the process of thinking—exhibit a far greater degree of independence in regard to cognitive issues than in regard to value issues.

Normative abstractions (such as "justice," for instance) stand on a higher, more advanced level of the hierarchy of man's concepts than do many (though obviously not all) of his cognitive abstractions; the conceptual chain that connects normative abstractions to their base in perceptual reality is long and complex. This fact is experienced by many men as fearsome and discomfiting: it demands a stronger commitment to the efficacy of their own mind than they possess.

Further—and this consideration is especially crucial—the fear of relying on the judgment of one's own mind is felt most acutely in the realm of values because of the direct consequences of one's judgments for one's own life and well-being. The evaluative errors that men make affect them personally far more often—and far more devastatingly—than do most of their cognitive errors. To assume responsibility for choosing the values that guide one's life, the principles by which to act, the goals in which to seek happiness—to make such judgments alone, relying solely upon one's own reason and understanding—is to practice the ultimate form of intellectual independence, the one most dreaded by the overwhelming majority of men. (Such intellectual independence, it should be mentioned, does not forbid the possibility of *learning* from other men, but it forbids the *substituting* of their judgment for one's own.)

Still another reason why the fear of independence is most intense in the sphere of value-judgments is the fact that independence in this area is most likely to bring a person into conflict with other men. Cognitive differences do not necessarily generate personal animosity among men; value differences commonly do, particularly when basic issues are involved. Therefore, independence in the sphere of value-judgments is more demanding psychologically.

Since a social form of existence is proper to man, since he has many benefits to derive from living among and dealing with his fellow men (benefits relative, among other things, to the superior manner of survival possible to him under a division of labor)—it should be recognized that the desire to have a harmonious and benevolent relationship with his fellow men is a rational one; it is not, per se, a breach of proper independence. It becomes such a breach only if and when a man subordinates his mind and judgment to that desire—i.e., if he places that desire above his perception of reality. If and when the price of "harmony" with his fellow men becomes the surrender of his mind, a psychologically healthy man does not pay it; nothing can be a benefit to him at that cost.

For some of the persons who dread intellectual self-reliance, there is still another motive involved. The process of rational thought and judgment is, necessarily, a process that a man performs alone. Men can learn from one another, but they cannot *share* the act of thinking; it is an individual, solitary process, not a social one. There are men who dread independent thought and judgment precisely for this reason: it makes them aware of their own separateness as living entities, it makes them aware of the respect in which every man necessarily *is* an island unto himself; it makes them aware of the responsibility they must bear for their own existence; it forces them to experience the fact that they are not and cannot be merely indeterminate constituents of a vast social ooze; it forces them to feel alienated, cut off, disconnected, rootless and shapeless; it forces them to face their own *being* and thus to confront the terror of their own state of *non*being.

To think, to judge, to choose one's values, is to be *individuated,* to create a distinct, personal *identity.* But there are men who, in their deepest emotions, do not *want* personal identity—however, much they may scream to their psychiatrists that they are tormented by a sense of inner emptiness.

This psychology represents the most profound form of rebellion against one's nature as man—more specifically, against the responsibility of a volitional (self-directed and self-regulating) consciousness—which means: the attempt to escape the responsibility of being human.

Fear of intellectual independence can exist in various degrees of intensity. What are its consequences when it is the dominant element in a person's psychology?

There is no escape from the facts of reality, no escape from man's nature or the manner of survival his nature requires. Every living species that possesses awareness can survive only by the guidance of its consciousness; *that* is the role and function of consciousness in a living organism. If (in effect) a person rejects his distinctive form of consciousness, if he decides that thinking is too much effort and/or that choosing the values needed to guide his actions is too frightening a responsibility—then, if he wants to survive and to function in the world, he can do so only by means of the minds of others: by means of *their* conclusions, *their* judgments, *their* values.

He knows, consciously or subconsciously, that he does not know what to do and that knowledge is required to make decisions in the face of the countless alternatives that confront him every day of his life. But *others* seem to know how to live and function, so the only way to exist, he feels, is to follow their lead and live by their knowledge; *they* know—they will spare him the effort and the risk; *they* know—somehow they possess control of that mysterious unknowable: reality.

He does not begin by choosing to be an intellectual dependent; he begins by failing to assume the responsibility of thinking and judging on his own; then he is *forced* into the position of a dependent. He is led to shape his soul in the image of a parasite inconceivable in any other living species: not a parasite of body, but of *consciousness.*

A man of self-esteem and sovereign consciousness deals with reality, with nature, with an objective universe of facts; he holds his mind as his tool of survival and develops his ability to think. But the psycho-epistemological dependent lives, not in a universe of facts, but in a *universe of people;* people, not facts, are *his* reality; people, not reason, are his tool of survival. It is on *them* that his consciousness must focus; reality is *reality-as-perceived-by-them;* it is *they* who he must understand or please or placate or deceive or maneuver or manipulate or obey. It is his success at this task that becomes the gauge of his efficacy—of his competence at living.

Having alienated himself from objective reality, he has virtually no other standard of truth, rightness, or personal worth. To grasp and successfully to satisfy the expectations, conditions, demands, terms, *values* of others, is experienced by him as his deepest, most urgent need. The temporary diminution of his anxiety, which the approval of others offers him, is his substitute for self-esteem.

This is the phenomenon that I designate as *"Social Metaphysics."*

"Metaphysics" is one's view of the nature of reality. To the psycho-epistemological dependent, reality (for all practical purposes) is *people:* in his mind, in his thinking, in the automatic connections of his consciousness, *people* occupy the place which, in the mind of a rational man, is occupied by reality.

Social metaphysics is the psychological syndrome that characterizes a person who holds the minds of other men, not objective reality, as his ultimate psycho-epistemological frame of reference.

Social Metaphysical Fear

It must be emphasized that the social metaphysician's dependence on other men is not, fundamentally, material or financial; it is deeper than any practical or tangible consideration; the material forms of parasitism and exploitation that some men practice are merely one of its consequences.

The basic dependence of the social metaphysician is psycho-epistemological; it is a parasitism of cognition, of judgment, of values—a wish to function within a context established by others, to live by the guidance of rules for which one does not bear ultimate intellectual responsibility—a parasitism of consciousness.

Since the social metaphysician's pseudo-self-esteem rests on his ability to deal with the-world-as-perceived-by-others, his fear of disapproval or condemnation is the fear of being pronounced inadequate to reality, unfit for existence, devoid of personal worth—a verdict he hears whenever he is "rejected."

The nonvenal, nonpractical nature of the social metaphysician's dependence is illustrated in the following example:

Consider the case of a social metaphysician who is a multimillionaire—and who is obsessively concerned with the question of what everyone thinks of him, even his office boy. He feels driven to win the office boy's approval or liking, he watches eagerly for any signs of a personal response, and any indication of the boy's indifference or dislike makes him feel anxious or depressed. He finds himself being compulsively "charming" in order to win the boy's admiration. He has nothing practical to gain from that boy's favor, neither money nor advice nor prestige nor business advantage; in any practical, business sense, the boy is his inferior; yet the multimillionaire feels that he must win the boy's affection. What significance, then, does the boy have for him? It is not the office boy as an actual person that he seeks to placate or charm, but the office boy as a symbol of other people, of any other people, of mankind at large. The implicit thought behind his compulsion is *not:* "This office boy is a potential provider who will take care of me and guide me"—but: "I am acceptable to other people. People who are non-me, approve of me, they regard me as a good human being."

In order to belong *with* others, the social metaphysician is willing to belong *to* them. Since, however, he is seeking a manner of survival improper to man by nature, since the intellectual sovereignty he has surrendered is an essential of mental health and self-esteem, he condemns himself to chronic insecurity, and to a fear of other men that is profoundly humiliating. The humiliation he endures—the sense of living under blackmail, in effect—is one of the most painful aspects of his plight.

The nature of his humiliation and fear, however, are seldom identified by him—because he would find it too degrading. Most often, he seeks to protect his pseudo-self-esteem by evading the humiliation and rationalizing the fear; he commonly attempts to justify his fear by an appeal to allegedly *"practical"* considerations, asserting that his fear is an appropriate response to an actual danger. This is one of the most prevalently used devices by which men seek to conceal their dread of independence and their moral cowardice.

The following examples illustrate this practice in various representative areas of life. They illustrate the manner in which men, prompted by a fear they dare not acknowledge and so cannot overcome, invent nonexistent dangers or grossly exaggerate minor ones, betray their own minds, sell out whatever authentic rationality they possess, contribute to the spread of values inimical to their own—and acquire a *vested interest* in believing that men are unavoidably evil, that human existence is evil, that the good has no chance on earth.

Consider the case of a professor of philosophy who is an atheist. He knows that the arguments for the existence of a God are thoroughly indefensible, he regards the notion of a supernatural being as irrational and destructive, he despises mysticism and considers himself an advocate of reason. Bu he evades the issue of atheism versus theism in his books and lectures, refuses to commit himself on the subject publicly, and, every Sunday, attends church with his parents and relatives.

He does not tell himself that his motive is fear, that he is terrified to stand alone against his family, friends, and colleagues, that violent arguments of any kind make him panicky—and that he desperately wants to feel "accepted." Instead, he tells himself that if he were to acknowledge his atheism, his career would be ruined (evading the fact that many professors are known atheists and their careers are unaffected by it). He tells himself that he is reluctant to cause pain to his elderly parents who are devoutly religious and who would be dismayed by his lack of faith (evading the fact that he is not obliged to "convert" his parents, merely to state his own convictions, and that a man who takes ideas seriously does not sacrifice his own judgments, which he knows to be rational, in order to placate people whose beliefs he knows to be irrational).

His rationalizations serve to shield him from a full recognition of his treason. But because it cannot be blanked out entirely, he is condemned to struggle against secret feelings of self-contempt—and he retaliates by cursing the malevolence of "the system" and of reality, since he cannot have his treason and his self-esteem, too.

Consider the case of a successful playwright who selects some important theme as the subject of a play, a theme requiring and deserving a serious dramatic presentation, and then realizes that his viewpoint will antagonize a great many people. He decides, therefore, to write the play as a comedy, making "good-natured fun" of the things he regards as evil, counting on his humor to prevent anyone from taking his views seriously and being offended or antagonized.

He does not tell himself that he dreads to be regarded as "unfashionable." Instead, he tells himself that serious plays dealing with controversial ideas are noncommercial—and dismisses the many exceptions as "freaks" requiring no explanation.

But he cannot entirely elude the knowledge that he has sold out the motive that prompted his desire to write the play in the first place. So he retaliates against his discomfiting sense of moral uncleanliness by cursing the "stupidity" and "bad taste" of the masses.

Consider the case of a scientist who despises the obscurantist jargon that is rampant in his profession, and the "postulates" underlying that jargon, who is rationally convinced that the theories of many of his most highly regarded colleagues are wrong. But he twists his brain to adopt that jargon in his own writings, dilutes his criticisms in every possible way, and strives to smuggle his own ideas into the minds of his readers in such a manner that no one will notice the extent of his departure from established belief.

He does not tell himself that he is afraid of being ridiculed as an "outsider," or that he abjectly hungers for the esteem of men he regards as pretentious incompetents. Instead, he tells himself that he is "playing it smart," that when he becomes famous *he* will be the term-setter, and that the "practical" way to become famous, to become a *successful* innovator, is to make himself indistinguishable from everyone else.

But he cannot entirely drown the knowledge that this was not the view of science with which he started, and that the youth who had been himself would find it strange to be told that devotion to truth is expressed by catering to falsehood. So he retaliates by cursing the malevolence of a universe in which the concept of a "fashionable innovator" is a contradiction in terms.

Consider, finally, the case of a businessman who recognizes that capitalism is the only rational and just social system. He knows the intelligence, independence, and dedication which industrial production requires, he knows that he *earns* his profits, he loves his work and is secretly proud of it. But he apologizes for his success publicly, contributes financially to intellectual organizations explicitly devoted to the destruction of businessmen, accepts the government's expropriation of his wealth and infringement of his rights without moral protest, and begs mankind at large to forgive him for the sin of possessing ability.

He does not tell himself that he is afraid to challenge the prevailing religion-derived value-system which damns his way of life as ignoble, selfish, and materialistic, even though that value-system has never made sense to him; he does not tell himself that he cannot bear to feel alienated from all those who support that value-system; he does not tell himself that the responsibility of passing independent judgments in the realm of *morality* fills him with dread. Instead, he tells himself that his policy is motivated solely by the desire to protect his business interests, that it is "good sense" not to antagonize government officials, that it is "shrewd public relations" to finance intellectuals of the statist persuasion, so they will see he is a "nice guy," that it is "bad business" to court unpopularity. His secret fear takes the form of imagining that the masses are unthinking brutes, that they are the ultimate masters of reality—they can kill him and take over his property whenever they wish—so they must be placated, they must be told that he works only to serve them, he must restrain them by assuring them that theirs is the right superseding all other rights. This, he tells himself, is "hard-headed realism."

But he cannot entirely escape the disquieting awareness somewhere within him that his appeasement is not prompted by the motives he names, that his "practicality" and "cynicism" are protective affectations masking something worse. So he retaliates by cursing human irrationality and the malevolence of a world which demands that he be concerned with moral issues.

To the extent that men irrationally surrender to fear, they increase the power of fear over their lives. More and more things acquire the power to *invoke* fear in them. Their self-confidence diminishes and their sense of danger grows. Social metaphysical fear is a cancer that either spreads or (if rationally resisted) contracts; but it does not stand still.

With every surrender to the consciousness of others, with every successive betrayal, the social metaphysician's sense of alienation from reality worsens and his sense of impotence finds confirmation. The shrinking remnants of his self-esteem are drained to appease an endless stream of blackmailers whose demands are inexhaustible—blackmailers who are any human consciousness but his own—blackmailers who, more often than not, are as afraid of *his* judgment as he is afraid of *theirs,* who are desperately seeking *his* approval, who are committing the same form of treason and enduring the same humiliation. The grim irony is that all sides involved assure themselves that the grotesque farce of their selfless existence is motivated by considerations of "practicality."

Social Metaphysical Types

"Social metaphysics" is a very broad classification; there are many different types of social metaphysicians. Certain traits or symptoms, however, are common to all social metaphysicians: (a) the absence of a firm, unyielding concept of existence, facts, reality, as apart from the judgments, beliefs, opinions, feelings of others; (b) a sense of fundamental helplessness or impotence, a feeling of *metaphysical* inefficacy; (c) a profound fear of other people, and an implicit belief that other people control that unknowable realm: reality; (d) a self-esteem—or, more precisely, a *pseudo*-self-esteem—

that is tied to and dependent on the responses of the "significant others"; (e) a tragic or malevolent sense of life, a belief that the universe is essentially inimical to one's interests. (This last symptom is not restricted exclusively to social metaphysicians.)

The most fundamental of these traits, the one that makes all the others inevitable, is: the absence of a firm, independent sense of *objective reality*.

This is the vacuum that is filled by the consciousnesses of others—and this is the void that is responsible for that desolate feeling of *alienation* which is every social metaphysician's chronic torture.

It is important to observe that the experience of self-alienation and the feeling of being alienated from reality, from the world around one, proceed from the same cause: one's default on the responsibility of thinking. The suspension of proper cognitive contact with reality and the suspension of one's ego are a single act. A flight from reality is a flight from self.

Since social metaphysics represents a flight from the responsibility of independent judgment (particularly in the realm of values), and represents an attempt to live through and by others—the most common and easily identifiable type of social metaphysician is the person whose values and view of life are a direct reflection and product of his particular culture or subculture. This is the person who, today, is sometimes described as a "conformist." I shall designate this type as the *Conventional* social metaphysician.

This is the person who accepts the world and its prevailing values ready-made; his is not to reason why. What is true? What others say is true. What is right? What others believe is right. How should one live? As others live. Why does one work for a living? Because one is *supposed* to. Why does one get married? Because one is *supposed* to. Why does one have children? Because one is *supposed* to. Why does one go to church? Oh, please don't start discussing religion, you might offend someone.

This is George F. Babbitt, this is Peter Keating, this is the Organization Man. This is the person for whom reality "*is*" the world as interpreted by the "significant others" of his social environment—the person whose sense of identity and personal worth is *explicitly* a function of his ability to satisfy the values, terms, and expectations of those omniscient and omnipresent "others." I am "as you desire me"—such is the formula of his existence, such is the "genetic code" controlling his soul's development.

The Conventional social metaphysician is the type of man who lends surface credibility to the doctrine of environmental determinism. Such a man *is* the product of his background—but through his own default.

In a culture where science is held as a value, such a man may become a scientist; if scientists are expected (occasionally and within limits) to think independently and sometimes challenge the views of their colleagues, he may do it; he may take pains to be an "individualist" and may actually discover new knowledge. If he is taught that the day of the lone innovator is past and that all future scientific progress depends on "teamwork," then he will seek to establish his qualifications as a scientist, not through the productive quality of his thinking, but through his expertise at "human relations."

In a culture where initiative, ambition, and business ability are held as values, he may enter business and perhaps function productively; he may even succeed in making a fortune. In a culture where these things are *dis*valued, he may go to Washington instead.

In a culture such as the present one, with its disintegrating values, its intellectual chaos, its moral bankruptcy—where the familiar guideposts and rules are vanishing, where the authoritative mirrors reflecting "reality" are splintering into a thousand unintelligible subcults, where "adjustment" is becoming harder and harder—the Conventional social metaphysician is the first to run to a psychiatrist, crying that he has lost his identity, because he no longer knows unequivocally what he is supposed to do and be.

This is the type of man without whom no dictatorship could establish itself or remain in existence. He is the man who, in a society moving toward statism, "swims with the current"—and is carried into the abyss. He is the man who, in response to advance signs of danger, closes his eyes—lest he be compelled to pass independent *value-judgments* and to recognize that his world is not safe, that action and protest are demanded of him, that the policies and goals of his leaders are evil, that *the "significant others" are wrong.* In the midst of atrocities, he tells himself that the authorities "must have their reasons"—in order to escape the terror of knowing to whom and to what he has surrendered his existence. It is this same man who—usually when it is too late—will sometimes rebel in hysterical indignation, when the atrocities have come too close and cannot be evaded any longer, and he may die senselessly, in effectual protest, screaming at the malevolent omnipotence of the enemy, and wondering who or what had made the enemy's power possible.

There are, of course, immense differences among Conventional social metaphysicians—differences in their intelligence, honesty, ambition, ability, and independence (within the limits of "the system"). And, in a culture that contains a diversity of values and models, there are significant differences in the discrimination and judgment exercised by Conventional social metaphysicians with regard to their choice of authorities.

The Conventional type is the most blatant and uncomplicated species of social metaphysician; he represents the paradigm case, so to speak—the basic pattern, example, or prototype that serves as a reference-point with regard to which other species of social metaphysicians may be understood.

A psychologically healthy man of sovereign consciousness bases his self-esteem on his rationality: on his dedication to knowing what is true and what is right in fact and in reality, and on acting consistently with his knowledge. A social metaphysician, in contradistinction, substitutes the consciousnesses of others for reality, as the realm and object of his ultimate concern; his pseudo-self-esteem depends on grasping, and acting in accordance with, what others *believe* to be true and right; thus, the approval he elicits from others becomes the gauge and proof of his efficacy and worth. But success is not guaranteed to him; here, too, as in dealing with objective reality, effort, struggle, risk and the possibility of failure are unavoidably involved. The Conventional type is not undisturbed by this, but he accepts it. What, however, if a social metaphysician feels inadequate to this task, just as he feels inadequate to dealing with reality? What if he finds the challenge and the demands too overwhelming? Then a *new* line of neurotic defenses and self-deceptive practices may be developed, to protect his pseudo-self-esteem against collapse. This is the phenomenon that one may observe in another type of social metaphysician: the *Power-seeker.*

In this type, fear of others is especially pronounced; he finds his fear intolerable—and his reaction is an overriding emotion of *hatred.* The hatred is aimed at those who invoke his fear. Resentment and hostility are his dominant emotional traits. (These emotions, of course, usually are operative in the Conventional social metaphysician also, but they do not play the same central role in his motivation, they are not the motor of his development and goals.)

To this type, the Conventional social metaphysician's path to pseudo-self-esteem is too frighteningly precarious; the spectre of possible failure and defeat looms too large to be endurable. The Power-seeking social metaphysician feels too unsure of his ability to gain the love and approval he desires; his sense of inferiority is overwhelming. And the humiliation of his dependence—of his *unrequited* dependence, so to speak—infuriates him. He longs for an escape from the uncertainty of "free market" social metaphysical competition, where he must win men's *voluntary* esteem. He wants to deceive, to manipulate, to coerce the minds of others; to leave them no choice in the matter. He wants to reach a position where he can *command* respect, obedience, love.

As an example, consider King Frederick William of Prussia, who would beat his subjects while shouting at them: "You must not fear me, you must love me!"

This is the psychology of any dictator from Hitler to Stalin to Khrushchev to Castro to Mao. This is the man whose formula is: "If you can't join them, lick them."

The hatred that such men feel toward other human beings extends ultimately to reality as such, to a universe which does not allow them to have their irrationality and their self-esteem too, a universe which inexorably links irrationality to pain and guilt. To defeat the reality they have never chosen to grasp, to defy reason and logic, to *succeed* at the irrational, *to get away with it*—which means: to make their will omnipotent—becomes a burning lust, a lust to experience the only sort of "efficacy" they can project. And since, for social metaphysicians, reality means other people, the goal of their existence becomes to impose their will on others, to compel others to provide them with a universe in which the irrational will work.

The extent of such men's alienation from reality, the extent to which objective facts have no status in their consciousness, may be observed in the following spectacle: a brute standing on the balcony of his palace, the blood of millions dripping from his fingers, beaming down at a ragged mob gathered there to honor him—the brute knowing that the scene is a fraud of his own staging, that the mob is there solely by virtue of his soldiers' bayonets—but his chest swelling in satisfaction nonetheless, while, self-hypnotized, he basks in the warmth of his victims' "adoration." (This is the creature whom other social metaphysicians, in their own alienation from reality, call *practical.*)

Fear is the emotion which Power-seeking social metaphysicians understand best, the emotion on which they are authorities—by introspection. Fear is the social atmosphere in which they feel most at home, and the absence of fear in any person they deal with robs them of their delusion of efficacy; their sense of personal identity tends to evaporate in such a person's presence. One can manipulate uncertainty and self-doubt; one cannot manipulate self-esteem.

While social metaphysicians of the Power-seeking variety will often be attracted to the political or military sphere, the type may be found in every profession and on every level of society—from the corporation president who promotes his executives, not according to their ability, but according to their capacity for obsequiousness—to the professor who enjoys undercutting the intellectual self-confidence of his students, by tossing off incomprehensible contradictions as knowledge—to the vicious little sadist browbeating her troop of Girl Scouts. Differences in ambition, skill, and interests obviously are relevant to the range of one's power seeking.

Also, there is the matter of *opportunity.* In a politically free society, the Power-seeking type is severely limited in opportunities for "self-expression." But in a statist society, or in a society moving toward statism, formerly repressed and inhibited Power-seekers start crawling from under rocks in startling numbers.

Faced with the question, "What am I to do with my life?" or "What will make me happy?"—the Conventional social metaphysician seeks the answer among the standard values of his culture: respectability, financial success, marriage, family, professional competence, prestige, etc.

Faced with the question, "How am I to make my existence endurable?"—the Power-seeking social metaphysician seeks the answer in aggressive and destructive action aimed at the external object of his fear: other people.

While his desire is to control the consciousnesses of others, he does not necessarily resort to physical force, even when opportunities exist. Manipulation, trickery, and deceit are often chosen by him, not as *adjuncts* to coercion, but as preferred *alternatives*. There are several reasons for this. First, not all men of this type have the "stomach" for physical violence: they cannot bear the vision of themselves resorting to such means. Second, devices such as manipulation and deceit do not ordinarily entail the physical risks and dangers inherent in the use of violence. Third, to some Power-seekers, these nonviolent devices represent a *superior* form of efficacy, a more "intellectual" form, so to speak. But what must be recognized is that these devices spring from the same root as the impulse to violence: the desire to bypass and overcome the *voluntary* judgment of others, to affect others through the imposition of one's own will, *against* their desires, knowledge, and interests—to gain a sense of triumph by cheating reason and reality. The desire to manipulate other men is the desire to manipulate reality and to make one's wishes omnipotent.

Consider, now, the psychology of the *Spiritual* social metaphysician. This type does not seek to please and placate people in the manner of a Conventional social metaphysician, or to gain power over them like a Power-seeker. This type often does virtually nothing at all. His chief virtue, he proclaims or implies, is that he is too good for this world. He must not be expected to confirm to conventional standards. He must not be expected to achieve anything *tangible*. His friends and acquaintances must love and respect him, not for anything he does—*doing* is so vulgar—but for what he is. What *is* he? Not everything can be communicated, after all. Some things—the important things—can only be *felt*.

To put it another way: the Spiritual social metaphysician's claim to esteem rests on his alleged possession of a superior kind of *soul*— a soul that is not his mind, not his thoughts, not his values, not anything specifiable, but an ineffable composite of undefinable longings, incommunicable insights, and impenetrable mystery.

So long as the influence of mysticism falls as a shadow across our culture, this sort of "solution" to the problem of self-esteem will attract a certain number of social metaphysicians. It spares them the necessity of effort or struggle (except, of course, the dreadful struggle to preserve this fraud *in their own eyes*). They know that the inferiority feelings of their fellow social metaphysicians offer them a "market" for their Spiritual role.

The "market" is a limited one, however; and it is distressingly unpredictable. The Spiritual type has an answer to this, i.e., he has his rationalization ready. If and when he fails to receive the acceptance and esteem he craves, he explains to himself that people are not fine enough to appreciate the "real" him. He may even prefer to be alone, to avoid people—the better to dream, undisturbed and unchallenged, about how he would be admired and loved if only people knew what he was "really" like, deep inside. (It should be added that there are moments when the thought of people knowing what he is *really* like fills him with terror.) An overactive fantasy-life is often characteristic of this type: he sees himself as a religious saint, or an inspired statesman, or a renowned poet, or (forgetting that he is supposed to be spiritual) a sexually irresistible Don Juan.

The extreme case of this mentality, carried to the edge of psychosis (and sometimes beyond), is a *sub*type which may be designated as the *Religious fanatic* social metaphysician. This type of person can disassociate himself from the human race altogether, he may become a hermit or anchorite—with *God* as his "significant other," as the object of his social metaphysical attachment. Having despaired of impressing his fellow men, it is God whom he seeks to impress. Since God cannot frown at him, or snub him socially, or inquire as to why he doesn't get a job, the Religious fanatic type is free to imagine that God is smiling down at him, blessing and protecting him, responding to the true nobility of his soul, which everyone on earth is too superficial or corrupt to do.

Then there is the *Independent* social metaphysician. This is the counterfeit individualist, the man who rebels against the status quo for the sake of being rebellious, the man whose pseudo-self-esteem is tied to the picture of himself as a defiant nonconformist.

This is the "rebel" who fulfills his concept of profundity and self-expression by proclaiming regularly that "Everything stinks." This is the nihilist, this is the hippie, this is the nonobjective "artist," this is the "individualist" who proves it by scorning money, marriage, jobs, baths, and haircuts. This is the son who leaves home to join the anarchist movement, because his father suggested to him that perhaps it is time to start earning a living, now that he, the son, is approaching forty.

Overwhelmed by feelings of inadequacy in relation to the conventional standards of his culture, this type of person retaliates with the formula "Whatever is, *is wrong.*" Overwhelmed by the belief that no one can possibly like or accept him, he goes out of his way to insult people—lest they imagine that he desires their approval. Overwhelmed with humiliation at feeling himself an outcast, he struggles to conquer his sense of nonidentity by maintaining that to be an outcast is proof of one's superiority.

The fact that he evades is that there are *two* opposite reasons why a man may be "outside" of society: because his standards are *higher* than those of society—or because they are *lower;* because he is above society—or below it; because he is too good—or not good enough.

To the Independent social metaphysician, existence is a clash between his whims and the whims of others. Reason, objectivity, reality as such have no meaning to him, no importance inside his mind.

While he may profess devotion to some particular idea or goal, or even posture as a dedicated crusader, his primary motivation is negative rather than positive; he is *against* rather than *for.* He does not originate or struggle for positive values of his own, he merely rebels against the values and standards of others—as if the *absence* of passive conformity, rather than the *presence* of independent, rational judgment, were the hallmark of self-reliance and spiritual sovereignty. It is by means of this delusion that he seeks to escape the fact of his inner emptiness.

The Independent social metaphysician is the brother-in-spirit of the Power-seeker. Often, it is merely the accident of historical circumstances that determines whether a social metaphysician becomes one type or the other. Naziism and communism, for instance, attracted many Independent social metaphysicians who made an instantaneous and effortless transition to the psychology of the Power-seeking type; they found a form of "togetherness" for which they were eagerly willing to relinquish their "independence."

In a culture where rationality, productiveness, and simple sanity are dominant values, if only on a common sense level, social metaphysicians of the Independent type tend to remain on the fringes of society. But in a culture such as ours, the pressure result-ing from the intellectual vacuum can fling them up from their cel-lars to the pinnacles of prestige, in an extended "Fools' Day" orgy. Then one sees the triumphant spread of pretentiously eccentric mediocrity, one sees the drunken glorification of unconsciousness; one sees unintelligible splashes of paint, representing nothing, dis-played on the walls of famous museums; one seeks unkempt young men, in denims and T-shirts, lecturing on Zen Buddhism in dis-tinguished universities; one sees whims for the sake of whims, absurdity for the sake of absurdity, destruction for the sake of destruction, becoming *fashionable.*

When and to the extent that this occurs, the Independent social metaphysicians involved may react in one of several ways. They may switch to the role of Conventional social metaphysi-cians, eager to be respectable conformists within the context of their newly established subculture, and may then proceed to sneer at all those who do not "belong." Or: They may switch to the psy-chology of the open Power-seekers, struggling to be accepted as leaders of the new elite, scheming and manipulating in order to protect their positions, trembling lest their status be usurped by more effective or aggressive rivals. Or: Feeling too insecure to strive for *any* fixed position within *any* subculture, they may aban-don the system or movement that they themselves helped to launch, and adopt some *new* posture that will *guarantee* their role as outcasts, so that they will never have to endure the anticipatory panic of possible rejection.

There is, finally, a type of social metaphysician that differs in important respects from all the foregoing varieties I have described. I call this type: the *Ambivalent* social metaphysician.

This is the person who, notwithstanding a major psycho-epistemological surrender to the authority of others, has still pre-served a significant degree of intellectual sovereignty. While no one, not even the most abject conformist, can renounce his mind completely, the Ambivalent type retains a far greater measure of authentic independence than any other species of social meta-physician.

His intellectual self-abdication is far more limited; it tends to center on that most sensitive area in which all social metaphysicians are especially vulnerable: the realm of values.

The Ambivalent type seldom dares to question the fundamental values of his social environment, but he is often indifferent to these values, paying them only perfunctory respect. In the areas of life to which these values pertain, he does not assert counter-values of his own, he merely withdraws, surrendering those aspects of reality to others. He tends to restrict his activity and concern to the sphere of his work, where his self-reliance and sovereignty are greatest.

His bondage to social metaphysics is revealed in his quietly persistent sense of alienation from reality, in his lack of confidence and freedom with regard to passing value-judgments, in his implicit belief that the world is controlled by others, that others possess a knowledge forever unknowable to him, and in his humiliating desire for "approval" and "acceptance." His superiority to other social metaphysicians is evidenced, not only by his greater independence, but also by his desire to *earn*, through objective achievements, the esteem he longs for, by his relative inability to find real pleasure in an admiration not based on standards he can respect— and by his tortured disgust at his own fear of the disapproval of others. Often, he tries to fight his fear, refusing to act on or surrender to it, exercising immense will power and discipline—but never winning his battle fully, never setting himself free, because he does not go to the roots of his problem, does not identify the psycho-epistemological base of his betrayal, does not accept full and ultimate intellectual responsibility for his own life and goals.

Among this type, one will find men of distinguished achievements and outstanding creative originality—whose reason and tragedy lie in the contrast between their private lives and their lives as creators. These are the men who have the courage to challenge the *cognitive* judgments of world figures, but lack the courage to challenge the *value*-judgments of the folks next door.

It must be understood that none of the social metaphysical types I have described are intended to represent mutually exclusive categories; any particular social metaphysician may possess characteristics of several types. The purpose of such a typological description is to isolate, by a process of abstraction, *certain dominant trends* among social metaphysicians, and to make those trends intelligible motivationally.

The forms that social metaphysics can take are virtually unlimited. But if one grasps the basic *principles* involved, one will be better able to understand the appalling consequences to which social metaphysics leads, socially and existentially. It has been barely possible here to hint at those consequences. The full story cannot be told in so brief a discussion. But it is written in blood across the pages of history.

Chapter Eleven

Self-Esteem and Romantic Love

The Principle of Psychological Visibility

The two sources of greatest potential happiness for man are productive work and romantic (sexual) love.

Through the productive use of his mind, man gains control over his existence and experiences the pleasure and pride of efficacy. Through romantic love, man gains the ultimate emotional reward of his efficacy and worth—of his efficacy and worth not merely as a producer, but wider: as a person—the reward and celebration of himself and of what he has made of himself, i.e., of the kind of character and soul he has created.

The experience of romantic love answers a profound psychological need in man. But the nature of that need cannot be understood apart from an understanding of a wider need: man's need of human companionship—of human beings he can respect, admire, and value, and with whom he can interact intellectually and emotionally. What is the root of the desire for human companionship? Why is man motivated to find human beings he can value and love?

Virtually everyone regards the desire for companionship, friendship, love, as a self-evident primary—in effect, as an irreducible fact of human nature, requiring no explanation. Sometimes, a pseudo-explanation is offered, in terms of an alleged "gregarious instinct" which man is said to possess. But this illuminates nothing; explanation via instincts is merely a device to conceal ignorance. Psychologists, to date, have contributed nothing to our understanding of this subject.

Man's desire for human companionship may be explained *in part* by the fact that living and dealing with other men in a social context, trading goods and services, etc., afford man a manner of survival immeasurably superior to that which he could obtain alone on a desert island or on a self-sustaining farm. Man obviously finds it to his interest to deal with men whose values and character are like his own, rather than with men of inimical values and character. And, normally, man develops feelings of benevolence or affection toward men who share his values and who act in ways that are beneficial to his existence.

It should be apparent, however—from observation and by introspection—that practical, existential considerations such as these are not sufficient to account for the phenomenon in question; and that the desire for and experience of friendship and love reflect a distinct *psychological* need. Everyone is aware, introspectively, of the desire for companionship, for someone to talk to, to be with, to feel understood by, to share important experiences with—the desire for *emotional closeness* with another human being. What is the nature of the psychological need that generates this desire?

I shall begin by giving an account of two events that were crucial in leading me to the answer—because I believe this will help the reader to understand the issues which the problem involves.

One afternoon, while sitting alone in my living room, I found myself contemplating with pleasure a large philodendron plant standing against a wall. It was a pleasure I had experienced before, but suddenly it occurred to me to ask myself: What is the nature of this pleasure? What is its cause?

The pleasure was not primarily esthetic: were I to learn that the plant was artificial, its esthetic characteristics would remain the same, but my response would change radically; the special pleasure I experienced would vanish. Essential to my enjoyment was the knowledge that the plant was healthily and glowingly *alive*. There was the feeling of a bond, almost of a kind of kinship, between the plant and me; in the midst of inanimate objects, we were united in the fact of possessing life. I thought of the motive of people who, in the most impoverished conditions, plant flowers in boxes on their window sills—for the pleasure of watching something grow. *What is the value to man of observing successful life?*

Suppose, I thought, one were left on a dead planet where one had every material provision to ensure survival, but where nothing was alive; one would feel like a metaphysical alien. Then suppose one came upon a living plant; surely one would greet the sight with eagerness and pleasure. *Why?*

Because—I realized—all life, life by its very nature, entails a struggle, and struggle entails the possibility of defeat; and man desires, and finds pleasure in seeing, concrete instances of successful life, as confirmation of his knowledge that successful life is possible. It is, in effect, a *metaphysical* experience. He desires the sight, not as a means of allaying doubts or of reassuring himself, but as a means of experiencing and confirming on the perceptual level, the level of immediate reality, that which he knows conceptually.

If such is the value that a plant can offer to man, I wondered, then cannot the sight of another human being offer man a much more intense form of that experience? This is surely relevant to the psychological value that human beings find in one another.

The next crucial step in my thinking occurred on an afternoon when I sat on the floor playing with my dog—a wire-haired fox terrier named Muttnik.

We were jabbing at and boxing with each other in mock ferociousness; what I found delightful and fascinating was the extent to which Muttnik appeared to grasp the playfulness of my intention: she was snarling and snapping and striking back while being unfailingly gentle in a manner that projected total, fearless trust. The event was not unusual; it is one with which most dog-owners are familiar. But a question suddenly occurred to me, of a kind I had never asked myself before: Why am I having such an enjoyable time? What is the nature and source of my pleasure?

Part of my response, I recognized, was simply the pleasure of watching the healthy self-assertiveness of a living entity. But that was not the essential factor causing my response. The essential factor pertained to the *interaction* between the dog and myself—the sense of interacting and communicating with a living *consciousness*.

Suppose I were to view Muttnik as an automaton without consciousness or awareness, and to view her actions and responses as entirely mechanical; then my enjoyment would vanish. The factor of consciousness was of primary importance.

Then I thought: Suppose I were left on an uninhabited island; would not the presence of Muttnik be of enormous value to me? Obviously it would. Because she could make a practical contribution to my physical survival? Obviously not. Then what value did she have to offer? Companionship. A conscious entity with whom to interact and communicate—as I was doing now. *But why is that a value?*

The answer to this question—I realized—would explain much more than the attachment to a pet; involved in this issue is the psychological principle that underlies man's desire for *human* companionship: the principle that would explain why a conscious entity seeks out and values other conscious entities, *why consciousness is a value to consciousness.*

When I identified the answer, I called it "the Muttnik principle"—because of the circumstances under which it was discovered. Now let us consider the nature of this principle.

My feeling of pleasure in playing with Muttnik contained a particular kind of self-awareness, and *this* was the key to understanding my reaction. The self-awareness came from the nature of the "feedback" Muttnik was providing. From the moment that I began to "box," she responded in a playful manner; she conveyed no sign of feeling threatened; she projected an attitude of trust and pleasurable excitement. Were I to push or jab at an inanimate object, it would react in a purely mechanical way; it would not be responding to *me;* there could be no possibility of it grasping the *meaning* of my actions, of apprehending my *intentions,* and of guiding its behavior accordingly. It could not react to my psychology, i.e., to my mental state. Such communication and response is possible only among conscious entities. The effect of Muttnik's behavior was to make me feel *seen,* to make me feel *psychologically visible* (at least, to some extent). Muttnik was responding to me, not as to a mechanical object, but as to a *person.*

What is significant and must be stressed is that Muttnik was responding to me as a person in a way that I regarded as objectively *appropriate,* i.e., consonant with my view of myself and of what I was conveying to her. Had she responded with fear and an attitude of cowering, I would have experienced myself as being, in effect, *mis-perceived* by her, and would not have felt pleasure.

Now, why does man value and find pleasure in the experience of self-awareness and psychological visibility that the appropriate response (or "feedback") from another consciousness can evoke?

Consider the fact that normally man experiences himself as a *process*—in that consciousness itself is a process, an activity, and the contents of man's mind are a shifting flow of perceptions, thoughts, and emotions. His own mind is not an unmoving entity which man can contemplate objectively—i.e., contemplate as a direct object of awareness—as he contemplates objects in the external world.

He has, of course, a sense of himself, of his own identity, but it is experienced more as a feeling than a thought—a feeling which is very diffuse, which is interwoven with all his other feelings, and which is very hard, if not impossible, to isolate and consider by itself. His "self-concept" is not a single concept, but a cluster of images and abstract perspectives on his various (real or imagined) traits and characteristics, the sum total of which can never be held in focal awareness at any one time; that sum is *experienced,* but it is not *perceived* as such.

In the course of a man's life, his values, goals, and ambitions are first conceived in his mind, i.e., they exist as data of consciousness, and then—to the extent that his life is successful—are translated into action and objective reality; they become part of the "out there," of the world that he perceives. They achieve expression and reality in material form. This is the proper and necessary pattern of man's existence. Yet a man's most important creation and highest value—his character, his soul, his psychological self—can never follow this pattern in the literal sense, can never exist apart from his own consciousness; it can never be perceived by him as part of the "out there." But man *desires* a form of objective self-awareness and, in fact, *needs* this experience.

Since man is the motor of his own actions, since his concept of himself, of the person he has created, plays a cardinal role in his motivation—he desires and needs the fullest possible experience of the reality and objectivity of that person, of his self.

When man stands before a mirror, he is able to perceive his own face as an object in reality, and he finds pleasure in doing so, in contemplating the physical entity who is himself. There is a value in being able to look and think: "That's me." The value lies in the experience of objectivity.

Is there a mirror in which man can perceive his *psychological* self? In which he can perceive his own soul? Yes. The mirror is another consciousness.

Man is able, alone, to know himself conceptually. What another consciousness can offer is the opportunity for man to experience himself perceptually.

To a very small extent, that was the opportunity afforded me by Muttnik. In her response, I was able to see reflected an aspect of my own personality. But a human being can experience this self-awareness to a full and proper extent only in a relationship with a consciousness like his own, a consciousness possessing an equal range of awareness, i.e., another human being.

A man's intelligence, his psycho-epistemology, his basic premises and values, his sense of life, are all made manifest in his personality. "Personality" is the externally perceivable sum of all those psychological traits or characteristics which distinguish one man from another. A man's psychology is expressed through his behavior, through the things he says and does, and through the way he says and does them. It is in this sense that a man's self is an object of perception to others. When others react to a man, to their view of him and of his behavior, their reaction (which begins in their consciousness) is expressed through *their* behavior, through the things they say and do relative to him, and through the way they say and do them. If their view of him is consonant with his own, and is, accordingly, transmitted by their behavior, he feels perceived, he feels psychologically visible— and he experiences a sense of the objectivity of his self and of his psychological state; he perceives the reflection of himself in their behavior. It is in this sense that others can be a psychological mirror.

Just as there are many different aspects of a man's personality and inner life, so a man may feel visible in different respects in different human relationships. He may experience a greater or lesser degree of visibility, over a wider or narrower range of his total personality—depending on the nature of the person with whom he is dealing and on the nature of their interaction.

Sometimes, the aspect in which a man feels visible pertains to a basic character trait; sometimes, to the nature of his intention in performing some action; sometimes, to the reasons behind a particular emotional response; sometimes, to an issue involving his sense of life; sometimes, to a matter concerning his activity as a producer; sometimes, to his sexual psychology; sometimes, to his esthetic values.

All the forms of interaction and communication among people—intellectual, emotional, physical—can serve to give a man the perceptual evidence of his visibility in one respect or another; or, relative to particular people, can give him the impression of invisibility. Most men are largely unaware of the process by which this occurs; they are aware only of the results. They are aware that, in the presence of a particular person, they do or do not feel "at home," do or do not feel a sense of affinity or understanding or emotional attunement.

The mere fact of holding a conversation with another human being entails a marginal experience of visibility—if only the experience of being perceived as a conscious entity. However, in a close human relationship, with a person one deeply admires and cares for, one expects a far more profound visibility, involving highly individual and intimate aspects of one's inner life.

A significant mutuality of intellect, of basic premises and values, of fundamental attitude toward life, is the precondition of that projection of mutual visibility which is the essence of authentic friendship. A friend, said Aristotle, is another self. It was an apt formulation. A friend reacts to a man as, in effect, the man would react to himself in the person of another. Thus, the man perceives himself through his friend's reaction. He perceives his own person through its consequences in the consciousness (and, as a result, in the behavior) of the perceiver.

This, then, is the root of man's desire for companionship and love: the desire to perceive himself as an entity in reality—to experience the perspective of objectivity—through and by means of the reactions and responses of other human beings.

The principle involved ("the Muttnik principle")—let us call it "the *Visibility* principle"—may be summarized as follows: Man desires and needs the experience of self-awareness that results from perceiving his self as an objective existent—and he is able to achieve this experience through interaction with the consciousness of other living entities.

In any given relationship, the extent to which a man achieves this experience depends, crucially, on two factors:

1. The extent of the mutuality of mind and values that exists between himself and the other person.

2. The extent to which his self-image corresponds to the actual facts of his psychology; i.e., the extent to which he knows himself and judges himself correctly; i.e., the extent to which his inner view of himself is consonant with the personality projected by his behavior.

As an example of the first of these factors, suppose that a self-confident man encounters a highly anxious and hostile neurotic; he sees that the neurotic reacts to him with unprovoked suspiciousness and antagonism; the image of himself reflected by the neurotic's attitude is, in effect, that of a brute advancing menacingly with a club; in such a case, the self-confident man would not feel visible; he would feel bewildered and mystified or indignant at being so grossly misperceived.

This is one of the most tragic and painful ways in which a psychologically healthy person, especially vulnerable when he is young, can be victimized by less healthy persons and given a bewilderingly irrational impression of the human realm. Not only are his virtues unrecognized and unappreciated, but worse: *he is penalized for them*. This is often one of the most vicious by-products of neurosis. The healthy person is made the innocent target for envy, resentment, antagonism—for responses from other people that bear no intelligible relationship to the qualities he exhibits—and he usually has no way to suspect that the animosity he encounters is a reaction, not to anything bad in him, but to the good.

As an example of the second factor, suppose a man is inclined to rationalize his own behavior and to support his pseudo-self-esteem by means of totally unrealistic pretensions. His self-deceiving image of the kind of person he is conflicts radically with the actual self conveyed by his actions. The consequence is that he feels chronically frustrated and chronically invisible in his human relationships—because the "feedback" he receives is not compatible with his pretensions.

Sometimes, in the case of interaction between two neurotics, a kind of pseudo-visibility can be mutually projected—in a situation where each participant supports the pretensions and self-deceptions of the other, in exchange for receiving such support himself. The "trade" occurs, of course, on a subconscious level. This pattern often underlies neurotic love relationships.

The desire for visibility is usually experienced by men as the desire for understanding, i.e., the desire to be understood by other human beings. If a man is happy and proud of some achievement, he wants to feel that those who are close to him, those he cares for, understand his achievement and its personal meaning to him, understand and attach importance to the reasons behind his emotions. Or, if a man is given a book by a friend and told that this is the kind of book he will enjoy, the man feels pleasure and gratification if his friend's judgment proves correct— because he feels visible, he feels understood, Or, if a man suffers over some personal loss, it is of value to him to know that his plight is understood by those close to him, and that his emotional state has reality to them. It is not blind "acceptance" that a normal person desires, nor unconditional "love," but *understanding*.

The overwhelming majority of contemporary psychologists regard man, in effect, as a social metaphysician by nature who needs the approval of others in order to approve of himself. But it would be a gross error to confuse the motives of the social metaphysician, which are pathological, with a healthy man's desire for visibility.

A psychologically healthy man does not depend on others for his self-esteem; he expects others to *perceive* his value, not to *create* it. Unlike the social metaphysician, he does not desire approval indiscriminately or for its own sake; the admiration of others is of value and importance to him only if he respects the standards by which others judge him and only if the admiration is directed at qualities which he himself regards as admirable. If other men give authentic evidence of understanding and appreciating him, *they* rise in his estimation; his estimate of himself does not change. He desires the experience of living in a rational and just social environment, where the responses he elicits from other men are logically related to his own virtues and achievements. He knows the truth about his own character and actions, conceptually; he wants to experience it, perceptually, through and by means of its consequences in persons who share his values.

As for social metaphysicians, it is not *visibility* they seek from others, but *identity* (plus the kind of pseudo-visibility indicated above).

People who have an "act," people who assume different personalities in different encounters, sentence themselves to live with a devastating contradiction. As human beings, they cannot escape the need for visibility—but, as neurotic "role-players," they dread being understood, i.e., being perceived correctly. Often, they secretly despise those who are taken in by their act, and they long subconsciously for someone whom they will not be able to deceive. At the same time, they do everything possible to avoid the perceptive glance of the person for whom their act does not work. If a man wishes to be authentically visible to others, *he must be willing to be visible to himself.*

This last has important relevance to a more innocent kind of person than the role-player. Consider the problem of the individual who—because of despair, or moral confusion, or self-doubt, or fear of being impractical and unrealistic—tends to repress his virtues and value-aspirations, and to submerge his own idealism (Chapter Five). Such a person does not feel visible to himself (he is *not* visible to himself)—and the protective shell of remoteness, resignation, and unresponsiveness to life, under which his actual soul is hiding, makes him invisible to others. Until and unless he releases that soul—which means: until and unless he identifies his values, grants them the sanction of moral objectivity, and gives them appropriate, objective expression in action—he will inevitably experience a sense of frustration and impoverishment in his human relationships. The act of giving objective expression to his values does not guarantee that he will be visible to others, since that depends, in part, on *their* values; but the failure to give such objective expression does guarantee that he will be invisible.

The desire for visibility does not mean that a psychologically healthy man's basic preoccupation, in any human encounter, is with the question of whether or not he is properly appreciated.

When a man of self-esteem meets a person for the first time, his primary concern is not, "What does he think of me?"—but rather, "What do I think of him?" His primary concern, necessarily, is with his own judgment and evaluation of the facts that confront him.

Entailed by man's desire to see his values objectified in reality is the desire to see his own values embodied in the person of others, to see human beings who face life as he faces it. That sight offers man a reaffirmation of his own view of existence.

In a relationship with a person he admires, a major source of pleasure to man is the process of communicating his estimate, making his admiration objective, projecting that the other person is visible to him. This is an important form of making his own self objective, of giving existential reality to his own values, of experiencing himself as an entity—through an act of self-assertiveness.

As was indicated above, a man can feel visible in different respects and to varying degrees in different human relationships. A relationship with a casual stranger does not afford man the degree of visibility he experiences with an acquaintance. A relationship with an acquaintance does not afford man the degree of visibility he experiences with an intimate friend.

But there is one relationship which is unique in the depth and comprehensiveness of the visibility it entails: romantic love.

Romantic Love

Contained in every human being's self-concept is the awareness of being male or female. One's sexual identity is normally an integral and intimate part of one's experience of personal identity. No one experiences oneself merely as a human being, but always as a male human being or a female human being. (When a person lacks a clear sense of sexual identity, his condition is recognized as being pathological.)

While one's sexual identity (one's masculinity or femininity) is rooted in the facts of one's biological nature, it does not consist merely of being physically male or female; it consists of the way one psychologically *experiences* one's maleness or femaleness. More broadly, it consists of one's personal psychological traits *qua* man or woman.

For example, if a man is characteristically honest in his dealings with people, this trait pertains to his psychology as a human being; it is not a sexual characteristic. If, on the other hand, he feels confident in his sexual role relative to women, this trait pertains to his psychology specifically as a man.

What, then, are the various psychological attributes whose sum constitutes one's specifically psycho-sexual identity, i.e., one's psychological identity as a man or as a woman?

One's psycho-sexual identity (one's sexual personality) is the product and reflection of the manner in which one responds to one's nature as a sexual being—just as one's personal identity, in the wider sense, is the product and reflection of the manner in which one responds to one's nature as a human being.

To what extent is one aware of oneself as a sexual entity? What is one's view of sex and of its significance in human life? How does one feel about one's own body? (This does not mean: how does one appraise one's body esthetically?—but rather: is one's body experienced as a value, as a source of pleasure?) How does one view the opposite sex? How does one feel about the body of the opposite sex? How does one identify the respective sexual roles of man and woman? How does one evaluate one's own sexual role—and does one feel confident in regard to it? It is his answers to such questions that determine (for good or for bad) a human being's sexual psychology.

A person's attitude toward these issues is not formed in a psychological vacuum. On the contrary: in sex, more than in any other realm, the total of one's premises and psychology tend to be involved. The single most pertinent factor in determining a person's sexual attitudes is the general level of his self-esteem: the higher the level of self-esteem, the stronger the likelihood that his responses to his own sexuality will be appropriate, i.e., that he will exhibit a healthy sex psychology.

A healthy masculinity or femininity is the consequence and expression of a rationally affirmative response to one's own sexual nature. This entails: a strong, affirmative awareness of one's own sexuality; a positive (fearless and guiltless) response to the phenomenon of sex; a perspective on sex that sees it as integrated to one's mind and values (*not* as a dissociated, mindless, and meaningless physical indulgence); a positive and self-valuing response to one's own body; a strong, positive response to the body of the opposite sex; a confident understanding, acceptance, and enjoyment of one's own sexual role.

This last point requires elaboration. The difference in the male and female sexual roles proceeds from differences in man's and woman's respective anatomy and physiology. Physically, man is the bigger and stronger of the two sexes; his system produces and uses more energy; and he tends (for physiological reasons) to be physically more active. Sexually, his is the more active and dominant role; he has the greater measure of control over his own pleasure and that of his partner; it is he who penetrates and the woman who is penetrated (with everything this entails, physically and psychologically). While a healthy aggressiveness and self-assertiveness is proper and desirable for both sexes, man experiences the essence of his masculinity in the act of romantic dominance; woman experiences the essence of her femininity in the act of romantic surrender.

Both roles require strength and self-confidence. A self-doubting man experiences fear of romantic self-assertiveness; a self-doubting woman experiences fear of romantic surrender. An unconfident woman fears the challenge of masculine strength; an unconfident man fears the challenge of the woman's expectation that he be strong.

Healthy masculinity requires a self-confidence that permits the man to be free, uninhibited, and benevolently self-assertive in the role of romantic initiator and aggressor. Healthy femininity requires a self-confidence that permits the woman to be free, uninhibited, and benevolently self-assertive in the role of challenger and responder to the man.

(The foregoing is intended only as a general indication of the masculine and feminine sex roles, not as an exhaustive analysis; the latter is outside the scope of this discussion.)

Just as one's sexual personality is essential to one's sense of oneself, so it is essential to that which one wishes to objectify and to see reflected or made visible in human relationships. The experience of full visibility and full self-objectification entails being perceived, and perceiving oneself, not merely as a certain kind of human being, but as a certain kind of man or woman.

This applies to persons with a neurotic sex psychology as much as to persons whose sex psychology is normal. For instance, the relationship of a sadist and masochist rests on the fact that each senses and responds positively to the weaknesses, flaws, secret doubts, and neurotic fears of the other. A major difference, however, is that, unlike a healthy couple, the sadist and masochist would dread to conceptualize and face consciously the nature of that which is being made visible between them.

From the above discussion, it should be clear why the optimal experience of visibility and self-objectification requires interaction with a member of the opposite sex. A close friend of the same sex, with whom one enjoys a mutuality of mind and values, perceives and responds to those traits which pertain to one's psychology *qua* human being, but not *qua* sexual being. One's sexual personality can be perceived and appreciated *abstractly* by one's friend, but it cannot be of great *personal* importance to him. A member of the opposite sex, with whom one enjoys a strong mutuality of mind and values, is capable of perceiving and personally responding to one in *both* areas, i.e., *qua* human being and *qua* sexual being. The difference in the way one is viewed from the perspective of the same sex and from the perspective of the opposite sex is thus crucial to the issues of experiencing full visibility.

Romantic love involves one's sense of visibility, not merely as a human being, but as a *man* or a *woman*.

It must be stressed that this experience of full visibility exists only as a *potential* in relation to the opposite sex, not as an automatic actuality. Whether or not a man and woman of the same basic values and sense of life will respond fully and personally to each other depends on many factors, such as the context or circumstances in which their relationship occurs, the nature of their respective interests, the presence or absence on either side of emotional involvements elsewhere, the presence or absence of repression in one or both of them, etc.

Further, a man and woman may be in love while not enjoying a full unity of mind and values, if there are major and basic areas of affinity and mutuality between them. Even if they do not feel optimally visible to each other, they may feel visible to a significant and enjoyable extent.

Love is an emotional response that involves two basic, related aspects: one regards the loved object as possessing or embodying qualities that one values highly—and, as a consequence, one regards the loved object as a (real or potential) source of pleasure. This applies to any category of love, not only romantic love.

In the case of romantic love, which is the most intense positive emotional response one human being can offer another, one sees the loved object as possessing or embodying one's *highest* values, and as being crucially important to one's personal happiness. "Highest," in this context, does not necessarily mean noblest or most exalted; it means: most important, in terms of one's personal needs and desires and in terms of that which one most wishes to find and experience in life. Further, one sees the loved object as being crucially important to one's *sexual* happiness. This last is one of the defining characteristics of romantic love.

More than any other relationship, romantic love involves the objectification of one's *self-value.* (I am speaking of genuine romantic love, not its counterfeit, infatuation; infatuation is an exaggerated, out-of-context response which consists of selectively focusing on one or two aspects of a total personality, ignoring or being oblivious to the rest, and responding as though the person were only those particular aspects.) Romantic love involves *fundamental* visibility. The essence of the romantic love response is: "I see you as a person, and because you are what you are, I desire you for my sexual happiness."

To understand why this is the most profound personal tribute one person can pay another, and why romantic love involves the most intense expression and objectification of one's self-value, we must consider certain facts about the nature and meaning of sex.

Of all the pleasures that a person can experience, sex is, potentially, the most intense. There are other pleasures that can last longer across time, but none that is comparable in strength and intensity. Further, sex is a pleasure, not of the body alone nor of the mind alone, but of the *person*—of the total entity. The pleasure of eating or walking or swimming, for instance, is essentially physical; psychological factors are involved, but the pleasure is primarily of the body. On the other hand, the enjoyment of productive work or of a stimulating discussion or of an artistic performance is essentially intellectual; it is a pleasure of the mind. But sex is unique among pleasures in its integration of body and mind: it integrates perceptions, emotions, values, and thought—it offers an individual the most intense form of experiencing his own total being, of experiencing his deepest and most intimate sense of his *self*. (Such is the *potential* of sex, when and to the extent that the experience is not diluted and undercut by conflict, guilt, alienation from one's partner, etc.)

In sex, one's own person becomes a direct, immediate source, vehicle, and embodiment of pleasure. And since pleasure is experienced by man as the good (Chapter Five), sex offers him the most intense and immediate form of experiencing himself as good, as a value. And further: sex offers man the most intense and immediate form of experiencing *life* as a value.

His conviction that he is competent to live and worthy of living (his self-esteem) exists in a man's mind as an abstraction; its meaning is that he is competent to achieve his values, and therefore to achieve happiness, and that he is worthy of doing so. The pleasure he experiences in the act of sex is the direct, immediate, sensory confirmation and reaffirmation of that conviction.

His conviction that life is a value, that life is worth living, exists in a man's mind as an abstraction; its meaning is the conviction that the nature of life is such that happiness is possible; that, by the nature of existence, happiness is within his power to achieve. The pleasure he experiences in the act of sex is the direct, immediate, sensory confirmation and reaffirmation of that conviction.

Thus, sex is the ultimate form in which man experiences *perceptually* that he is good and that life is good.

In sex, more than in any other activity, man experiences the fact of being *an end in himself* and of feeling that the purpose of life is happiness. (Even if the motives that lead a person to a particular sexual encounter are neurotic, and even if, immediately afterwards, he is tortured by shame or guilt—so long as and to the extent that he is able to enjoy the sex act, life is asserting itself within him, the principle that a human being is an end in himself is asserting itself.) In sex, man escapes from any malevolent feeling of life's futility or drudgery, of his own senseless servitude to incomprehensible ends, which, unfortunately, most men experience too often. Thus, sex is the highest form of *selfishness* in the noblest sense of that word.

In light of the above, it is not difficult to understand why, throughout the centuries, the mystic-religionist enemies of man, of man's mind, of his self-esteem and of his life on earth, have been so violently hostile to the phenomenon of human sexuality.

The celebration of self and of life is so implicit in the act of sex that the person who lacks the self-esteem which such a celebration requires and implies often feels driven to fake it, to enact a neurotic substitute: to go through the motions of sex, not as an expression of his sense of self-value and of the value of life, but as a means of gaining a momentary feeling of personal worth, a momentary amelioration of despair, an escape from anxiety.

In the act of sex, the participants experience a unique and intense form of self-awareness—a self-awareness that is generated both by the sex act itself and by the verbal-emotional-physical interaction between them. The nature of the self-awareness, in any given experience, is crucially conditioned by the nature of the interaction, by the degree and kind of visibility they project and are made to feel. If and to the extent that the parties involved enjoy a strong sense of spiritual affinity (by "spiritual," I mean: pertaining to one's mind and values) and, further, a sense that their sexual personalities are harmoniously complementary—the result is the deepest possible experience of self, of being spiritually as well as physically naked, and of glorying in that fact. Conversely, if and to the extent that the parties involved feel spiritually and/or sexually alienated and estranged, the result is that the sexual experience is felt as autistic (at best), or frustratingly "physical," or degradingly meaningless.

Sex affords an individual the most intensely pleasurable form of self-awareness. In romantic love, when a man and woman project that they desire to achieve this experience by means of each other's person, *that* is the highest and most intimate tribute a human being can offer or receive, *that* is the ultimate form of acknowledging the value of the person one desires and of having one's own value acknowledged. It is in this sense that romantic love involves an intense objectification of one's self-value; one sees that value reflected and made visible in the romantic response of one's partner.

A crucial element involved in this experience is the perception of one's efficacy as a source of pleasure to the being one loves. One feels that it is one's *person*, not merely one's body, that is the cause of the pleasure felt by one's partner. One feels, in effect: "Because I am what I am, I am able to cause her (or him) to feel the things she (or he) is feeling." Thus, one sees one's own soul—and its value—in the emotions on the face of one's partner.

If sex involves an act of self-celebration—if, in sex, one desires the freedom to be spontaneous, to be emotionally open and uninhibited, to assert one's right to pleasure and to flaunt one's pleasure in one's self—then the person one most desires is the person with whom one feels freest to *be* oneself, the person whom one (consciously or subconsciously) regards as one's proper psychological mirror, the person who reflects one's deepest view of oneself and of life. *That* is the person who will allow one to experience optimally the things one wishes to experience in the realm of sex.

Most people experience great difficulty in identifying the cause of their romantic-sexual choices, not only because most people are poor introspectors, but also because the factors that bring about a (healthy or neurotic) romantic attraction between two individuals are enormously complex. "A mutuality of mind and values" is a very wide abstraction. What, more specifically, does it entail?

To answer that question, we must consider a concept that is basic to an understanding of romantic love: the concept of "sense of life."

Romantic Affinity

A "sense of life" is the emotional form in which a person experiences his deepest view of existence and of his own relationship to existence.

It is, in effect, the emotional corollary of a metaphysics—of a personal metaphysics—reflecting the subconsciously integrated sum of a person's broadest and deepest (implicit) conclusions about the world, about life and about himself.

The formation of a sense of life begins in early childhood, long before the child is able to think about the world and himself in philosophical terms. The conscious philosophical convictions he acquires later may or may not be in accord with his sense of life; his explicit, avowed philosophy may give articulate, conceptual expression to his sense of life, may alter or modify it, or may be in unrecognized contradiction to it—depending on such factors as how rational he is, how conceptually reflective about his own life, how well-integrated psychologically.

In the course of his development from childhood, a human being encounters certain fundamental facts of reality—facts about the nature of existence and the nature of man—to which he can respond in a variety of ways and with varying degrees of rationality and realism. It is the cumulative sum of these responses that constitutes a person's distinctive sense of life.

For example, it is an inescapable fact of reality that *thinking* is a necessity of man's existence, i.e., that man requires knowledge and that the acquisition of knowledge requires the effort or conceptual thought. The position a young person takes on this issue is not arrived at by explicit decision nor by a single choice. It is arrived at by the cumulative implication of a long series of choices and responses in the face of specific situations involving the need to think.

A young person may respond positively and healthily, learning to take an active pleasure in the exercise of his mind. Or he may approach intellectual effort grudgingly and dutifully, viewing it, in effect, as a "necessary evil." Or he may regard intellectual effort with lethargic resentment or fear, viewing it as an unfair burden and imposition, and determine to avoid it whenever possible. What gradually forms and hardens in his psychology is a trend, a policy, a habit—a position or premise *by implication*. It is in this manner that all sense-of-life attitudes are formed.

There are many issues involved in a person's sense of life; they include, but are not limited to, the following:

It is a fact of reality, as I have stressed throughout this book, that man is neither omniscient nor infallible. A young person discovers, very early, not only that his knowledge must be acquired by process of thought, but that there is no guarantee, in any given case, that his effort will necessarily and automatically be successful. He may accept the responsibility of thought and judgment willingly, realistically, and fearlessly, fully prepared to bear the consequences of his conclusions (and subsequent actions), recognizing that no rational alternative to his policy is possible. Or he may react with fear and with a longing to escape responsibility—by shrinking the area of his thought and action so as to minimize the "risks" entailed by possible errors, and/or by passing to others the responsibility he dreads, living off their thoughts, their judgments, their values.

It is a fact of reality that success is not automatically guaranteed to a man, not only in the pursuit of knowledge, but in the pursuit of *any* value. A young person comes to realize, implicitly or explicitly, that life involves a process of struggle, and struggle entails the possibility of failure and defeat. He may respond assertively and eagerly to the challenges of existence. Or he may tend to withdraw from them, regarding the necessity of struggle and the uncertainty of success as, in effect, a metaphysical tragedy.

It is a fact of reality that man must live long-range, that he must project his goals into the future and work to achieve them, and that this demands of him the ability and willingness, when and if necessary, to defer immediate pleasures and to endure unavoidable frustrations. A person may accept this fact realistically and unself-pityingly, preserving his ambition for values. Or he may rebel against this fact, stamping his foot at reality, in effect, and seeking only the sort of values that can be attained easily and swiftly, in resentment against a universe that does not grant omnipotence to his desires.

It is a fact of reality that, in the course of his life, a human being will inevitably experience some degree of suffering; the degree may be great or small, depending on many factors; what is not inevitable, however, is the status that he will ascribe to his suffering, i.e., the significance he will give it in his life and in his view of existence. A person may preserve an unclouded sense of the value of existence, no matter what adversity or suffering he encounters; he may preserve the conviction that happiness and success are the normal and natural, and that pain, defeat, disappointment are the abnormal and accidental, the metaphysically *unimportant*—just as we rationally view health, not disease, as man's normal state. Or he may decide that suffering and defeat are the essence of existence—that happiness and success are the temporary, abnormal, and accidental.

It is a fact of man's nature that he is a being of volitional consciousness, that he has the capacity to be rational or irrational; every human being encounters some degree of irrationality in some of the people around him, which causes him suffering. A person may identify the fact that irrationality is *wrong*, that it represents an aberration, a departure from reality. Or he may conclude (in the form of an emotional generalization) that *he* is wrong in expecting people to be rational, and may surrender to a malevolent view of the universe, to the conclusion that man is, for all practical purposes, *inherently* irrational.

It is in the nature of a living organism that it must act to preserve its own life and well-being; it is in the distinctive nature of man that he must *choose* to value his own life and happiness sufficiently to generate the thought and action they require: for man, the process is not automatic. A person may develop the life-assertive selfishness proper to a living being; he may form a solemn ambition to achieve happiness, an intransigent loyalty to his own values, which entails a proud refusal to treat them as an object of renunciation or sacrifice. Or, fearing the effort, the responsibility, the integrity, the courage that such selfishness (and self-value) require, he may begin the process of giving up his soul before it is even fully formed; he may surrender his aspirations, his happiness, his values, not to some tangible beneficiary, but to his own nameless, unidentified lethargy or apprehension.

Such are some of the basic issues involved in a person's sense of life; the list is far from exhaustive. It should be mentioned that matters of *degree* are involved in sense-of-life issues; any of the possible responses can be maintained with varying degrees of intensity and consistency.

The cumulative result of such responses is generalized feeling about oneself, about existence, and about one's relationship to existence. A person's sense of life can reflect an unbreached self-esteem and an undiluted sense of the value of existence, the conviction that the universe is open to the efficacy of one's thought and effort—or it can reflect the torture of self-doubt and the anxiety of feeling that one lives in a universe which is unintelligible and hostile. It can reflect a view of life as exaltation or a view of life as tragic doom—a view of life as adventure or a view of life as frustration—a view of life as beauty or a view of life as sordid senselessness. It can embody eagerness and self-confidence—or muted, wistful longing—or anguished, tragic defiance—or gentle, uncomplaining resignation—or aggressive impotence.

A person's sense of life is of crucial importance in the formation of his basic values, since all value-choices rest on an implicit view of the being who values and of the world in which he must act. A person's sense of life underlies all his other feelings, all his emotional responses—like the leitmotif of his soul, the basic theme of his personality.

This is particularly evident in the sphere of his romantic-sexual responses.

Just as one's own sense of life can be very difficult to isolate and identify conceptually, so it is very difficult to isolate and identify the sense of life of another human being, because it colors the entire personality. However, in romantic relationships, the affirmative response of each party to the sense of life of the other is crucial to the experience of love and to the projection of mutual visibility. In romantic love, one feels implicitly: "He (or she) sees life as I do. He (or she) faces existence as I face it. He (or she) experiences the fact of being alive as I experience it."

There are many ways in which a sense-of-life affinity is communicated; perhaps the rarest is by explicit, conceptual statement. Two people discover their affinity by learning of each other's values and disvalues—and by such means as observing each other's manner of talking, of smiling, of standing, of moving, of expressing emotions, of reacting to events, etc. They discover it by the way they react to each other, by the things that are said and by the things that are not said, by the explanations it is not necessary to give, by sudden, unexpected signs of mutual understanding.

One of the most eloquent signs of a sense-of-life affinity is common likes and dislikes in the field of art; art is a sense-of-life realm, more explicitly than any other human activity; and an individual's sense of life is crucial in determining his artistic responses.

Two individuals' discussion of their respective ideas is not unimportant; it can be very important, indeed; but mere abstract, intellectual agreement on particular subjects is not sufficient by itself to establish an authentic sense-of-life affinity.

Without a significant sense-of-life affinity, no fundamental and intimate experience of visibility is possible. One may be admired for some particular quality of qualities, by a person with an alien sense of life, but one's feeling of gratification, if any would be extremely limited; one would sense that the basic frame of reference of the other person, the basic context from which one is being viewed and appraised, is different from one's own, and that the admiration does not mean what it would mean in one's own context.

For example, suppose that a person with a self-confident affirmative sense of life, engaged in some difficult and challenging pursuit, is admired by a person whose own sense of life is defiantly tragic—so that the admiration projected is for the image of a heroic but doomed martyr. The recipient of such admiration would not feel properly visible, because the image would clash with his own nontragic sense of himself.

In romantic love, optimally experienced, one is admired for the things one wishes to be admired for, and—equally important—in a way and from a perspective that is in accord with one's view of life. *That* is *full* visibility.

A person's sense of life can be better (more appropriate to reality) or worse than his conscious philosophical convictions; in other words, a person's psychology can be healthier or less healthy than his philosophy. As a consequence of the fact that a person's sense of life and avowed philosophy may be inconsistent, and of the fact that a sense of life can be very hard to identify, people are often tempted to feel that love is inexplicable, that it is "just there," that it is not susceptible to rational analysis. An individual may be at a loss to explain why he feels uniquely visible, uniquely in emotional accord, with one particular person and not with another (who, on the surface, may appear to be an equally plausible romantic partner).

In the case of a romantic relationship between two people who are highly neurotic, a further obstacle to the understanding of the grounds of their attachment is the fact that they experience a strong resistance to identifying the nature of the emotional universe they share; they do not care to know of what elements their common sense of life is made.

Regardless, however, of whether a romantic relationship is healthy or neurotic (or both in part), the key to understanding that relationship is through an understanding of the participants' sense of life, and of the unique self-experience which the relationship affords them. If a person wishes to identify the ultimate grounds of his romantic feeling for another human being, the questions to ask and answer are:

What does this relationship make me feel about myself? What is the distinctive nature of the self-experience it produces in me? And why? What attitudes, characteristics, and actions of the person I love are essential in giving me this experience?

The answers to these questions will tell a person a great deal, not only about the nature of his romantic feeling, but also about the nature of his self-esteem and about his deepest image of himself.

| **Psychotherapy**

Thinking and Psychotherapy

Psychotherapy is the treatment of mental disorders by psychological means.

As I propose to make clear, psychotherapy is properly to be conceived as a process of education through which the patient is (a) led to understand the deficiencies in his method of thinking, and the errors in his values and premises, that underlie his problems; and (b) taught how to improve the efficacy of his thinking processes, and to replace irrational values and premises with rational ones.

When interviewing a new patient, it is my policy to tell him the following, in effect: "I see psychotherapy as involving three elements or forces. There is I, the psychotherapist. There is the 'you' who has a psychological problem. There is the 'you' who is rational enough to recognize the existence of the problem and to want to conquer it. Psychotherapy is an alliance of the therapist with the rational 'you'—against the 'you' who has the problem."

Thus the patient is required to maintain a highly active role in the process of his own treatment; he is required to become, in effect, a co-psychotherapist. He is not indulged in the delusion that he can be cured while maintaining an attitude of mental passivity (the same passivity, in most cases, that was a crucial cause of his neurosis).

For the patient to take a usefully active part in the process of his own treatment, it is often necessary that, on the road to self-understanding and self-improvement, he be taught a good deal about psychology—about how the mind functions, about the nature and conditions of healthy self-esteem, about the cause of pathological anxiety, about the relationships among anxiety, defense values, and neurotic symptoms. Since a patient tends to regard his problems and his mental processes as unique, *sui generis,* he does not think about them abstractly and objectively, and thus is incapable of correcting them. He must learn to recognize the wider psychological principles operative within his mind; he must acquire a conceptual perspective from which to view himself.

One of the first and crucially important facts a patient must learn, when he enters therapy, is the relationship between his mind and his emotions. Commonly, he suffers from the feeling that his painful emotions are incomprehensible; he feels like an impenetrable mystery to himself. Therefore, one of the therapist's first tasks is to help the patient to understand that his problems are solvable, that his emotions have intelligible causes. If the patient is led to understand the relation that exists between his emotions and his values (and between his values and his thinking or nonthinking), this understanding (even if, initially, it is only generalized and abstract) can be highly therapeutic. It can give him confidence that his problems can be solved.

A patient is strongly inclined to regard his neurotic emotions and desires as an integral and inherent component of his personal identity. "My (anxious or depressed or hostile or masochistic or homosexual) feelings, *c'est moi.*" This attitude is obviously refractory to therapy. It is necessary to establish in the patient's consciousness a sense of "psychological distance" between his mind or ego and his unhealthy emotions and desires, so that he can begin to think about them with objectivity and detachment. The more clearly he understands that his feelings, however long he may have experienced them, are *not* part of his nature, the more he will be motivated to identify the ideational roots of his feelings, to untangle the causal factors involved and effect a *change* in his emotional responses.

It is worth observing, in this connection, that both the religious doctrine of Original Sin and the Freudian theory of an id are disastrously harmful psychologically. Aside from the fact that they are groundless and offensive to reason, they tend to confirm the patient's hopeless, deterministic feelings about himself and his problems. They also tend to support the patient's inclination to passivity and resignation, on the premise of "I can't help it." Men *can't* help it—if they are taught and if they accept a view of emotions that amounts to the medieval notion of demonology. This is the view that must be challenged and repudiated.

Just as a patient must learn not to regard his emotions as irreducible primaries, so he must learn not to regard his manner of thinking—is psycho-epistemology—as an irreducible primary. The task of instilling this awareness is often exceptionally difficult: there is nothing a man is so likely to regard as irreducibly and unalterably "himself" as his manner of thinking—not the content of his thinking, but the method. Nevertheless, to teach the patient *a new method of thinking* is one of the prime tasks to which a truly effective psychotherapy must address itself—building on the foundation of whatever elements of a rational psycho-epistemology the patient already possesses.

Consider, for example, the case of a man who habitually avoids thinking about the causes of any emotion or desire that he suspects to be irrational, immoral, or unrealistic; he seeks to deny the existence of such feelings by means of such devices as evasion and repression; if and when the feelings persist past his attempts to throttle them, he sabotages his consciousness further by surrendering to them blindly, ignoring his reason and intelligence, and resorting to additional devices of self-deception, such as self-justifying rationalizations. The emotional result is a state of pathological anxiety. While a therapist might conceivably be able to ameliorate his patient's anxiety by dealing with some of the specific irrationalities that triggered it off, the basic problem cannot be solved, the patient cannot be brought to psychological health, unless his condition is attacked *fundamentally*, i.e., in terms of his psycho-epistemology.

There are two categories of psycho-epistemological problems which are virtually universal among patients, and which need to be dealt with explicitly and in depth by the psychotherapist. The first of these is the patient's failure to think in principles about himself and his difficulties, his tendency to regard his emotions, reactions, and general psychological state as unrelated to any wider principles or to any abstract knowledge he possesses. The second of these problems is the patient's susceptibility to being motivated by fear, in the process of thinking about himself, his life, and his actions.

For example, a patient may know, abstractly, that emotions are not tools of cognition, are not criteria of truth or falsehood, right or wrong. But this knowledge does not stop his tendency to function, in particular cases, on the implicit premise that if he desires or fears something intensely, his emotion must be warranted and may serve as a valid guide to action. His abstract knowledge does not stop this tendency because he does not apply that knowledge to himself. He must be taught to do so. Or, a patient may be engaging in a course of action that he would identify as flagrantly irrational and neurotic were he to observe it in someone else. But he exempts himself from any such conclusions, on the basis of his vague feeling that in some unspecified way he is "different," i.e., there are special "extenuating circumstances" in his case. He must be led to understand the self-deception he is practicing.

As to the problem of motivation by fear, I have given many examples of it in preceding chapters. In choosing his actions and goals, in deliberating the question of what constitutes his self-interest in various situations, a patient is very commonly influenced by his fears: fear of failure, fear of shaking his self-esteem (or pseudo-self-esteem), fear of provoking disapproval, fear of jeopardizing his precarious sense of "security." The therapist must first discover the nature of the specific fears and how they operate to disintegrate a particular patient's psycho-epistemology, then work at communicating this knowledge to the patient, so that the patient becomes more sensitive to the mechanics of his own mental processes and is better able to catch his errors while they are occurring and to reorient his thinking in a more realistic direction.

In untangling the roots of his patient's problems, the therapist will find that he must constantly move back and forth between psycho-epistemological errors and emotional or motivational conflicts, i.e., between his patient's method of thinking and his mistaken values and premises. A relationship of reciprocal causation exists between the spheres of cognition and evaluation. Just as rational thinking encourages the formation of rational values, and the formation of rational values encourages rational thinking—so unhealthy thinking tends to result in unhealthy values, and unhealthy values tend to result in unhealthy thinking.

Emotional and motivational (i.e., value) disturbances tend to *worsen* existing psycho-epistemological errors and, often, to create *new* psycho-epistemological errors. For example, the anxiety produced by unhealthy cognitive practices leads to additional and often worse evasions, repressions, rationalizations, flights from reality into fantasy, etc.—which aim at diminishing the anxiety. Or, when a sufferer from neurotic depression, passively under the sway of his emotions, distorts his perceptions of reality in such a way as to find evidence of his worthlessness and depravity elsewhere, his psycho-epistemology is deteriorating under the impact of his depression.

On the other hand, unhealthy psycho-epistemology leads to unhealthy motivation, i.e., to the selection of irrational values; and the pursuit of irrational values, because they *are* irrational, necessitates further psycho-epistemological self-sabotaging, further cognitive disintegration, which leads to the pursuit of irrational values, etc. For example, a person whose "thinking" is dominated by social-metaphysical considerations may be led to accept an entirely specious set of values, as in the case of the boy who, growing up in a bad neighborhood, becomes a criminal; and the irrationality inherent in his criminal pursuits leads to a further corruption of his thinking processes which makes it possible for worse and worse crimes to be acceptable to him.

A person's view and estimate of himself—his self-concept and self-evaluation—are, as we have seen, the vital center of his psychology: they are the motor of his behavior. In attempting to understand his patient's problems and to help solve them, the psychotherapist must constantly relate psycho-epistemological and motivational (or emotional) disorders to the nature of the patient's self-esteem.

If, for example, a patient typically evades, represses, rationalizes in a certain area of his life—the therapist must ask: What purpose does this serve relative to the maintenance of the patient's self-esteem (or pseudo-self-esteem)? If, as a consequence of self-sabotaging psycho-epistemological practices, the patient's thinking is hopelessly ineffectual in certain areas—how does that fact affect his sense of himself? If a patient is torn by desires that are flagrantly irrational and self-destructive—what is the specific self-esteem deficiency or area of self-doubt that blinds him and makes him unable to relinquish such desires? If a patient permits himself to be pushed into irrational behavior by the pressure of irrational

desires or fears—what are the consequences for his already inadequate self-esteem? What specific self-doubts are his neurotic
defenses designed to protect? How does this view and estimate of
himself relate to his values and goals in the spheres of work and
human relationships? How does it affect his sexual psychology?
The detailed working out, with the patient, of the answers to such
questions, is basic to the process of effective psychotherapy.

Consider the case of a man who enters psychotherapy with the
following dual complaint: he is unhappy and frustrated in his work
and he is unhappy and frustrated in his marriage; he does not
know why. Investigation reveals that the patient is a social metaphysician; that he selected his particular career under the pressure
of his parents' urging, without any first-hand interest or desire on
his own part; and that he selected the girl who was to become his
wife by an essentially similar process: she was generally regarded
as the most attractive and desirable girl among his circle of friends
and acquaintances, so that winning her was perceived by him as a
great personal triumph. Twice during his marriage, as a blind
attempt at self-assertiveness, he has deceived his wife in affairs with
other women; the women meant nothing to him and the net effect
of the experiences was to raise the level of his anxiety. He feels
increasingly haunted by a sense of inner emptiness and futility, the
sense of attaining nothing, enjoying nothing, *being* nothing.

In the treatment of such a patient, one of the therapist's chief
tasks is to make the patient aware of the psycho-epistemological
processes by which his values and goals were chosen: the reliance
on the terms, expectations, beliefs, standards of his "significant others," the substitution of the minds of those others for his own, the
craving for approval and status as the regulator of his "thinking"
(which means: the destruction of thinking); the fear of independence that lay behind the early surrender of his intellectual autonomy; and the devastating consequences for his self-esteem, not only
of his initial surrender, but of its implementation across the years,
via his attempts to deal with reality second-hand, i.e., by means of
the minds of others. The patient has to be led to understand in
what way his initial default on the responsibility of independence
generated the sense of insecurity that pushed him into the position of a psycho-epistemological dependent; the process by which
each new act of surrender to the minds of others carried him

farther and farther away from reality and thus lower and lower in his own estimation; the way in which the betrayal of his autonomy and thus of his self-esteem inevitably strengthened his craving for social metaphysical "approval"—so that his problem became, in effect, self-perpetuating. He has to be led to understand that his defiantly unthinking attempt at "independence," by means of his infidelities, represents not authentic, healthy self-assertiveness but only another form of capitulation and self-surrender: *his* thoughts, *his* values, were not involved; he had nothing of his own to express or to seek; he was not acting *for* himself but only *against* others, the omnipresent others whom he sees no way to escape; he is still a "stranger and afraid in a world [he] never made."

This leads us to the question: Is a patient's *understanding* of the nature and origins of his problems all that is required to produce a cure? The answer is: No, it is *not* all that is required; it is essential, but it is only a first step.

The patient's basic disorder was caused by his failure to perform a certain category of mental action: that of independent thought, judgment, evaluation in regard to himself, his life, and the world around him; the failure to direct his mind to the task of understanding the facts of reality. The action on which he defaulted is psycho-epistemological, and the result is his lack of self-esteem and his social-metaphysical dependency. Until and unless that default is corrected *in action* (meaning: until and unless he learns to use his mind properly and to be guided by it in his behavior), his problem cannot be dealt with effectively and eliminated. This requires the slow, laborious, painful, halting, doubt-ridden process of learning to look at reality through his own eyes, to judge the things he sees, to draw his own conclusions as honestly and rationally as he is able—and to act accordingly. This is the only way he can acquire the self-esteem he lacks.

While not all neurotics are social metaphysicians, the therapist will find that the majority of his patients are, to some extent—and that to guide such patients to intellectual autonomy is one of the most challenging, difficult, and complex tasks of psychotherapy. I will mention only two of the commonest problems the therapist may expect to encounter, because they illuminate the kind of psycho-epistemological retraining that is necessary.

First: the therapist must be prepared to deal with and correct a policy that is virtually universal among social metaphysicians in their first attempts at independence: their tendency to rely on their emotions as the sole form of autonomy known to them. Attempting to break out of the frame of reference of their "significant others," social metaphysicians often begin by feeling that they have nothing with which to defy their authorities except their own chaotic emotions—and so they pursue any desire, without concern for its rationality or validity, provided it is *not* sanctioned by those authorities. They tend to see life as a conflict between *their* desires and the desires of *others*. Their concern is only: By whose wishes shall I be guided—mine or other people's? Such a policy, however, leaves them as cut off from reality as they were before; it does not solve the problem of their alienation from reality, it merely changes the form of the alienation; and, consequently, it does nothing to build an authentic self-esteem and self-reliance. If a patient is to acquire healthy independence, genuine independence, it is his mind he must learn to assert, not his feelings divorced from his mind.

Second: it is virtually inevitable that, in the process of seeking to free himself from his "significant others," the patient will replace the authority of those "others" with that of the therapist; he will be "rational" and "independent" in order to win his therapist's approval. The therapist must constantly be on guard against this trend, and must make the patient fully aware of it. Often, however, the following kind of complication arises. The patient finds himself in a situation where he has rationally (and correctly) decided that he should take a certain action, but he is also aware that, in taking it, he will win approval from his therapist and that that consideration is immensely attractive to him; the question then arises in his mind whether he should take the action, in view of the presence of social metaphysical elements in his motivation. In such cases, he must be taught to understand that if he is rationally convinced that a given action is right, appropriate to the facts of reality, he should take that action regardless of whether or not other, nonrational considerations are also operative in his psychology. Consider the alternative: if he avoids performing an action he knows to be right, in order to thwart any social metaphysical impulses within him, then he is still placing other considerations above reason and reality; he is still being manipulated by his social metaphysical problem, in his very effort to defy it. A patient cannot reasonably proceed on the premise that if any projected action of his might elicit approval (which he still neurotically craves), then he will abstain from taking that action, irrespective of how rational the action might be in its own terms. He can eliminate his social metaphysical impulses only by eliminating the self-doubt that is their cause; and he can eliminate his self-doubt only by learning to form and to act on his independent, rational judgment.

Values and Psychotherapy

The belief that moral values are the province of faith and that no rational, scientific code of ethics is possible, has had disastrous effects in virtually every sphere of human activity. But the consequences of this belief have been particularly acute for the science of psychology.

Central to the science of psychology is the issue or problem of motivation. The key to motivation lies, as we have seen, in the realm of values. Within the context of his inherent needs and capacities as a specific kind of living organism, it is a man's premises—specifically his value-premises—that determine his actions and emotions.

The existence of neurosis, of mental and emotional disturbances, is, I submit, one of the most eloquent proofs that man *needs* an integrated, objective code of moral values—that a haphazard collection of subjective or collective whims and precepts will not do—that a rational ethical system is as indispensable to man's psychological survival as it is to his existential survival.

The paradox—and the tragedy—of psychology today is that *values* is the one issue specifically banned from its domain.

The majority of psychologists—both as theoreticians and as psychotherapists—have accepted the premise that the realm of science and the realm of ethics are mutually inimical, that morality is a matter of faith, not of reason, that moral values are inviolately subjective, and that a therapist must cure his patients without appraising or challenging their fundamental moral beliefs.

It is this premise that must be challenged.

Guilt, anxiety, and self-doubt—the neurotic's chronic complaints—entail *moral* judgments. The psychotherapist must deal with such judgments constantly. The conflicts that torture patients are *moral* conflicts: Is sex evil, or is it a proper human pleasure?—Is the profit motive evil, or do men have the right to pursue their own interests?—Must one love and forgive everybody, or is it ever justifiable to feel violent indignation?—Must man blindly submit to the teachings of his religious authorities, or dare he subject their pronouncements to the judgment of his own intellect?—Is it one's duty to remain with the husband or wife one no longer loves, or is divorce a valid solution?—Should a woman regard motherhood as her noblest function and duty, or may she pursue an independent career?—Is man "his brother's keeper," or does he have the right to live for his own happiness?

It is true that patients frequently repress such conflicts and that the repression constitutes the major obstacle to the conflict's resolution. But it is not true that merely bringing such conflicts into conscious awareness guarantees that the patients will resolve them. The answers to moral problems are not self-evident; they require a process of complex philosophical thought and analysis.

Nor does the solution lie in instructing the patient to "follow his deepest feelings." That frequently is the policy that brought him to disaster in the first place. Nor does the solution lie in "loving" the patient, and, in effect, giving him a moral blank check (which is one of the approaches most commonly advocated today). Love is not a substitute for reason, and the suspending of all moral estimates will not provide the patient with the code of values that his mental health requires. The patient feels confused, he feels uncertain of his judgment, he feels he does not know what is right or wrong; if the therapist, to whom the patient has come for guidance, is professionally *committed* to not knowing, the impasse is total.

To the extent that the therapist acts on the principle that he must be silent in moral issues, he passively confirms and sanctions the monopoly on morality held by mysticism—more specifically, by religion. Yet no conscientious therapist can escape the knowledge that religious teachings frequently are instrumental in *causing* the patient's neurosis.

In fact, there is *no way* for a psychotherapist to keep his own moral convictions out of his professional work. By countless subtle indications he reveals and makes the patient aware of his moral estimates—through his pauses, his questions, his tone of voice, the things he chooses to say or not to say, the emotional vibrations he projects, etc. But because—for both parties—this process of communication is subconscious, the patient is being guided emotionally rather than intellectually; he does not form an independent, self-conscious appraisal of the therapist's value-premises; he can only accept them, should he accept them at all, on *faith*, by *feeling*, without reasons or proof, if the issues are never named explicitly. This makes of the therapist, in effect, a religious authority—a *subliminal* religious authority, as it were.

A therapist who approaches moral problems in this manner will, most commonly, encourage conformity to and acceptance of the prevailing moral beliefs of the culture, without regard for the question of whether or not those beliefs are compatible with psychological health. But even if the values such a therapist communicates are rational, the method of "persuasion" is not—and thus fails to bring the patient any closer to authentic, *independent* rationality.

A code of ethics or morality is a code of values to guide one's choices and actions.

Effective psychotherapy requires a conscious, rational, scientific code of ethics—a system of values based on the facts of reality and geared to the needs of man's life on earth.

As I have discussed in an earlier book, it is my conviction that Ayn Rand has provided such a code of ethics in her philosophy of Objectivism.[1] For a detailed presentation of the Objectivist ethics, the reader is referred to Miss Rand's novel *Atlas Shrugged* and to her collection of essays on ethics, *The Virtue of Selfishness*.

It is not my purpose, in this context, to provide a detailed exposition of the Objectivist ethics, but rather (a) to present the base or foundation of this system of ethics, i.e., the method of deriving and justifying the Objectivist standard of value; (b) to indicate the general direction of this ethics; and (c) to juxtapose it with traditional religious ethics, with reference to the consequences of each system for mental health.

Objectivism does not begin by taking the phenomenon of "values" as a given; i.e., it does not begin merely by observing that men pursue various values and by assuming that the first question of ethics is: What values ought man to pursue? It begins on a far deeper level, with the question: What are values and why does man need them? What are the facts of reality—the facts of existence and of man's nature—that necessitate and give rise to values?

"A 'value' is that which one acts to gain and/or keep."[2] A value is the object of an action. "'Value' presupposes an answer to the question: of value to whom and for what? 'Value' presupposes a standard, a purpose, and the necessity of action in the face of an alternative. Where there are no alternatives, no values are possible."[3] An entity who—by its nature—had no purposes to achieve, no goals to reach, could have no values and no need of values. There would be no "for what." An entity incapable of initiating action, or for whom the consequences would always be the same, *regardless* of its actions—an entity *not confronted with alternatives*— could have no purposes, no goals, and hence no values. Only the existence can make purpose—and therefore values—possible and necessary.

> There is only one fundamental alternative in the universe: existence or non-existence—and it pertains to a single class of entities: to living organisms. The existence of inanimate matter is unconditional, the existence of life is not: it depends on a specific course of action. Matter is indestructible, it changes its form, but it cannot cease to exist. It is only a living organism that faces a constant alternative: the issue of life or death. Life is a process of self-sustaining and self-generated action. If an organism fails in that action, it dies; its chemical elements remain, but its life goes out of existence. It is only the concept of 'Life' that makes the concept of 'Value' possible. It is only to a living entity that things can be good or evil.[4]

It is only a living entity that can have needs, goals, *values*—and it is only a living entity that can generate the actions necessary to achieve them.

A plant does not possess consciousness; it can neither experience pleasure and pain nor have the concepts of life and death; nevertheless, plants can die; a plant's *life* depends on a specific course of action.

A plant must feed itself in order to live; the sunlight, the water, the chemicals it needs are the values its nature has set it to pursue; its life is the standard of value directing its actions. But a plant has no choice of action; there are alternatives in the conditions it encounters, but there is no alternative in its function: it acts automatically to further its life, it cannot act for its own destruction.[5]

Animals possess a primitive form of consciousness; they cannot know the issue of life and death, but they can know pleasure and pain; an animal's life depends on actions automatically guided by its sensory mechanism.

An animal is equipped for sustaining its life; its senses provide it with an automatic code of action, an automatic knowledge of what is good for it or evil. It has no power to extend its knowledge or to evade it. In conditions where its knowledge proves inadequate, it dies. But so long as it lives, it acts on its knowledge, with automatic safety and no power of choice, it is unable to ignore its own good, unable to decide to choose the evil and act as its own destroyer.[6]

Given the appropriate conditions, the appropriate physical environment, all living organisms—with one exception—are set by their nature to originate automatically the actions required to sustain their survival. The exception is *man.*

Man, like a plant or an animal, must act in order to live; man, like a plant or an animal, must gain the values his life requires. But man does not act and function by automatic chemical reactions or by automatic sensory reactions; there is no physical environment on earth in which man could survive by the guidance of nothing but his involuntary sensations. And man is born without innate ideas; having no innate knowledge of what is true or false, he can have no innate knowledge of what is good for him or evil. *Man has no automatic means of survival.*

Man's basic means of survival is his mind, his capacity to reason. "Reason is the faculty that identifies and integrates the material provided by man's senses."[7]

For man, survival is a question—a problem to be *solved.* The perceptual level of his consciousness—the level of passive sensory awareness, which he shares with animals—is inadequate to solve it. To remain alive, man must *think*—which means: he must exercise the faculty which he alone, of all living species, possesses: the faculty of abstractions, of *conceptualizing*. The *conceptual* level of consciousness is the human level, the level required for man's survival. It is upon his ability to think that man's life depends.

> But to think is an act of choice. The key to . . . "human nature" . . . is the fact that *man is a being of volitional consciousness*. Reason does not work automatically; thinking is not a mechanical process; the connections of logic are not made by instinct. The function of your stomach, lungs or heart is automatic; the function of your mind is not. In any hour and issue of your life, you are free to think or to evade that effort. But you are not free to escape from your nature, from the fact that *reason* is your means of survival—so that for *you*, who are a human being, the question "to be or not to be" is the question "to think or not to think."[8]

A being of volitional consciousness, a being without innate ideas, must discover, by a process of thought, the goals, the actions, the values on which his life depends. He must discover what will further his life and what will destroy it. If he acts against the facts of reality, he will perish. If he is to sustain his existence, he must discover the *principles of action* required to guide him in dealing with nature and with other men. His need of these principles is his need of a code of values.

Other species are not free to *choose* their values. Man is. "A code of values accepted by choice is a code of morality."[9]

The reason of man's need for morality determines the purpose of morality as well as the standard by which moral values are to be selected. Man needs a moral code in order to live; that is the purpose of morality—for every man as an individual. But in order to know what are the values and virtues that will permit him to achieve that purpose, man requires a standard. Different species achieve their survival in different ways. The course of action proper to the survival of a fish or an animal, would not be proper to the survival of man. Man must choose *his* values by the standard of that which is required for the life of a *human being*—which means: he must hold *man's life* (man's survival *qua* man) as his standard of value. Since reason is man's basic tool of survival, this means: the life appropriate to a rational being—or: that which is required for the survival of man *qua* rational being.

"All that which is proper to the life of a rational being is the good; all that which destroys it is the evil."[10]

To live, man must think, he must act, he must *produce* the values his life requires. This, metaphysically, is the *human* mode of existence.

Thinking is man's basic virtue, the source of all his other virtues. Thinking is the activity of perceiving and identifying that which exists—of integrating perceptions into concepts, and concepts into still wider concepts, of constantly expanding the range of one's knowledge to encompass more and more of reality.

Evasion, the refusal to think, the willful rejection of reason, the willful suspension of consciousness, the willful defiance of reality, is man's basic vice—the source of all his evils.

Man, like every other living species, has a specific manner of survival which is determined by his nature. Man is free to act against the requirements of his nature, to reject his means of survival, his mind; but he is not free to escape the consequence: misery, anxiety, destruction. When men attempt to survive, not by thought and productive work, but by parasitism and force, by theft and brutality, it is still the faculty of reason that they are secretly counting on: the rationality that some moral man had to exercise in order to create the goods which the parasites propose to loot or expropriate. Man's life depends on thinking, not on acting blindly; on achievement, not on destruction; nothing can change that fact. Mindlessness, passivity, parasitism, brutality are not and cannot be principles of survival; they are merely the policy of those who do not wish to face the issue of survival.

"Man's life" means: life lived in accordance with the *principles* that make man's survival *qua* man possible.

Just as man is alive, physically, to the extent that the organs within his body function in the constant service of his life, so man is alive, as a total entity, to the extent that his *mind* functions in the constant service of his life. The mind, too, is a vital organ—the one vital organ whose function is *volitional*. A man encased in an iron lung, whose own lungs are paralyzed, is not dead; but he is not liv-

ing the life proper to man. Neither is a man whose *mind* is volitionally paralyzed.

If man is to live, he must recognize that facts are facts, that A is
A, that *existence exists*—that reality is an absolute, not to be evaded
or escaped—and that the task of his mind is to perceive it, that this
is his primary responsibility. He must recognize that his life requires
the pursuit and achievement of rational values, values consonant
with his nature and with reality—that life is a process of self-sustaining and self-generated action. He must recognize that *self*-value
is the value without which no others are possible, but it is a value
that has to be earned—and the virtue that earns it, is thinking.

> To live, man must hold three things as the supreme and ruling val-
> ues of his life: Reason—Purpose—Self-esteem. Reason, as his only
> tool of knowledge—Purpose, as his choice of the happiness which
> that tool must proceed to achieve—Self-esteem, as his inviolate cer-
> tainty that his mind is competent to think and his person is worthy
> of happiness, which means: is worthy of living.[11]

The cardinal principle at the base of the Objectivist ethical system is the statement that "it is only the concept of 'Life' that makes
the concept of 'Value' possible. It is only to a living entity that
things can be good or evil." This is the identification that cuts
through the Gordian knot of past ethical theorizing, that dissolves
the mystical fog in the field of morality, and refutes the contention
that a rational morality is impossible and that values cannot be
derived from facts.

It is the nature of living entities—the *fact* that they must sustain
their life by self-generated action—that makes the existence of *values* possible and necessary. For each living species, the course of
action required is specific; what an entity *is* determines what it
ought to do.

By identifying the context in which values arise existentially,
Objectivism refutes the claim—especially prevalent today—that the
ultimate standard of any moral judgment is "arbitrary," that *normative* propositions cannot be derived from *factual* propositions.
By identifying the genetic roots of "value" epistemologically, it
demonstrates that *not* to hold man's life as one's standard of moral
judgment is to be guilty of a logical contradiction. It is only to a

living entity that things can be good or evil; life is the basic value that makes all other values possible; the value of life is not to be justified by a value beyond itself; to demand such justification—to ask: Why *should* man choose to live?—is to have dropped the meaning, context, and source of one's concepts. "Should" is a concept that can have no intelligible meaning, if divorced from the concept *and value* of life.

If life—existence—is *not* accepted as one's standard, then only one alternative standard remains: *non*existence. But nonexistence—death—is not a standard of value: it is the negation of values. The man who does not wish to hold life as his goal and standard is free not to hold it; but he cannot claim the sanction of reason; he cannot claim that his choice is as valid as any other. It is not "arbitrary," it is not "optional," whether or not man accepts his nature as a living being—just as it is not "arbitrary" or "optional" whether or not he accepts reality.

What are the major virtues man's survival requires, according to the Objectivist ethics? Rationality—Independence—Honesty—Integrity—Justice—Productiveness—Pride.

Rationality is the unreserved commitment to the perception of reality, to the acceptance of reason as an absolute, as one's only guide of knowledge, values, and action. Independence is reliance upon one's own mind and judgment, the acceptance of intellectual responsibility for one's own existence. Honesty is the refusal to seek values by faking reality, by evading the distinction between the real and the unreal. Integrity is loyalty *in action* to the judgment of one's consciousness. Justice is the practice of identifying men for what they *are*, and treating them accordingly—of rewarding the actions and traits of character in men which are pro-life and condemning those which are anti-life. Productiveness is the act of supporting one's existence by translating one's thought into reality, of setting one's goals and working for their achievement, of bringing knowledge or goods into existence. Pride is *moral ambitiousness,* the dedication to achieving one's highest potential, in one's character and in one's life—and the refusal to be sacrificial fodder for the goals of others.

If life on earth is the standard, then it is not the man who *sacrifices* values who is moral, but the man who *achieves* them; not the man who renounces, but the man who creates; not the man who forsakes life, but the man who makes life possible.

The Objectivist ethics holds that man—every man—is an end in himself, not a means to the ends of others. *He is not a sacrificial animal.* As a living being, he must exist for his own sake, neither sacrificing himself to others not sacrificing others to himself. The achievement of his own happiness is man's highest moral purpose.

To live for his own happiness imposes a solemn responsibility on man: he must learn what his happiness objectively requires. It is a responsibility that the majority of men have failed to assume. No belief is more prevalent—or more disastrous—than that men can achieve their happiness by the pursuit of any random desires they experience. The existence of such a profession as psychotherapy is an eloquent refutation of that belief. Happiness is the consequence of living the life proper to man *qua* rational being, the consequence of pursuing and achieving consistent, life-serving values.

Thus, Objectivism advocates an ethics of *rational self-interest.*

Only reason can judge what is or is not objectively to man's self-interest; the question cannot be decided by feeling or whim. To act by the guidance of feelings and whims is to pursue a course of self-destruction; and self-destruction is not to man's self-interest.

To think is to man's self-interest; to suspend his consciousness, is not. To choose his goals in the full context of his knowledge, his values, and his life, is to man's self-interest; to act on the impulse of the moment, without regard for his long-range context, is not. To exist as a productive being, is to man's self-interest; to attempt to exist as a parasite, is not. To seek the life proper to his nature, is to man's self-interest; to seek to live as an animal, is not.

Such is the base of the Objectivist ethics.

We have seen that self-esteem is the hallmark of mental health. It is the consequence, expression, and reward of a mind fully committed to reason. Commitment to reason is commitment to the maintenance of a full intellectual focus, to the constant expansion of one's understanding and knowledge, to the principle that one's actions must be consistent with one's convictions, that one must never attempt to fake reality, or place any consideration above reality, that one must never permit oneself contradictions—that one must never attempt to subvert or sabotage the proper function of consciousness.

In order to deal with reality successfully—to pursue and achieve the values which his life requires—man needs self-esteem; he needs to be confident of his efficacy and worth. Anxiety and guilt, the antipodes of self-esteem and the insignia of mental illness, are the disintegrators of thought, the distorters of values and the paralyzers of action. When a man of self-esteem chooses his values and sets his goals, when he projects the long-range purposes that will unify and guide his actions, it is like a bridge thrown to the future, across which his life will pass, a bridge supported by the conviction that his mind is competent to think, to judge, to value, and that *he* is worthy of enjoying values.

As I have stressed earlier (Chapter Seven), this sense of control over reality, of control over one's own existence, is not the result of special skills, ability, or knowledge. It is not dependent on *particular* successes or failures. It reflects one's *fundamental* relationship to reality, one's conviction of *fundamental* efficacy and worthiness. It reflects the certainty that, in essence and in principle, one is *right* for reality.

It is this psychological state that traditional morality makes impossible, to the extent that a man accepts its tenets. And this is one of the foremost reasons why a psychotherapist cannot be indifferent to the question of moral values in his work.

Neither mysticism nor the creed of self-sacrifice is compatible with mental health or self-esteem. These doctrines are destructive existentially *and psychologically.*

1. The maintenance of his life and the achievement of self-esteem require of man the fullest exercise of his reason—but morality, men are taught, rests on and requires *faith.*

Faith is the commitment of one's consciousness to beliefs for which one has no sensory evidence or rational proof.

When a man rejects reason as his standard of judgment, only one alternative standard remains to him: his feelings. A mystic is a man who treats his feelings as tools of cognition. Faith is the equation of *feeling* with *knowledge.*

To practice the "virtue" of faith, one must be willing to suspend one's sight and one's judgment; one must be willing to live with the unintelligible, with that which cannot be conceptualized or integrated into the rest of one's knowledge, and to induce a trance-like illusion of understanding. One must be willing to repress one's critical faculty and hold it as one's guilt; one must be willing to drown any questions that rise in protest—to strangle any thrust of reason convulsively seeking to assert its proper function as the protector of one's life and cognitive integrity.

All of man's knowledge and all his concepts have a hierarchical structure. The foundation and starting point of man's thinking are his sensory perceptions; on this base, man forms his first concepts, then goes on building the edifice of his knowledge by identifying and integrating new concepts on a wider and wider scale. If man's thinking is to be valid, this process must be guided by *logic*, "the art of non-contradictory identification"[12]—and any new concept man forms must be integrated without contradiction into the hierarchical structure of his knowledge. *To introduce into one's consciousness a major and fundamental idea that cannot be so integrated, an idea not derived from reality, not validated by a process of reason, not subject to rational examination or judgment—and worse: an idea that clashes with the rest of one's concepts and understanding of reality—is to sabotage the integrative function of consciousness, to undercut the rest of one's convictions and kill one's capacity to be certain of anything.*

There is no greater self-delusion than to imagine that one can render unto reason that which is reason's and unto faith that which is faith's. Faith cannot be circumscribed or delimited; to surrender one's consciousness by an inch is to surrender one's consciousness in total. Either reason is an absolute to a mind or it is not—and if it is not, there is no place to draw the line, no principle by which to draw it, no barrier faith cannot cross, no part of one's life faith cannot invade; then one remains rational only until and unless one's *feelings* decree otherwise.

Faith is a malignancy that no system can tolerate with impunity; and the man who succumbs to it will call on it in precisely those issues where he needs his reason most. When one turns from reason to faith, when one rejects the absolutism of reality, one undercuts the absolutism of one's consciousness—and one's mind becomes an organ one cannot trust any longer. It becomes what the mystics claim it to be: a tool of distortion.

2. Man's need of self-esteem entails the need for a sense of control over reality—but no control is possible in a universe which,

by one's own concession, contains the supernatural, the miraculous, and the causeless, a universe in which one is at the mercy of ghosts and demons, in which one must deal, not with the *unknown,* but with the *unknowable;* no control is possible if man proposes, but a host disposes, no control is possible if the universe is a haunted house.

3. His life and self-esteem require that the object and concern of man's consciousness be reality and this earth—but morality, men are taught, consists of scorning this earth and the world available to sensory perception, and of contemplating, instead, a "different" and "higher" reality, a realm inaccessible to reason and incommunicable in language, but attainable by revelation, by special dialectical processes, by that superior state of intellectual lucidity known to Zen-Buddhists as "No-Mind," or by death.

There is only one reality—the reality knowable to reason. And if man does not choose to perceive it, there is nothing else for him to perceive; if it is not of this world that he is conscious, then he is not conscious at all.

The sole result of the mystic projection of "another" reality is that it incapacitates man psychologically for this one. It was not by contemplating the transcendental, the ineffable, the undefinable— it was not by contemplating the nonexistent—that man lifted himself from the cave and transformed the material world to make a human existence possible on earth.

If it is a virtue to renounce one's mind, but a sin to use it; if it is a virtue to approximate the mental state of a schizophrenic, but a sin to be in intellectual focus; if it is a virtue to denounce this earth, but a sin to make it livable; if it is a virtue to mortify the flesh, but a sin to work and act; if it is a virtue to despise life, but a sin to sustain and enjoy it—then no self-esteem or control or efficacy are possible to man, *nothing* is possible to him but the guilt and terror of a wretch caught in a nightmare universe, a universe created by some metaphysical sadist who has cast man into a maze where the door marked "virtue" leads to self-destruction and the door marked "efficacy" leads to self-damnation.

4. His life and self-esteem require that man take pride in his power to think, pride in his power to live—but morality, men are taught, holds pride, and specifically intellectual pride, as the gravest of sins. Virtue begins, men are taught, with humility: with

the recognition of the helplessness, the smallness, the impotence of one's mind.

Is man omniscient?—demand the mystics. Is he infallible? Then how dare he challenge the word of God or of God's representatives, and set himself up as the judge of—anything?

Intellectual pride is not—as the mystics imply it to be—a pretense at omniscience or infallibility. On the contrary, precisely because man must *struggle* for knowledge, precisely because the pursuit of knowledge requires an *effort*, the men who assume this responsibility properly feel pride.

Sometimes, colloquially, pride is taken to mean a pretense at accomplishments one has not in fact achieved. But the braggart, the boaster, the man who affects virtues he does not possess, is not proud; he has merely chosen the most humiliating way to reveal his humility.

Pride (as an emotional state) is one's response to one's power to achieve values, the pleasure one takes in one's own efficacy. And it is this that mystics regard as evil.

But if doubt, not confidence, is man's proper moral state; if self-distrust, not self-reliance, is the proof of his virtue; if fear, not self-esteem, is the mark of perfection; if guilt, not pride, is his goal—then mental illness is a moral ideal, the neurotics and psychotics are the highest exponents of morality, and the thinkers, the achievers, are the sinners, those who are too corrupt and too arrogant to seek virtue and psychological well-being through the belief that they are unfit to exist.

Humility is, of necessity, the basic virtue of a mystical morality: it is the only virtue possible to men who have renounced the mind.

Pride has to be earned; it is the reward of effort and achievement; but to gain the virtue of humility, one has only to abstain from thinking—nothing else is demanded—and one will feel humble quickly enough.

5. His life and self-esteem require of man loyalty to his values, loyalty to his mind and its judgments, loyalty to his life—but the essence of morality, men are taught, consists of self-sacrifice; the sacrifice of one's mind to some higher authority, and the sacrifice of one's values to whomever may claim to require it.

It is not necessary, in this context, to analyze the almost countless evils entailed by the precept of self-sacrifice. Its irrationality and destructiveness have been thoroughly exposed by Ayn Rand in *Atlas Shrugged*. But there are two aspects of the issue that are especially pertinent to the subject of mental health.

The first is the fact that *self*-sacrifice means—and can only mean—mind-sacrifice.

A sacrifice means the surrender of a higher value in favor of a lower value or of a nonvalue. If one gives up that which one does not value in order to obtain that which one does value—or if one gives up a lesser value in order to obtain a greater one—this is not a sacrifice, but a *gain*.

All of man's values exist in a hierarchy; he values some things more than others; and, to the extent that he is rational, the hierarchical order of his values is rational: he values things in proportion to their importance in serving his life and well-being. That which is inimical to his life and well-being, that which is inimical to his nature and needs as a living being, he disvalues.

Conversely, one of the characteristics of mental illness is a distorted value structure; the neurotic does not value things according to their objective merit, in relation to his nature and needs; he frequently values the very things that will lead him to self-destruction. Judged by *objective* standards, he is engaged in a chronic process of self-sacrifice.

But if sacrifice is a virtue, it is not the neurotic but the rational man who must be "cured." He must learn to do violence to his own rational judgment—to reverse the order of his value hierarchy—to surrender that which his mind has chosen as the good—to turn against and invalidate his own consciousness.

Do mystics declare that all they demand of man is that he sacrifice his *happiness*? To sacrifice one's happiness is to sacrifice one's desires; to sacrifice one's desires is to sacrifice one's values; to sacrifice one's values is to sacrifice one's judgment; to sacrifice one's judgment is to sacrifice one's mind—and it is nothing less than this that the creed of self-sacrifice aims at and demands.

If his judgment is to be an object of sacrifice—what sort of efficacy, control, freedom from conflict, or serenity of spirit will be possible to man?

The second aspect that is pertinent here, involves not only the creed of self-sacrifice but *all* the foregoing tenets of traditional morality.

An irrational morality, a morality set in opposition to man's nature, to the facts of reality and to the requirements of man's survival, necessarily forces men to accept the belief that there is an inevitable clash between the moral and the practical—that they must choose either to be virtuous or to be happy, to be idealistic or to be successful, but they cannot be both. This view establishes a disastrous conflict on the deepest level of man's being, a lethal dichotomy that tears man apart; it forces him to choose between making himself *able* to live and making himself *worthy* of living. Yet self-esteem and mental health require that he achieve *both*.

If man holds life as the good, if he judges his values by the standard of that which is proper to the existence of a rational being, then there is no clash between the requirements of survival and of morality—no clash between making himself able to live and making himself worthy of living; he achieves the second by achieving the first. But there is a clash, if man holds the renunciation of this earth as the good, the renunciation of life, of mind, of happiness, of self. Under an anti-life morality, man makes himself worthy of living to the extent that he makes himself unable to live—and to the extent that he makes himself able to live, he makes himself unworthy of living.

The answer given by many defenders of traditional morality is: "Oh, but people don't have to go to extremes!"—meaning: "We don't expect people to be *fully* moral. We expect them to smuggle *some* self-interest into their lives. We recognize that people have to live, after all."

The defense, then, of this code of morality is that few people will be suicidal enough to attempt to practice it consistently. *Hypocrisy* is to be man's protector against his professed moral convictions. What does *that* do to his self-esteem?

And what of the victims who are insufficiently hypocritical?

What of the child who withdraws in terror into a private universe because he cannot cope with the ravings of parents who tell him that he is guilty by nature, that his body is evil, that thinking is sinful, that question-asking is blasphemous, that doubting is depravity, and that he must obey the orders of a supernatural ghost because if he doesn't, he will burn forever in hell?

Or the daughter who collapses in guilt over the sin of not wanting to devote her life to caring for the ailing father who has given her cause to feel only hatred?

Or the adolescent who flees into homosexuality because he has been taught that sex is evil and that women are to be worshipped, but not desired?

Or the businessman who suffers an anxiety attack because, after years of being urged to be thrifty and industrious, he has finally committed the sin of succeeding, and is now told that it shall be easier for the camel to pass through the eye of a needle than for a rich man to enter the kingdom of heaven?

Or the neurotic who, in hopeless despair, gives up the attempt to solve his problems because he has always heard it preached that this earth is a realm of misery, futility, and doom, where no happiness or fulfillment is possible to man?

If the advocates of these doctrines bear a grave moral responsibility, there is a group who, perhaps, bears a graver responsibility still: the psychologists and psychiatrists who see the human wreckage of these doctrines, but who remain silent and do not protest—who declare that philosophical and moral issues do not concern them, that science cannot pronounce value judgments—who shrug off their professional obligations with the assertion that a rational code of morality is impossible, and, by their silence, lend their sanction to spiritual murder.

The Danger of Authoritarianism

Mental health requires of man that he place no value above perception, i.e., no value above consciousness, i.e., no value above reality.

If the patient is to be cured of his neurosis, he must learn to distinguish between a *thought* and a *feeling*, between a *fact* and a *wish*, and to recognize that nothing but destruction can result from sacrificing one's sight of reality to any other consideration. He must learn to seek his sense of self-esteem in the productive use of his mind, in the achievement of rational values, on whatever his level of ability. He must learn that the approval of others cannot be a substitute for self-esteem, and that only anxiety is possible to those who attempt such a substitution. He must learn not to be afraid to question and challenge the prevalent beliefs of his culture. He must learn to reject the claims of those who demand his agreement *on faith*. He must learn to fight for his own happiness and to deserve it. He must learn that the irrational *will not work*—and that so long as any part of him desires it, that desire is the cause of his suffering.

He must learn to live as a rational being—and for guidance at this task, he needs a code of rational moral principles. This is the reason I consider the Objectivist ethics indispensable to the practice of psychotherapy.

It is necessary, at this point, to enter a note of caution with regard to the manner in which moral principles are communicated to patients.

There is a radical difference between *directive* therapy, in which the therapist accepts the responsibility of his role as educator—and *authoritarian* therapy, in which the therapist preaches, propagandizes, intimidates, cajoles, and otherwise attempts to pressure the patient into accepting certain views.

Authoritarianism in the name of reason, or for the patient's "own good," is a contradiction in terms. The fact that a patient has psychological problems does not mean that the therapist is entitled to treat him with less than full intellectual respect. It is often all too easy, granted the nature of the therapist's position and the patient's self-doubt, for the therapist to use subtle forms of intimidation to compel acceptance of his own moral or philosophical beliefs. Such a practice is counter to the entire nature and intention of the therapeutic enterprise. If a therapist is to help his patient, what he needs is the patient's rational understanding, not his blind faith. A therapist is a scientist, not a witch doctor.

It would be an error, I should mention, to assume that the danger of authoritarianism is peculiar to therapists who accept the necessity and responsibility of dealing with values in their practice. Witch-doctory is fully as prevalent, if not more prevalent, among the type of therapist who eschews the issue of values. Freudians in particular are notorious in this regard.[13]

Therapeutic Techniques

It is outside the scope of this book to enter into a detailed discussion of the techniques of psychotherapy. I may make that the subject of a future work. Here I shall confine myself to a few general observations about more technical aspects of therapy.

1. I have found it immensely helpful to have patients do written "homework" assignments during the progress of therapy. At the end of the first interview, the patient is almost always asked to write a paper covering (a) the history and development of his personal problems, from childhood on; (b) what he believes his problems to be at present; (c) what he hopes to achieve through therapy. Following this, the patient may be assigned additional papers dealing with his educational and career autobiography, his sexual autobiography, relationships with parents and friends, etc. Such assignments, of course, are intended to be a supplement to history-making, not a substitute for it. They often provide valuable additional information. Further, the patient usually finds that the task of putting his life and problems down on paper helps him to achieve an objective perspective.

It is often desirable to have the patient write reports on his understanding of the things he is learning in therapy and on how he believes his new understanding is affecting him intellectually, emotionally, and behaviorally. This can be especially helpful in group therapy, as a means of helping the therapist to remain informed about the state and progress of each patient. Another value of such papers is that they act as a corrective to any inclination on the part of the therapist to believe that the patient understands more than he in fact understands. They also act as a corrective to any impulse on the part of the patient to confine his thinking about his problems to the time spent in therapy.

2. In view of the central and basic role which repression plays in the formation (as well as the sustaining) of psychological problems, one of the therapist's most important tasks is to guide the patient through the process of de-repression. I have indicated (Chapter Six) some of the evidences of the presence of repression: contradictions between a person's verbally expressed beliefs and his emotions and behavior, or between his emotions and his behavior, or among his emotions themselves, or among his actions themselves.

It is in seeking to understand and bring to light the patient's actual beliefs and feelings, when they have been repressed, that the therapist's skills are especially tested. He requires the full power of his perceptiveness, his emotional sensitivity, his ability to grasp implications in his patient's statements to which the patient may be oblivious. Often, for example, the patient is telling the thera-pist one story with his words and an entirely different story with his body, with his breathing, his movements, his posture, the pupils of his eyes, etc. The therapist must continually work at improving his skill at the art of question-asking, which is surely the most power-ful technique at his command. The art consists first, of course, of knowing what questions to ask, but also of knowing when to ask them and in what manner. An effective therapist strives to create an atmosphere in which the patient is able to feel, in effect: Here, in this room, I can say *anything*. This is accomplished, not by the therapist projecting an attitude of all-embracing warmth, forgive-ness, and "love," but rather projecting an attitude of respectful, benevolent *interest*, a sense of profound *relaxation* and the convic-tion that truth, whatever it may be, need not ever be frightening, that liberation can be achieved only by facing *facts*.

I regret that there is not space here to amplify my conviction that the therapist's ability to remain deeply relaxed while working, and to manifest his inner state to the patient, is one of his most important technical assets. Authentic relaxation on the part of a therapist forbids the kind of stony, emotionally frozen remoteness or pedantic impersonality which many inexperienced or insecure therapists adopt as a protective façade. Professional effectiveness does not require such a façade and is, in fact, impeded by it, since it prevents proper rapport between therapist and patient, and obstructs free emotional communication on the part of the patient.

I can only mention, in passing, that hypnosis is another pow-erful tool for penetrating repressive barriers. Hypnosis can enable a patient to achieve a level of greatly enhanced mental concentra-tion in which forgotten or repressed material becomes accessible to him. Every therapist should acquire skill in the art of question-asking under hypnosis, in hypnotic age-regression, and in other related techniques.[14]

I have said that the therapist must acquire the skill of question-asking. Part of that skill consists of learning the questions he must teach the patient to ask himself. It is astonishing how seldom a patient who is seeking to de-repress his emotions thinks of asking himself: What do I want? This is, perhaps, the most important ques-tion a person can ask himself—and the therapist should teach his patient to ask it, and keep asking it, day after day, week after week, month after month, about every conceivable aspect of his life. What do I want to accomplish in my career? Where do I want to be, professionally, ten years from now? What do I want to feel about my work? What do I want others to appreciate in my work? What qualities do I want to find in friends? What qualities do I want to find in a romantic partner? What do I want to feel in regard to a romantic partner? What do I want to be made to feel sexually? How do I want to spend my time with my friends and loved ones? What do I want to find, and to experience, in the books I read?— in the movies I see?—in the music I listen to?

Most patients initially experience considerable difficulty in answering such questions (except, perhaps, in vague and useless generalities). But if he is encouraged to persist, to go on asking them until the answers begin to come, the patient will be led to identify not only his desires (i.e., his values), but also and equally importantly, his frustrations, his disappointments, his hurts and grievances. The number of such questions to be asked are almost without limit; above, I have indicated only a few.

3. There are two categories in which it is useful to have the patient organize his problems. Some of the patient's problems may be susceptible to immediate partial or total correction, by alterations in his behavior in issues which are subject to his direct volitional control—for example, lying, physically abusing one's child, sexual promiscuity, failing to seek a job, seeking escape from one's problems by excessive socializing, etc. Other problems are clearly not correctable merely by an act of choice or decision—for example, feelings of anxiety or depression, inappropriate sexual desires, difficulty in thinking clearly, psychosomatic illness, etc. Sometimes a patient needs help in determining in which category a given problem belongs. (Not all problems readily fit exclusively into either category; mildly compulsive behavior, for instance, represents a borderline case.)

A plan should be worked out whereby the patient will proceed, across a specified period of time, to alter those aspects of his behavior which he recognizes to be within his direct control. The confidence that results from his rational regulation of his behavior in such areas helps him in working on those problems requiring more intensive therapy.

With regard to these latter problems, it is important for the patient to be very specific in identifying the therapeutic goals he wants to attain. Sometimes, this task is relatively easy, as when the goal is simply, say, to become heterosexual rather than homosexual, or to be free of migraine headaches, or to lose weight. Often, however, the patient's problems are more diffuse, he has vague feelings of anxiety or depression, he suffers a general lack of self-confidence, he complains that his life has no direction or purpose. In such cases, it is important to help him formulate as specifically as possible the conditions that would have to be satisfied in order for him to regard himself as "cured." He should be led to formulate specific goals, psychological and/or existential, toward which he is to work. Otherwise, therapy can become a diffuse, interminable process.

At each step of the way, throughout therapy, it is important for the patient's self-esteem and progress that he take whatever actions are volitionally possible to him with regard to the correction of his problems. Problems are not solved all at once; they are solved step by step. In the slow, difficult process of helping a patient build self-confidence and self-respect, one must do everything possible to help him avoid repeating the errors that led to his neurotic condition. Problems are not *created* all at once; they are created step by step; and then they are sustained and reinforced year after year, by endless repetitions of the kinds of self-defeating practices I have discussed throughout this book. The patient must be made aware of the things he does that he could avoid doing, which serve to keep his problems alive. He must be made aware of, and encouraged to take, the opposite kinds of actions, so that the process can be reversed.

For example, suppose that for many years a person has tended to retreat from any challenge or difficulty that seemed at all threatening. As an adult he is passive, withdrawn, self-doubting, ineffective. The therapist cannot demand of him that he immediately undertake major projects or responsibilities that clearly are light-years beyond the range of his present level of confidence. So one begins by encouraging him to set a series of modest goals, goals that do constitute a challenge for him and invoke some degree of fear—but a fear that is manageable, a fear he has the power to work his way through and to overcome. The patient thus acquires the strength and confidence to move on to more demanding goals.

As we have discussed, many elements are involved in therapy: helping the patient to identify his feelings and desires, teaching him more effective ways of thinking, leading him to understand his conflicts, etc. Nevertheless, it is vital to keep the patient thinking of his problems in terms of *action*. By what *actions* (psycho-epistemological or existential) did he contribute to the creation of his problem? By what *action* does he sustain it? By what *actions* can he reverse the process? By what *actions* can he move towards the attainment of the kind of life he wants?

4. This leads us to a principle which is closely related to the above. One of the commonest mistakes made by patients is an attitude which amounts to the following: *After* I have learned to understand myself thoroughly, *after* all my emotional problems are solved and all my fears vanquished, *then* I will be able to act differently than I act now.

The mistake here is in failing to recognize that one's behavior must be modified *during* the process of therapy, *as* one learns. Otherwise, one's learning avails one very little. Many patients claim to have derived all sorts of benefits from therapy, to have been given invaluable insights—but it is obvious that they are behaving exactly as they behaved before entering therapy. In such cases, it is difficult to say in what way therapy benefited them or if it actually did. The truth is that, unless the patient modifies his behavior as he learns, his emotional problems will not be solved and his fears will not be vanquished.

The ultimate test of cure or improvement is: What is the patient doing differently than he did before? At each step of therapy the patient should be encouraged to translate into action whatever new understanding he has achieved. The action may consist of taking a new job, or working harder at the present one, or dealing differently with his children, or speaking more openly about his emotions to his wife, or curtailing his temper, or preparing and following a budget, or going back to school, or breaking with undesirable companions, or speaking up in defense of his convictions at a social gathering, etc. Such practices will have a beneficial effect on his self-esteem which, coupled with the further understanding he attains in therapy, will enable him subsequently to introduce additional modifications into his behavior.

5. The question is often asked: To what extent is it necessary to analyze childhood experiences in order to resolve the psychological problems of an adult? I do not believe there is any general answer to this question that will fit all cases. There are some problems that can be corrected without ever exploring the patient's childhood; in other cases, extensive exploration and analysis is needed.

Where an analysis of childhood experiences is appropriate, the patient must be taught to recognize that it is not the experiences as such that are generating his problem, nor even the initial conclusions he drew from those experiences, but rather the fact that he keeps reinforcing those conclusions every day of his adult life. There are persons who begin telling themselves that they are worthless at the age of three, and go on telling it to themselves every day thereafter into their thirties or forties. On the other hand, there are persons who draw mistaken conclusions about themselves or about life at an early age, but later revise those conclusions as a result of new thinking and, perhaps, additional evidence, and who, therefore, escape painful experiences with no enduring harm.

However, instructive and valuable it may be for the patient to learn how his problems began, and it *can* be valuable and instructive, he must still learn what he is doing *in the present* to keep his problems alive. There is nothing he can do about his past actions. The solution lies in what he does about his present and future actions—in the new conclusions he forms, the new psycho-epistemological policies he adopts, the new values he acquires, the new goals he elects to pursue.

Conclusion

In our analysis of needs (Chapter Two), I discussed the fact that the frustration of a need does not necessarily result in the immediate or direct death of the organism: it can result instead in a general lowering of the ability of an organism to function, a diminution of the organism's effectiveness and power. This is applicable to psychological needs in general and to the need of self-esteem in particular.

Obviously, patients do not normally *die* from a deficiency of self-esteem (although sometimes they do, as in suicide or other forms of self-destruction), but the extent of that deficiency is the extent of their inability to *live*. That ability or inability is measured in terms of a man's capacity to optimize his intellectual and creative potential, to translate that potential into productive achievement, to function effectively and unimpededly on the emotional as well as on the intellectual level, to love and to give objective expression to his love, to explore the challenges and reap the rewards that human existence offers to man.

If a patient must be taught that the frustrations, the despair, the wreckage of his life are ultimately traceable to his deficiency of self-esteem and to the policies that led to that deficiency, it is equally imperative that he be taught the solution: that supreme expression of selfishness and self-assertiveness which consists of holding his self-esteem as his highest value and most exalted concern—and of knowing that each struggling step upward, taken in the name of that value, carries him further from the bondage to his past suffering and closer to the sunlight reality of the human potential.

Epilogue
Working with Self-Esteem in Psychotherapy

When I began practicing psychotherapy in the 1950s, I became convinced that low self-esteem was a common denominator in most, if not all, of the varieties of personal distress I encountered in my practice. I saw low self-esteem as both a predisposing causal factor of psychological problems and a consequence. This Epilogue briefly outlines (1) what self-esteem is, (2) why the need for it is urgent, (3) what its attainment depends on, and (4) how the clinician can nurture it in psychotherapy.

Some clients' problems are direct expressions of underdeveloped self-esteem. Examples include shyness, timidity, and fear of self-assertion, intimacy, or human relationships; another example is the lack of participation in life. Other issues can be understood as consequences of denying poor self-esteem, that is, as defenses against the reality of the problem. Examples of such defenses include controlling and manipulative behavior, obsessive-compulsive rituals, inappropriate aggressiveness, fear-driven sexuality, and destructive forms of ambition. All of these consequences are driven by the desire to experience efficacy, control, and personal worth. Problems that manifest as poor self-esteem also contribute significantly to the continuing deterioration of self-esteem.

A primary task of psychotherapy is to help strengthen self-esteem. I believe that self-esteem can and should be addressed explicitly and that it should set the context for the entire therapeutic enterprise. Even when the client is not working on self-esteem issues directly—even when therapy is focused or aimed at solving specific problems—problem solving can be accomplished by framing or contextualizing the process so that it strengthens self-esteem explicitly.

Almost all therapeutic orientations help clients confront previously avoided conflicts or challenges. My technique differs in that I typically ask questions like, "How do you feel about yourself when you avoid an issue that you know, at some level, needs to be dealt with?" Another question is, "How do you feel about yourself when you master your avoidance impulses and confront the threatening issue?" In other words, I frame the process in terms of its consequences for self-esteem. I want clients to notice how their choices and actions affect their experience of themselves.

Definition of Self-Esteem

I define *self-esteem* as the experience of being competent to cope with the basic challenges of life and of being worthy of happiness. It consists of two components: (1) *self-efficacy*—confidence in one's ability to think, learn, choose, and make appropriate decisions, and, by extension, to master challenges and manage change—and (2) *self-respect*—confidence in one's right to be happy and, by extension, confidence that achievement, success, friendship, respect, love, and fulfillment are appropriate for oneself.

To illuminate this definition, consider the following. If a client feels inadequate to face the challenge of life or lacks fundamental self-trust or confidence in his or her mind, a clinician would recognize the presence of a self-esteem deficiency, no matter what other assets the client possesses. The same would be true if a client lacks a basic sense of self-respect, feels unworthy of the love or respect of others, feels unentitled to happiness, or is fearful of asserting thoughts, wants, or needs.

Self-efficacy and self-respect are the dual pillars of healthy self-esteem; if either is absent, self-esteem is impaired. They are the defining characteristics of the term because of their fundamentality; they represent not derivative or secondary meanings of *self-esteem* but its essence.[1]

The Need for Self-Esteem

How people experience themselves affects every moment of their existence. Their self-evaluation is the basic context in which they act and react, choose their values, set their goals, and meet the challenges of life. Their responses to events are shaped in part by who and what they think they are—how competent and worthy they perceive themselves to be. Of all the judgments they pass in life, none is more important than the judgment they pass on themselves.

To say that self-esteem is a basic human need is to say that it makes an essential contribution to the life process, that it is indispensable to normal and healthy development, that it has value for survival. Without positive self-esteem, psychological growth is stunted. Positive self-esteem operates, in effect, as the immune system of consciousness, providing resistance, strength, and a capacity for regeneration.

When self-esteem is low, resilience in the face of life's adversities is diminished. Clients with low self-esteem crumble before vicissitudes that a healthier sense of self could vanquish. They tend to be more influenced by the desire to avoid pain than to experience joy; negatives have more power over them than positives.

This does not mean that they are necessarily incapable of achieving real values. Some persons may have the talent and drive to achieve a great deal in spite of a poor self-concept. An example is a highly productive workaholic who is driven to prove his worth to, say, a father who predicted he would amount to nothing.

However, clients with low self-esteem will be less effective—less creative—than they might be; they will also be crippled in their ability to find joy in their achievements. Nothing they do will ever feel like enough.

Clients who do exhibit a realistic confidence in their mind and value—who feel secure within themselves—tend to experience the world as open to them and to respond appropriately to challenges and opportunities. Self-esteem empowers, energizes, and motivates. It inspires persons to achieve and allows them to take pleasure and pride in their achievements. It allows them to experience satisfaction.

High self-esteem seeks the challenge and stimulation of worthwhile and demanding goals. Reaching such goals nurtures healthy self-esteem. Low self-esteem seeks the safety of the familiar and undemanding, which in turn further weakens self-esteem.

The more solid a client's self-esteem, the better equipped that person is to cope with adversity in life. Such a client tends to be more ambitious, not necessarily in a career or a financial sense but in terms of hopes for experience in life—emotionally, intellectually, creatively, spiritually. The lower a client's self-esteem, the less that person aspires to and the less likely he or she is to achieve set goals.

Either path tends to be self-reinforcing and self-perpetuating. The person with higher self-esteem is more open and honest, and communications are more likely to be appropriate, which reinforces a positive self-concept. The person with lower self-esteem is more evasive, and communications are likely to be inappropriate. This can happen because of uncertainty about his or her own thoughts and feelings or fear of the listener's response, or both. This, in turn, further diminishes a positive experience of self.

The higher the client's self-esteem, the more disposed he or she is to form nourishing rather than toxic relationships. Vitality and expansiveness in others are naturally more appealing to persons of good self-esteem than are emptiness and dependency.[2] Those with healthier self-esteem are more inclined to treat others with respect, benevolence, good will, and fairness. Such persons do not tend to perceive others as a threat, and self-respect is the foundation of respect for others.

Roots of Self-Esteem

On what does healthy self-esteem depend? What factors have an impact? There is reason to believe that we may come into this world with certain inherent differences that make it easier or harder to attain healthy self-esteem—differences pertaining to energy, resilience, disposition to enjoy life, and so on. I suspect that in future years we will learn that genetic inheritance is an important contributing factor in the ability to develop a healthy self-concept.

Upbringing, of course, is critical to self-esteem development. No one can say how many persons suffer ego damage in their early years, before the ego is fully formed; in such cases, it may be all but impossible for healthy self-esteem to emerge later without intense psychotherapy. Research suggests that one of the best ways to have good self-esteem is to have parents who model healthy self-esteem, as Coopersmith's *The Antecedents of Self-Esteem* demonstrates.[3]

Children who have the best chance of acquiring the foundation for healthy self-esteem tend to have parents who

- Raise them with love and respect
- Allow them to experience consistent and benevolent acceptance
- Give them the supporting structure of reasonable rules and appropriate expectations
- Do not assail them with contradictions
- Do not resort to ridicule, humiliation, or physical abuse as a means of controlling them
- Project that they believe in the child's competence and goodness

However, no research has ever found the result of healthy parenting to be inevitable. Coopersmith's work, for example, clearly showed that it is not. His study provided examples of adults who appeared to have been raised superbly by the standards listed and yet became insecure, self-doubting adults. And many people emerge from appalling backgrounds but do well in school, form stable and satisfying relationships, have a powerful sense of their own value and dignity, and, as adults, satisfy any rational criterion of good self-esteem.

Although we may not know all the biological or developmental factors that influence self-esteem, we know a good deal about the specific (volitional) practices that can raise or lower it. We know that an honest commitment to understanding inspires self-trust and that an avoidance of the effort has the opposite effect. We know that people who live mindfully feel more competent than those who live mindlessly. We know that integrity engenders self-respect and that hypocrisy does not. We "know" all this implicitly, although it is astonishing how rarely psychologists discuss such matters. Clinicians cannot work on self-esteem directly because self-esteem is a consequence—a product of internally generated practices. If clinicians understand what those practices are, they can work with others to facilitate or encourage their actualization. Interventions can be designed with that end in view. But the practices themselves can arise only within the client, and only the client can cause them.

The Six Pillars of Self-Esteem

What then are these practices? More than three decades of study have convinced me that six practices are crucial and fundamental. When these six practices are absent, self-esteem necessarily suffers. To the extent that they are an integral part of a person's life, self-esteem is strengthened.

The Six Pillars of Self-Esteem

1. The Practice of Living Consciously
2. The Practice of Self-Acceptance
3. The Practice of Self-Responsibility
4. The Practice of Self-Assertiveness
5. The Practice of Living Purposefully
6. The Practice of Integrity

The Practice of Living Consciously

If clients' lives and well-being depend on the appropriate use of their consciousness, then the extent to which they honor "sight over blindness" is the single most important determinant of their self-efficacy and self-respect. One cannot feel competent in life while wandering around (whether at work dealing with superiors, subordinates, associates, and customers, or in marriages or in relations with one's children) in a self-induced mental fog. Those who attempt to exist unthinkingly and evade discomfiting facts suffer a deficiency in their sense of worthiness. They know their defaults, whether or not anyone else does.

A thousand times a day, each person must choose the level of consciousness at which to function. Gradually, over time, a person establishes a sense of the kind of person he or she is, depending on the choices made and the degree of rationality and integrity exhibited. If, at the end of therapy, a client functions no more consciously than at the beginning, we would have to question the efficacy of the therapeutic enterprise.

In therapy, one can encourage consciousness by

- Creating an environment in which thought and exploration are safe

- Using a wide repertoire of interventions that remove obstructions to awareness[4]
- Making the client aware of the self-destructive consequences of willful blindness[5]

Tom, age forty-four, who was the CEO of an insurance benefits business, said that his business was growing rapidly, that he needed to hire a new high-level consultant, and that he was afraid of hiring someone who might be more brilliant than himself. Rather than work on his problem in my office, I gave him a homework assignment: for the next two weeks, he was to write six to ten endings every day for the incomplete sentence, "If I bring a higher level of consciousness to my fear of hiring a brilliant consultant. . . . " At the end of two weeks, he reported that he had resolved the issue to his complete satisfaction; he proceeded to hire a brilliant consultant with whom he continues to have an outstanding working relationship.

The exercise I gave Tom stimulated, by its repetitiveness and by the implications of the words in the stem, his creativity and problem-solving abilities. A further benefit was that the solution was entirely his own, which enhanced his self-esteem.

The Practice of Self-Acceptance

At the deepest level, self-acceptance is the virtue of commitment to the value of one's own person. It is not the pretense at a self-esteem one does not possess but rather the primary act of self-value that serves as the basis for dedication to achieving self-esteem. It is expressed, in part, through the willingness to accept—to make real to oneself without denial or evasion—that we think what we think, feel what we feel, have done what we have done, and are what we are.

Self-acceptance is the refusal to regard any part of ourselves—our bodies, our fears, our thoughts, our actions, our dreams—as alien, as "not me." It is the willingness to experience rather than disown whatever the facts of one's being are at a particular moment. It is the refusal to engage in an adversarial relationship with oneself. It is the willingness to say of any emotion or behavior, "This is an expression of me—not necessarily an expression I like or admire but an expression of me nonetheless, at least at the time it occurred." It is the virtue of realism—of respect for reality—applied to the self. Thus if I am confronted with a mistake I have made, in accepting that it is mine, I am free to learn from it and do better in the future. I cannot learn from a mistake I cannot accept having made.

Self-acceptance is the precondition of change and growth. Mary, age thirty-nine—a lawyer—became indignant at the idea of self-acceptance and said, "I've got lousy self-esteem! And you're asking me to accept that?" I responded, "If you don't accept that you have the problem, how do you plan to solve it? Self-esteem begins with respect for reality."

Can therapy be called successful if the client fails to grow in self-acceptance? One of the ways we can teach self-acceptance in therapy is by dealing with total acceptance—no condescension, no sarcasm or ridicule, no quarreling with clients' feelings—absolute, relentless (and unsentimental) respect.

An important aspect of my work, unfortunately beyond the scope of this lesson, is the identification and integration of the client's subpersonalities.[6] This can be viewed as a field within the broader field of self-acceptance, but it is actually something of a specialty in its own right. Many clinicians have observed that whenever one learns to own and integrate a previously unrecognized or denied "part," one feels stronger and more complete; self-esteem is strengthened.

The Practice of Self-Responsibility

To feel competent to live and be worthy of happiness, the client needs to experience a sense of control over his or her existence. This requires that the client be willing to take responsibility for actions and the attainment of goals—which means taking responsibility for life and for well-being.

The practice of self-responsibility entails these realizations:

- I am responsible for the achievement of my desires.
- I am responsible for my choices and actions.
- I am responsible for the level of consciousness I bring to my work.

- I am responsible for the level of consciousness I bring to my relationships.
- I am responsible for my behavior with other people— coworkers, associates, customers, spouse, children, friends.
- I am responsible for how I prioritize my time.
- I am responsible for the quality of my communications.
- I am responsible for my personal happiness.
- I am responsible for choosing the values by which I live.
- I am responsible for raising the level of my self-esteem.

In my opinion, one of the most important moments in therapy occurs when clients finally realize (however this is achieved) that no one is coming: no one is coming to redeem their childhood; no one is coming to make them happy; no one is coming to rescue them. If they wish their life to improve, they will have to do something different themselves. One day in group therapy, a client with a sense of humor challenged me: "You always say that no one is coming. But you came!" "Correct," I admitted, "but I came to say that no one is coming."

The Practice of Self-Assertiveness

Self-assertiveness is the virtue of appropriate self-expression—of honoring one's needs, wants, values, and convictions and seeking rational forms for their expression in reality. Its opposite is the surrender to timidity, which consists of consigning oneself to a perpetual underground where everything that one is lies hidden or stillborn. The client who is not self-assertive usually seeks to avoid confrontation with someone whose values differ, or wants to please, placate, or manipulate someone, or is trying simply to "belong."

Healthy self-assertion entails the willingness to confront rather than evade the challenges of life and to strive for mastery. A client who expands the boundaries of his or her ability to cope also expands self-efficacy and self-respect. A continuing refrain in my work with clients is this: "Your wants are important. Your life is important. Whether or not you are happy is important."

This message (like everything else I do) is always underscored and amplified by sentence-completion exercises. The sentence stem, "If someone had taught me my wants were important. . . ."

typically elicits such endings as, "I'd care more about them; I'd take them more seriously; I'd think about them; I'd exert more energy on my own behalf; I'd be more assertive; I'd treat myself with more respect."

Repetitive exercises of this kind stimulate shifts of consciousness and behavior that are experienced by the client as originating entirely from within. Clients are helped to identify what their most important wants are and then to develop action plans for their attainment (if possible).

A typical group therapy exercise that I use asks all members of the group to identify some important desire in their life. Sitting in groups of three, they are asked to work with the question, "If I were to convert this desire into a conscious purpose, what would I need to do?" Action plans develop out of the group's brainstorming.

The Practice of Living Purposefully

Life has been defined as a process of self-sustaining and self-generated action. Purpose, then, is the very essence of the life process. Through our purposes, we organize our behavior, giving it focus and direction. Through our goals, we create the sense of structure that allows us to experience control over our existence. To live purposefully is to use our powers for the attainment of goals we have selected, such as studying, raising a family, earning a living, starting a business, bringing a new product into the marketplace, solving a scientific problem, or building a vacation home. Our goals lead us forward; they call for the exercise of our faculties and energize our existence.

To observe that purposefulness is essential to fully realized self-esteem should not be understood to mean that the measure of a client's worth is his or her external achievements. We admire achievements—in others and in ourselves—and it is natural and appropriate for us to do so. But this is not the same thing as saying that achievements are the real measure (or grounds) of self-esteem. The root of self-esteem is not external achievements but those internally generated practices that, among other things, make it possible to achieve.

By way of teaching purposefulness, I typically ask clients to explore the following ideas. If you were to operate 5 percent more

purposefully on the job, or in your marriage, or in your relationship with your children, or in therapy itself, what do you imagine
you might do differently? Would there be advantages for you in
doing that? What might the obstacles be? Would you be willing to
experiment for, say, thirty days with operating more purposefully
in order to discover what happens and whether you like it? (Why 5
percent? Because it is not intimidating. Anyone can accomplish
5 percent!)

The Practice of Integrity

As a person matures and develops values and standards (or absorbs
them from others), the issue of personal integrity assumes increasing importance in self-assessment. Integrity is the integration of
ideals, convictions, standards, beliefs, and behavior. When behavior is congruent with professed values (when ideal and practice
match), a person is said to have integrity. Those who behave in
ways that conflict with their own judgment of what is appropriate
lose face in their own eyes. If the policy becomes habitual, they
trust themselves less or cease to trust themselves at all.

When a breach of integrity wounds self-esteem, only the practice of integrity can heal it. At the simplest level, personal integrity
entails asking such questions as, "Am I honest, reliable, and trust-
worthy? Do I keep my promises? Do I do the things I say I admire
and avoid the things I say are despicable?"

To understand why lapses of integrity are detrimental to self-
esteem, consider what a lapse of integrity entails. If I act in contradiction to a moral value that someone else holds but that I do
not, I may or may not be wrong, but I cannot be faulted for having
betrayed my convictions. If, however, I act against what I myself
regard as right, that is, if my actions clash with my expressed values, then I act against my judgment. I betray my mind. Hypocrisy,
by its very nature, is self-invalidating. A default on integrity undermines me and contaminates my sense of self. It damages me as no
external rebuke or rejection can damage me.

Rebecca, age forty, was a physician with a suburban practice
affiliated with a small local hospital. If the combined days her
patients spent in the hospital annually passed a certain number,
the hospital rewarded Rebecca and her husband with a luxurious

cruise. When she knew their insurance was adequate, she often found herself recommending a longer hospital stay for her patients than was strictly necessary. She came to therapy because of mysterious bouts of anxiety and depression. "I've got a wonderful husband—we've got a great home and a great life—I don't know what's the matter with me."

When I learned of Rebecca's arrangement with the hospital, I inquired as to how she felt about it. Instantly she became defensive and, in fact, canceled her next two appointments. When she returned to my office, she complained of a new problem: insomnia. When I reopened the question of her dealings with the hospital, she said angrily, "Well, I suppose I do feel a little guilty, but it's stupid to feel guilty. I mean, who am I really hurting?"

Although symptoms such as Rebecca's could have many possible causes, I suspected her anxiety, depression, and insomnia were mostly rooted in this issue. She was violating her deep sense of right and wrong, and no rationalization could protect her self-esteem. Therapy did not proceed easily.

At one point Rebecca wondered aloud if perhaps she should drop therapy and attack her problem with tranquilizers and antidepressants. The breakthrough occurred when I proposed an experiment: "Would you be willing, for the next two months, to prescribe only hospital stays you're convinced are medically necessary? And let's see what happens." She agreed. Within ten days her symptoms began to disappear.

Psychologists do not talk much about integrity. In today's world, many people find the word incongruously old-fashioned. It does not sound scientific. And yet we do need principles to guide our lives, and the principles we accept must be reasonable because if we betray them, our self-esteem will suffer. Integrity is one of the guardians of mental health.

The Self-Esteem Sentence-Completion Program

Central to all of my work is a self-esteem-building program I designed that integrates the six pillars; I give it to most of my clients. Sentence-completion work is a deceptively simple yet uniquely powerful tool for raising self-understanding, self-esteem, and personal effectiveness. It rests on the premise that all of us have more knowledge than we normally are aware of; we have more wisdom than we use and more potential than is typically displayed in our behavior.

Sentence completion stimulates insight and integration and can be used for many different purposes. The purpose here is to use a thirty-week program to build self-esteem and, concurrently, to improve overall effectiveness at work and in relationships. A rather complex set of premises and assumptions about motivation are embedded in this exercise; during the course of therapy, most of these are made explicit sooner or later.

The procedure essentially consists of the client writing an incomplete sentence (a stem) and adding different endings; the sole requirement is that each ending be a grammatical completion of the sentence. The client should work as rapidly as possible, with no pauses to think. The therapist should tell the client that any ending is fine. The client can work with a notebook, typewriter, or computer.

First thing in the morning, before proceeding with the day's business, the client should sit down and write the first stem. Then as rapidly as possible and without pausing for reflection, the client should write as many endings for that sentence as possible in two or three minutes. The therapist should instruct the client not to worry about whether the endings are literally true, make sense, or are profound; the idea is to write *something*. The client should complete the remaining stems in the same fashion. The therapist should instruct the client to proceed with the day's business after all stems have been completed. The exercise should be completed every day, Monday through Friday for the first week, always before the start of the day's business. The client should not read what was written the day before. Naturally, there will be many repetitions, but new endings inevitably will occur.

In doing this exercise, clients should empty their mind of any expectation concerning what will happen or what is supposed to happen. The therapist should instruct clients to invent an ending if their mind goes absolutely blank but not to stop with the excuse that they cannot do the exercise. An average session should not take longer than ten minutes. If it takes much longer, the client is thinking (rehearsing, calculating) too much.

At some point each weekend, the client should reread what has been written for the week and then write a minimum of six endings for this stem: If any of what I wrote this week is true, it might be helpful if I. . . .

If the client finds this program helpful, it is often useful to start it over again. Some of my clients use this program three or four times, always with new results.

Discussion of Sentence Completion

When a client is given a sentence stem and asked to keep repeating it (either orally or in writing), the process tends to act as a stimulant to new associations and integrations, both of which lay the groundwork for subsequent shifts in feelings and behavior. It is not uncommon for a client to say something like, "My pattern became so clear to me and its futility or destructiveness so devastatingly obvious that I found I could no longer continue it. I had to try something different. I found myself driven to experiment with these new learnings."

The value of having a client work with the same set of stems for a week (or longer) is that the repetitiveness helps to counteract the inclination to dismiss unpleasant realities; it also encourages and facilitates absorption of the insights that "spontaneously" tend to surface. When working with sentence completion with the client in the office rather than as a homework assignment, the therapist should offer new stems that are inspired by significant endings to previous ones so that the client develops an awareness that goes progressively deeper.

For example, exploring the influence of a client's mother in his development, the therapist might offer a chain of stems as follows:

Mother was always. . . .

With Mother I felt. . . .

Mother always seemed to expect. . . .

One of the things I wanted from Mother and
    did not get was. . . .

Mother speaks through my voice when I tell myself. . . .

One of the ways I'm still trying to win Mother's love is. . . .

If it turns out I am more than my mother's child. . . .

I am becoming aware. . . .

This last stem often is used at the end of a chain to facilitate the integration and articulation of insights. Alternates to accomplish the same end include

I'm beginning to suspect. . . .

If any of what I'm saying is true. . . .

What I hear myself saying is. . . .

Conclusion

If a therapist perceives the building of self-esteem as central to his or her work, specific issues must be addressed. They can be summarized in the form of questions:

By what means do I propose to help my client live more consciously?

How will I teach self-acceptance?

How will I facilitate a higher level of self-responsibility and autonomy?

How will I encourage a higher level of self-assertiveness?

How will I inspire greater integrity in everyday living?

What can I do to nurture autonomy?

How can I contribute to my client's enthusiasm for life?

How can I help liberate blocked potentials?

How can I help my client free himself or herself from irrational fears?

How do I help my client free himself or herself from the lingering pain of old wounds and traumas?

How can I help my client recognize, accept, and integrate denied and disowned aspects of the self?

If one's aim is to build self-esteem in psychotherapy, perhaps the first step is to become aware that these are the questions the therapist needs to ask—and answer.

A Thirty-One-Week Sentence-Completion Exercise for Self-Esteem Enhancement

Week 1

If I bring more awareness to my life today. . . .

If I take more responsibility for my choices and actions today. . . .

If I pay more attention to how I deal with people today. . . .

If I boost my energy level by 5 percent today. . . .

Week 2

If I bring 5 percent more awareness to my important relationships. . . .

If I bring 5 percent more awareness to my insecurities. . . .

If I bring 5 percent more awareness to my deepest needs and wants. . . .

If I bring 5 percent more awareness to my emotions. . . .

Week 3

If I treat listening as a creative act. . . .

If I notice how people are affected by the quality of my listening. . . .

If I bring more awareness to my dealings with people today. . . .

If I commit to dealing with people fairly and benevolently. . . .

Week 4

If I bring a higher level of self-esteem to my activities today. . . .

If I bring a higher level of self-esteem to my dealings with people today. . . .

If I am 5 percent more self-accepting today. . . .

If I am self-accepting even when I make mistakes. . . .

If I am self-accepting even when I feel confused and overwhelmed. . . .

Week 5

If I am more accepting of my body. . . .

If I deny and disown my body. . . .

When I deny or disown my conflicts. . . .

If I am more accepting of all the parts of me. . . .

Week 6

If I wanted to raise my self-esteem today, I could. . . .

If I am more accepting of my feelings. . . .

When I deny and disown my feelings. . . .

If I am more accepting of my thoughts. . . .

When I deny and disown my thoughts. . . .

Week 7

If I am more accepting of my fears. . . .

When I deny and disown my fears. . . .

If I were more accepting of my pain. . . .

When I deny and disown my pain. . . .

Week 8

If I am more accepting of my anger. . . .

When I deny and disown my anger. . . .

If I am more accepting of my sexuality. . . .

When I deny and disown my sexuality. . . .

Week 9

If I am more accepting of my excitement. . . .

When I deny and disown my excitement. . . .

If I am more accepting of my intelligence. . . .

If I deny and disown my intelligence. . . .

Week 10

Self-responsibility to me means. . . .

If I take 5 percent more responsibility for my life and well-being. . . .

When I avoid responsibility for my life and well-being. . . .

If I take 5 percent more responsibility for the attainment of my goals. . . .

If I avoid responsibility for the attainment of my goals. . . .

Week 11

If I take 5 percent more responsibility for the success of my relationships. . . .

Sometimes I keep myself passive when I. . . .

Sometimes I make myself helpless when I. . . .

I am becoming aware. . . .

Week 12

If I take 5 percent more responsibility for my standard of living. . . .

If I take 5 percent more responsibility for my choice of companions. . . .

If I take 5 percent more responsibility for my personal happiness. . . .

If I take 5 percent more responsibility for the level of my self-esteem. . . .

Week 13

Self-assertiveness to me means. . . .

If I lived 5 percent more assertively today. . . .

If I treat my thoughts and feelings with respect today. . . .

If I treat my wants with respect today. . . .

Week 14

If (when I was young) someone had told me my wants really mattered. . . .

If (when I was young) I had been taught to honor my own life. . . .

If I treat my life as unimportant. . . .

If I were willing to say yes when I want to say yes and no when I want to say no. . . .

If I were willing to let people hear the music inside me. . . .

If I were to express 5 percent more of who I am. . . .

Week 15

Living purposefully to me means. . . .

If I bring 5 percent more purposefulness into my life. . . .

If I operate 5 percent more purposefully at work. . . .

If I operate 5 percent more purposefully in my relationships. . . .

If I operate 5 percent more purposefully in marriage. . . .

Week 16

If I operate 5 percent more purposefully with my children. . . .

If I were 5 percent more purposeful about my deepest yearnings. . . .

If I take more responsibility for fulfilling my wants. . . .

If I make my happiness a conscious goal. . . .

Week 17

Integrity to me means. . . .

If I look at instances where I find full integrity difficult. . . .

If I bring 5 percent more integrity into my life. . . .

If I bring 5 percent more integrity to my work. . . .

Week 18

If I bring 5 percent more integrity to my relationships. . . .

If I remain loyal to the values I believe are right. . . .

If I refuse to live by values I do not respect. . . .

If I treat my self-respect as a high priority. . . .

Week 19

If the child in me could speak, he or she would say. . . .

If the teenager I once was still exists inside of me. . . .

If my teenage self could speak he or she would say. . . .

At the thought of reaching back to help my child self. . . .

At the thought of reaching back to help my teenage self. . . .

If I could make friends with my younger selves. . . .

Week 20

If my child self felt accepted by me. . . .

If my teenage self felt I was on his or her side. . . .

If my younger selves felt I had compassion for their struggles. . . .

If I could hold my child self in my arms. . . .

If I could hold my teenage self in my arms. . . .

If I had the courage and compassion to embrace and love my
younger selves. . . .

Week 21

Sometimes my child self feels rejected by me when I. . . .

Sometimes my teenage self feels rejected by me when I. . . .

One of the things my child self needs from me and rarely gets is. . . .

One of the things my teenage self needs from me and hasn't gotten is. . . .

One of the ways my child self gets back at me for rejecting him
or her is. . . .

One of the ways my teenage self gets back at me for rejecting
him or her is. . . .

Week 22

At the thought of giving my child self what he or she needs from
me. . . .

At the thought of giving my teenage self what he or she needs
from me. . . .

If my child self and I were to fall in love. . . .

If my teenage self and I were to fall in love. . . .

Week 23

If I accept that my child self may need time to learn to trust
me. . . .

If I accept that my teenage self may need time to learn to trust
me. . . .

As I come to understand that my child self and my teenage self
are both part of me. . . .

I am becoming aware. . . .

Week 24

Sometimes when I am afraid I. . . .

Sometimes when I am hurt I. . . .

Sometimes when I am angry I. . . .

An effective way to handle fear might be to. . . .

An effective way to handle hurt might be to. . . .

An effective way to handle anger might be to. . . .

Week 25

Sometimes when I am excited I. . . .

Sometimes when I am turned on sexually I. . . .

Sometimes when I experience strong feelings I. . . .

If I make friends with my excitement. . . .

If I make friends with my sexuality. . . .

As I grow more comfortable with the full range of my
emotions. . . .

Week 26

When I think about becoming better friends with my child
self. . . .

When I think about becoming better friends with my teenage
self. . . .

As my younger selves become more comfortable with me. . . .

As I create a safe space for my child self. . . .

As I create a safe space for my teenage self. . . .

Week 27

Mother gave me a view of myself as. . . .

Father gave me a view of myself as. . . .

Mother speaks through my voice when I tell myself. . . .

Father speaks through my voice when I tell myself. . . .

Week 28

If I bring 5 percent more awareness to my relationship with my
mother. . . .

If I bring 5 percent more awareness to my relationship with my
father. . . .

If I look at my mother and father realistically. . . .

When I reflect on the level of awareness I bring to my
relationship with my mother. . . .

When I reflect on the level of awareness I bring to my relationship with my father. . . .

Week 29

At the thought of being free of Mother, psychologically. . . .

At the thought of being free of Father, psychologically. . . .

At the thought of belonging fully to myself. . . .

If my life really does belong to me. . . .

If I really am capable of independent survival. . . .

Week 30

If I bring 5 percent more awareness to my life. . . .

If I am 5 percent more self-accepting. . . .

If I bring 5 percent more self-responsibility to my life. . . .

If I operate 5 percent more self-assertively. . . .

If I live my life 5 percent more purposefully. . . .

If I bring 5 percent more integrity to my life. . . .

If I breathe deeply and allow myself to experience what self-esteem feels like. . . .

Notes

Introduction
   1. Branden, N. *Who Is Ayn Rand?* New York: Random House, 1962.

Chapter One
   1. Rand, A. *An Introduction to Objectivist Epistemology.* New York: The Objectivist, 1967, p. 52.
   2. Pratt, J. B. *Matter and Spirit.* New York: Macmillan, 1922, pp. 11–12.
   3. Blanshard, B. *The Nature of Thought.* New York: Macmillan, 1939, pp. 336–337.
   4. For a valuable discussion of Aristotle's views concerning consciousness and life, see John Herman Randall, Jr., *Aristotle* (New York: Columbia University Press, 1960).
   5. Roback, A. A. *History of American Psychology.* New York: Library Publishers, 1952.
   6. For an especially devastating critique, see Brand Blanshard, *The Nature of Thought.* Vol. 1. New York: Macmillan, 1939, pp. 313–340. See also: C. D. Broad, *The Mind and Its Place in Nature* (Paterson, N.J.: Littlefield, Adams and Co., 1960), pp. 612–624; Robert Efron, "The Conditioned Reflex: A Meaningless Concept," *Perspectives in Biology and Medicine,* 1966, *9,* pp. 488–514; Robert Efron, "Biology Without Consciousness—and Its Consequences," *Perspectives in Biology and Medicine,* 1967, *11,* pp. 9–36; Arthur Koestler, *The Ghost in the Machine* (New York: Macmillan, 1968), pp. 3–44.

Chapter Two
   1. See Freud, S. *Beyond the Pleasure Principle.* New York: Liveright, 1950.
   2. Quoted in Healy, Bronner, and Bowers, *The Structure and Meaning of Psychoanalysis.* New York: Knopf, 1930, p. 72.

3. James, W. *Principles of Psychology.* Vol. 2. New York: Dover Publications, 1950, p. 383.

4. McDougall, W. *An Introduction to Social Psychology.* New York: Barnes & Noble, University Paperbacks, 1960, p. 25.

5. Freud, S. *Collected Papers.* Vol. 4. New York: Basic Books, 1959, p. 64.

6. Discussing the invalidity of the attempt to define instinct as a compound reflex, neurologist Robert Efron writes: "A reflex is an automatic, involuntary action which occurs as a consequence of a stimulus to a receptor. It does not involve the faculty of consciousness. So-called instincts, on the other hand, clearly do involve and require the active participation of consciousness. This being the case, no reflex and no *series* of reflexes can ever produce, or be equated with, an 'instinct.'" [From a personal communication]

7. An excellent critique of "explanation via instincts" in animals may be found in Daniel S. Lehrman, "A Critique of Konrad Lorenz's Theory of Instinctive Behavior," *The Quarterly Review of Biology,* 1953, *28,* pp. 337–363. For good examples of the scientific methodology that is replacing "explanation via instincts," see Lehrman, "Hormonal Regulation of Parental Behavior in Birds and Infrahuman Mammals," in William C. Young (ed.), *Sex and Internal Secretions* (Baltimore: Williams and Wilkins Co., 1961), pp. 1268–1382.

Chapter Three

1. Adler, M. J. *The Difference of Man and the Difference It Makes.* New York: Holt, Rinehart & Winston, 1967.

2. *Ibid.,* p. 153.

3. *Ibid.*

4. Rand, A. *Introduction to Objectivist Epistemology.* New York: The Objectivist, 1967, p. 12.

5. *Ibid.,* p. 15.

6. *Ibid.,* p. 76.

7. Rand, A. *The Virtue of Selfishness.* New York: New American Library, 1964, p. 13.

Chapter Four

1. Rand, A. *Atlas Shrugged.* New York: Random House, 1957, p. 1012.

2. Taylor, R. *Metaphysics.* Englewood Cliffs, N.J.: Prentice Hall, 1963, p. 50.

3. Rand, A. *Atlas Shrugged.* New York: Random House, 1957, p. 1037. For a detailed exposition of this principle, see H.W.B. Joseph, *An Introduction to Logic* (New York: Oxford University Press, 1957), pp. 400–425.

4. Windelband, W. *A History of Philosophy*. Vol. 2. New York: Harper Torchbooks, 1958, p. 410.

Chapter Five
1. Rand, A. *The Virtue of Selfishness*. New York: New American Library, 1964, p. 5.
2. Quoted by Brand Blanshard in *Reason and Analysis* (LaSalle, Ill.: Open Court, 1962), p. 47.
3. Brill, A. A. *Lectures on Psychoanalytic Psychiatry*. New York: Vintage Books, 1955, pp. 42–43.

Chapter Six
1. The term was first used, in print, by Ayn Rand to designate a man's "method of awareness," in *For the New Intellectual* (New York: Random House, 1961), p. 18. However, the *concept* of "psycho-epistemology," as used in Objectivism and in Biocentric Psychology, was originated neither by Miss Rand nor by myself but by Barbara Branden who, in the mid-1950s, first brought this field of study to our attention and persuaded us of its importance.
2. Rand, A. *The Virtue of Selfishness*. New York: New American Library, 1964, p. 12.

Chapter Seven
1. For a partial anticipation of this concept of self-esteem, see Ayn Rand, *Atlas Shrugged* (New York: Random House, 1957), pp. 1018, 1056–1057.
2. *Ibid.*, p. 1013.
3. For a valuable discussion of this issue, see Betty Friedan, *The Feminine Mystique* (New York: W. W. Norton, 1963).
4. For a fuller discussion of this issue, see Ayn Rand, "Art and Sense of Life," *The Objectivist*, Mar. 1966, *5*(3).

Chapter Nine
1. James, W. (edited and with Introduction). *The Literary Remains of the Late Henry James*. Boston: Osgood, 1885, pp. 59–60.

Chapter Twelve
1. Branden, N. *Who Is Ayn Rand?* New York: Random House, 1962.
2. Rand, A. *The Virtue of Selfishness*. New York: New American Library, 1964, p. 5.
3. Rand, A. *Atlas Shrugged*. New York: Random House, 1957, p. 1012.

4. *Ibid.*, pp. 1012–1013.
5. *Ibid.*, p. 1013.
6. *Ibid.*
7. Rand, A. *The Virtue of Selfishness.* New York: New American Library, 1964, p. 13.
8. Rand, A. *Atlas Shrugged.* New York: Random House, 1957, p. 1012.
9. *Ibid.*, p. 1013.
10. *Ibid.*, p. 1014.
11. *Ibid.*, p. 1018.
12. *Ibid.*, p. 1016.
13. As to practitioners who subscribe to the Objectivist ethics and use it in their work, it is my observation that certain of them (by no means all) are unfortunately prone to moralistic pedantry in communications with their patients, and exhibit a tendency to treat their patients' inappropriate behavior not as an offense against the patients' own life and happiness, but, in effect, as an offense against an abstraction called "morality." Because of my long-standing association with Objectivism, I feel obliged to stress my unreserved opposition to this policy. It is entirely incompatible with the nature and spirit of the Objectivist ethics, and represents a residue of an older, religious way of thinking about morality.
14. Among the better works on clinical hypnosis, I would recommend: Milton H. Erickson, *Advanced Techniques of Hypnosis and Therapy,* Jay Haley (ed.) (New York: Grune and Stratton, 1967); Erickson, Herschman, and Secter, *The Practical Application of Medical and Dental Hypnosis* (New York: Julian Press, 1961); Lewis Wolberg, *Medical Hypnosis* (New York: Grune and Stratton, 1948); Andre M. Weitzenhoffer, *General Techniques of Hypnotism* (New York: Grune and Stratton, 1957); William S. Kroger, *Clinical and Experimental Hypnosis* (Philadelphia: J. B. Lippincott Co., 1963); Jerome M. Schneck, *Hypnosis in Modern Medicine* (Springfield, Ill.: Charles C. Thomas, 1953); Dave Elman, *Findings in Hypnosis* (Clifton, N.J.: Dave Elman, 1964). Not one of these authors, of course, is in full agreement with any other, nor am I in full agreement with any of them. But their books contain material of major value.

Epilogue
1. For a critique of other definitions, see Nathaniel Branden, *The Six Pillars of Self-Esteem* (New York: Bantam Books, 1995), pp. 305–308.

2.   Branden, N. *The Psychology of Romantic Love.* New York: Bantam Books, 1981.

3.   Coopersmith, S. *The Antecedents of Self-Esteem.* (2nd ed.) Palo Alto, Calif.: Consulting Psychologists Press, 1981, pp. 27–31.

4.   Branden, N. *The Disowned Self* (New York: Bantam Books, 1973); *How to Raise Your Self-Esteem* (New York: Bantam Books, 1987); *The Art of Self-Discovery* (New York: Bantam Books, 1993); *The Six Pillars of Self-Esteem* (New York: Bantam Books, 1995), *Honoring the Self: Personal Integrity and the Heroic Potentials of Human Nature* (Los Angeles: Jeremy P. Tarcher, Inc.).

5.   For specific exercises aimed at energizing consciousness, see Branden, *The Six Pillars of Self-Esteem* (New York: Bantam Books, 1995), pp. 84–89, 309–317.

6.   *Ibid.,* pp. 265–271.

Index

A

Actions: and causality, 57–61; conflicts between values and, 160–165; and emotions, 72–77; and mental illness, 100–101; modification of, during psychotherapy, 248; as necessity for survival, 17–18; required for cure in psychotherapy, 224–226; and values, 26, 47

Active cognitive integration, 41

Adler, Mortimer, 30–31

Admiration, as achieved pleasure, 136

Animals: as area of study in psychology, 5; biological basis of values and goals of, 66; instinct as determining behavior of, 25, 276n7; perceptual abstractions in, 30–31; primitive consciousness of, 230; psychological visibility in interaction with, 196–198

The Antecedents of Self-Esteem (Coopersmith), 254

Anxiety. *See* Pathological anxiety

Anxiety attacks, 154–155, 161–164. *See also* Pathological anxiety

Aristotle, 10, 45, 200

Art, as source of pleasure, 135–136

Associationism, and knowledge, 56

Atlas Shrugged (Rand), 228, 240

Authoritarianism, in psychotherapy, 242–243, 278n13

Awareness: conceptual level of, and volition, 43–44; consciousness as, 5–6, 8; degrees of, 79; of emotions, to avoid repression, 92; focal, 78, 79; as goal, 40–41, 43, 44; levels of, 41–42; psychology as concerned with living organisms exhibiting, 5–6; reasons for lack of, of values underlying emotions, 68–69. *See also* Self-awareness

Axiomatic concepts, 8

B

Behavior. *See* Actions

Behaviorism: on consciousness, 12–16; methodological, 12–13; radical, 12

Beliefs, erroneous, resulting in repression, 84–87

Beyond the Pleasure Principle (Freud), 22

Biocentric psychology, xv, 28–29

Biology, needs and capacities as concern of, 18

Branden, Barbara, 277n1

Brill, A. A., 85–86

C

Capacities: defined, 18; as fundamental concept in biology and psychology, 18; involved in transformation of needs into goals, 22–23

Causality, law of, 57–62; applied to man, 58–59, 60–61; applied to objects, 57–58, 59

Childhood experiences, analysis of, in psychotherapy, 249

Children: attitude of, toward fear, 119–121; parental behaviors promoting self-esteem in, 255; social environment of, and volition, 48–52

About the Author

WITH A PH.D. IN PSYCHOLOGY and a background in philosophy, Nathaniel Branden is a practicing psychotherapist in Los Angeles. He also does corporate consulting, conducting seminars, workshops, and conferences on the application of self-esteem principles and technology to the challenges of modern business.

He is the author of many books, including *The Six Pillars of Self-Esteem*, *The Art of Living Consciously*, and, most recently, *Self-Esteem at Work*, *A Woman's Self-Esteem*, and *My Years with Ayn Rand*. His books have been translated into eighteen languages, and there are more than 3.5 million copies in print.

In addition to his in-person practice, he consults worldwide over the telephone. He can be reached at his Los Angeles office in the following ways:

P.O. Box 2609
Beverly Hills, CA 90213
Telephone: (310) 274-6361
Fax: (310) 271-6808
E-mails: NathanielBranden@compuserve.com;
brandenn@pacbell.net
Web site: http://www.nathanielbranden.net